Home Landscaping

Other titles available in the *Home Landscaping* series:

CREATIVE
HOMEOWNER®

Home Landscaping Texas

Roger Holmes

&

Greg Grant

CREATIVE HOMEOWNER®, Upper Saddle River, New Jersey

Produced by WordWorks.

Editors: Roger Holmes and Greg Grant
Editorial consultant: Rita Buchanan
Creative Homeowner editor: Neil Soderstrom
Copyeditor: Sarah Disbrow
Design and layout: Deborah Fillion
Illustrators: Portfolio of Designs by Steve Buchanan;
    Guide to Installation by Michelle Angle Farrar, Lee Hov,
    Robert La Pointe, Rick Daskam, and Teresa Nicole Green
Indexer: Brigid A. O. Wilson
Cover design: Michelle Halko
Cover photo: Charles Mann; garden design by Mike Shoup, Antique Rose Emporium, Brenham, Texas

Printed in the United States of America

Current Printing (last digit)
10 9 8 7 6 5 4 3 2

Library of Congress Catalog Card Number: 2002110576
ISBN: 1-58011-144-0
CREATIVE HOMEOWNER®
A Division of Federal Marketing Corp.
24 Park Way
Upper Saddle River, NJ 07458
www.creativehomeowner.com

Safety First

Though all concepts and methods in this book have been reviewed for safety, it is not possible to overstate the importance of using the safest working methods possible. What follows are reminders—do's and don'ts for yard work and landscaping. They are not substitutes for your own common sense.

▲ *Always* use caution, care, and good judgment when following the procedures described in this book.

▲ *Always* determine locations of underground utility lines before you dig, and then avoid them by a safe distance. Buried lines may be for gas, electricity, communications, or water. Start research by contacting your local building officials. Also contact local utility companies; they will often send a representative free of charge to help you map their lines. In addition, there are private utility locator firms that may be listed in your Yellow Pages. *Note:* Previous owners may have installed underground drainage, sprinkler, and lighting lines without mapping them.

▲ *Always* read and heed the manufacturer's instructions for using a tool, especially the warnings.

▲ *Always* ensure that the electrical setup is safe; be sure that no circuit is overloaded and that all power tools and electrical outlets are properly grounded and protected by a ground-fault circuit interrupter (GFCI). Do not use power tools in wet locations.

▲ *Always* wear eye protection when using chemicals, sawing wood, pruning trees and shrubs, using power tools, and striking metal onto metal or concrete.

▲ *Always* read labels on chemicals, solvents, and other products; provide ventilation; heed warnings.

▲ *Always* wear heavy rubber gloves rated for chemicals, not mere household rubber gloves, when handling toxins.

▲ *Always* wear appropriate gloves in situations in which your hands could be injured by rough surfaces, sharp edges, thorns, or poisonous plants.

▲ *Always* wear a disposable face mask or a special filtering respirator when creating sawdust or working with toxic gardening substances.

▲ *Always* keep your hands and other body parts away from the business ends of blades, cutters, and bits.

▲ *Always* obtain approval from local building officials before undertaking construction of permanent structures.

▲ *Never* work with power tools when you are tired or under the influence of alcohol or drugs.

▲ *Never* carry sharp or pointed tools, such as knives or saws, in your pockets. If you carry such tools, use special-purpose tool scabbards.

The Landscape Designers

John S. Troy is a landscape architect in San Antonio. His firm, under his own name, was founded in 1981 and specializes in residential landscape design. His designs have appeared in numerous books and magazines and have won several awards from the Texas Chapter of the American Society of Landscape Architects. In 2001, *Garden Design* magazine presented him with a Golden Trowel Award. His designs, done with his associate designer Anne Solsbery, appear on pp. 32–35, 80–83, and 88–91.

Rosa Finsley founded King's Creek Gardens, a Cedar Hill nursery and landscape design firm, in 1970. She has designed residential, public, and commercial gardens throughout Texas, including the Historic River Link for the Riverwalk in San Antonio. She is known for her naturalistic designs. Cheryl Bryant assisted Rosa in the designs shown on pp. 40–43, 56–59, and 68–71.

Mark Bowen is a landscape designer and co-founder, in 1987, of the Houston-based landscape design/build firm Living Art Landscapes. He has served as president of the community gardening group Urban Harvest. He writes a weekly column for the Houston *Chronicle* and is the author of several books. His designs appear on pp. 20–23, 48–51, and 60–63.

Michael Parkey has been a landscape architect and designer of gardens in north Texas since 1983. His special interests are resource-efficient landscapes and the use of native plants in gardens and restored habitats. In addition to his Dallas-based practice, he lectures and writes about design and teaches courses at Southern Methodist University. He has received awards from the City of Dallas and the American Society of Landscape Architects. His designs appear on pp. 28–31, 76–79, and 84–87.

John Ahrens is principal at King's Creek Landscape Management in Austin. His firm has worked throughout the Texas Hill Country, Colorado, and in the Austin and San Antonio areas. The firm specializes in indigenous stone work and water features, as well as in landscapes that include mostly native and "Texas tough" naturalized plantings. Barry Landry, RLA, and Nena Scott assisted John with the designs that appear on pp. 44–47, 52–55, 72–75, and 96–99.

Mary Wilhite and **Sharon Lee Smith** are co-owners of Blue Moon Gardens, a nursery near Tyler. Founded in 1984, the nursery specializes in herbs, perennials, cottage flowers, and Texas natives. Active in numerous professional organizations, Mary also writes a gardening column for the Fort Worth *Star-Telegram* and articles for regional garden magazines. Sharon, a horticulture graduate of Stephen F. Austin University, features heirloom and native plants in her designs, and she enjoys creating spectacular container gardens. Their designs appear on pp. 24–27, 36–39, 64–67, and 92–95.

Contents

PORTFOLIO OF DESIGNS

GUIDE TO INSTALLATION

PLANT PROFILES

About This Book

Of all the home-improvement projects homeowners tackle, few offer greater rewards than landscaping. Paths, patios, fences, arbors, and, most of all, plantings can enhance home life in countless ways, large and small, functional and pleasurable, every day of the year. At the main entrance, an attractive brick walkway flanked by eye-catching shrubs and perennials provides a cheerful send-off in the morning and welcomes you home from work in the evening. A carefully placed grouping of small trees, shrubs, and fence panels creates privacy on the patio or screens a nearby eyesore from view. An island bed showcases your favorite plants, while dividing the backyard into areas for several different activities.

Unlike some home improvements, landscaping can be as rewarding in the activity as in the result. Planting and caring for lovely shrubs, perennials, and other plants can afford years of enjoyment. And for those who like to build things, outdoor construction projects can be especially satisfying.

While the installation and maintenance of plants and outdoor structures are within the means and abilities of most people, few of us are as comfortable determining exactly which plants or structures to use and how best to combine them. It's one thing to decide to dress up the front entrance or patio, another to come up with a design for doing so.

That's where this book comes in. Here, in the Portfolio of Designs, you'll find designs for 20 common home-landscaping situations, created by landscape professionals who live and work in Texas. Drawing on years of experience, these designers balance functional requirements and aesthetic possibilities, choosing the right plant or structure for the task, confident of its proven performance in similar landscaping situations.

Complementing the Portfolio of Designs is the Guide to Installation, the book's second section, which will help you install and maintain the plants and structures called for in the designs. The third section, Plant Profiles, gives information on all the plants used in the book. The discussions that follow take a closer look at each section; we've also printed representative pages of the sections on pp. 9 and 10 and pointed out their features.

Portfolio of Designs

This section is the heart of the book, providing examples of landscaping situations and solutions that are at once inspiring and accessible. Some are simple, others more complex, but each one can be installed in a few weekends by homeowners with no special training or experience.

For each situation, we present two designs, the second a variation of the first. As the sample pages on the facing page show, the first design is displayed on a two-page spread. A perspective illustration (called a "rendering") depicts what the design will look like several years after installation, when the perennials and many of the shrubs have reached mature size. (For more on how plantings change as they age, see "As Your Landscape Grows," pp. 16–17.) The rendering also shows the planting as it will appear at a particular time of year. ("Seasons in Your Landscape," pp. 12–15, takes a look at changes within a single year.) A site plan indicates the positions of the plants and structures on a scaled grid. Text introduces the situation and the design and describes the plants and projects used.

The second design, presented on the second two-page spread, addresses the same situation as the first but differs in one or more important aspects. It might show a planting suited for a shady rather than a sunny site, or it might incorporate different structures or kinds of plants to create a different look. As in the first design, we present a rendering, site plan, and written information, but in briefer form. The second spread also includes photographs of a selection of the plants featured in the two designs. The photos showcase noteworthy qualities—lovely flowers, handsome foliage, or striking form—that these plants contribute to the designs.

Installed exactly as shown here, the designs will provide years of enjoyment. But individual needs and properties will differ, and we encourage you to alter the designs to suit your site and desires. Many types of alterations are easy to make. You can add or remove plants and adjust the sizes of paths, patios, and arbors to accommodate larger or smaller sites. You can rearrange groupings and substitute favorite plants to suit your taste. Or you can integrate the design with your existing landscaping. If you are uncertain about how to solve specific problems or about the effects of changes you'd like to make, consult with staff at a local nursery or with a landscape designer in your area.

Guide to Installation

In this section you'll find detailed instructions and illustrations covering all the techniques you'll need to install any design from start to finish. Here we explain how to think your way through a landscaping project and anticipate the various steps. Then you'll learn how to do each part of the job: readying the site; laying out the design; choosing materials; addressing basic irrigation needs; building paths, trellises, or other structures; preparing the soil

Portfolio of Designs

First Design Option
An overview of the situation and the design.

Rendering
Shows how the design will look when plants are well established.

Plants & Projects
Noteworthy qualities of the plants and structures and their contributions to the design.

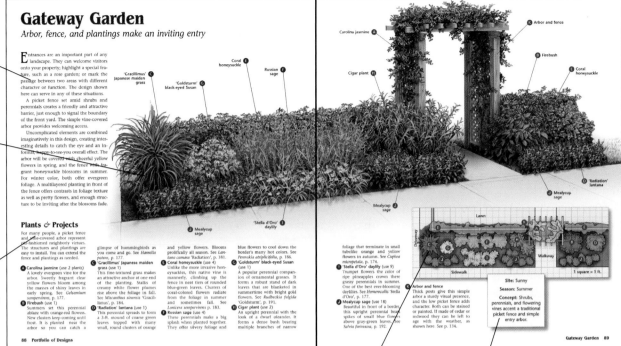

Second Design Option
Addressing the same situation as the first design, this variation may differ in design concept, site conditions, or plant selection.

Site Plan
Positions all plants and structures on a scaled grid.

Concept Box
Summarizes an important aspect of the design; tells whether the site is sunny or shady and what season is depicted in the rendering.

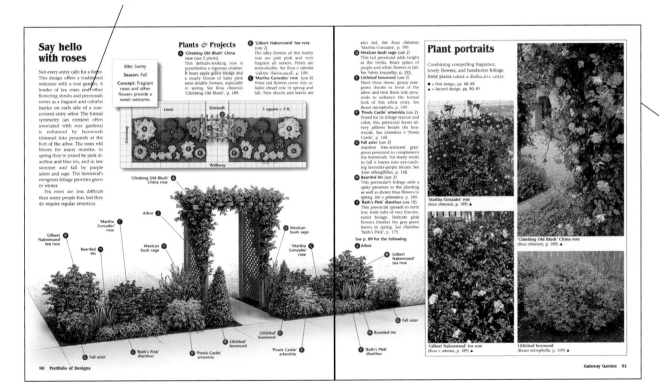

Plant Portraits
Photos of a selection of the plants used in both designs.

Guide to Installation

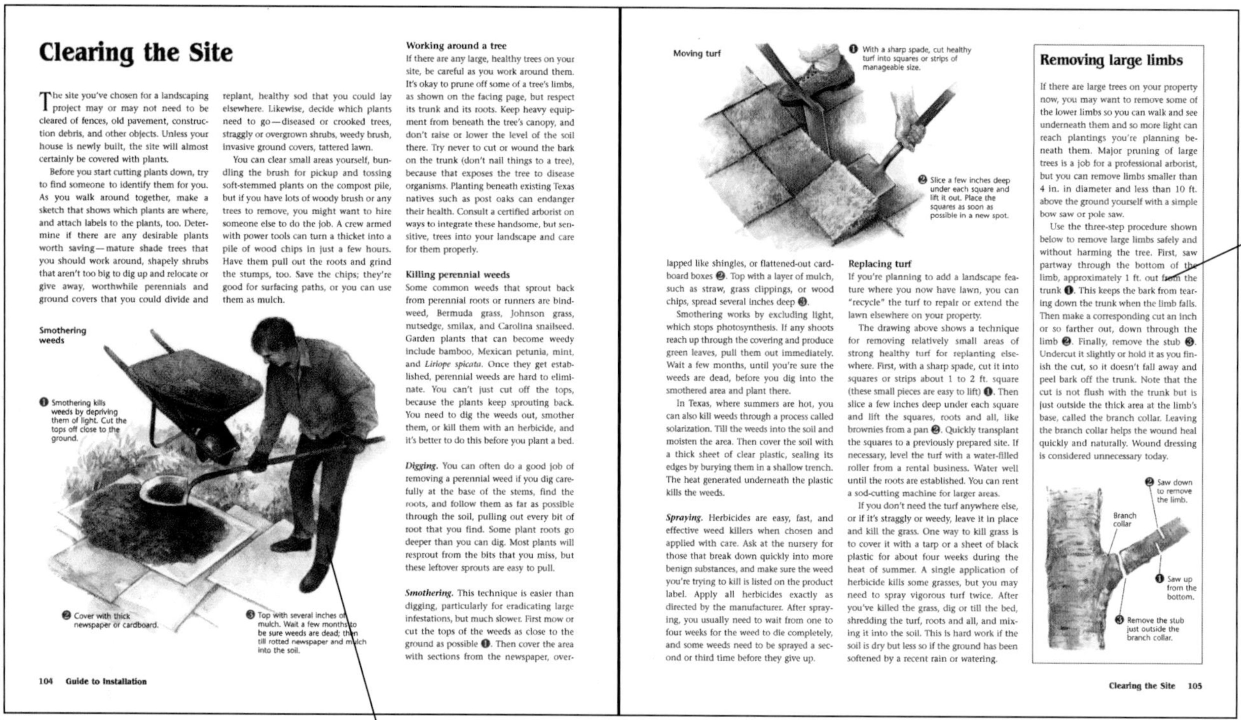

Clearing the Site

The site you've chosen for a landscaping project may or may not need to be cleared of fences, old pavement, construction debris, and other objects. Unless your house is newly built, the site will almost certainly be covered with plants.

Before you start cutting plants down, try to find someone to identify them for you. As you walk around together, make a sketch that shows which plants are where, and attach labels to the plants, too. Determine if there are any desirable plants worth saving—mature shade trees that you should work around, shapely shrubs that aren't too big to dig up and relocate or give away, worthwhile perennials and ground covers that you could divide and replant, healthy sod that you could lay elsewhere. Likewise, decide which plants need to go—diseased or crooked trees, straggly or overgrown shrubs, weedy brush, invasive ground covers, tattered lawn.

You can clear small areas yourself, bundling the brush for pickup and tossing soft-stemmed plants on the compost pile, but if you have lots of woody brush or any trees to remove, you might want to hire someone else to do the job. A crew armed with power tools can turn a thicket into a pile of wood chips in just a few hours. Have them pull out the roots and grind the stumps, too. Save the chips; they're good for surfacing paths, or you can use them as mulch.

Smothering weeds
❶ Smothering kills weeds by depriving them of light. Cut the tops off close to the ground.
❷ Cover with thick newspaper or cardboard.
❸ Top with several inches of mulch. Wait a few months to be sure weeds are dead; then till rotted newspaper and mulch into the soil.

Working around a tree

If there are any large, healthy trees on your site, be careful as you work around them. It's okay to prune off some of a tree's limbs, as shown on the facing page, but respect its trunk and its roots. Keep heavy equipment from beneath the tree's canopy, and don't raise or lower the level of the soil there. Try never to cut or wound the bark on the trunk (don't nail things to a tree), because that exposes the tree to disease organisms. Planting beneath existing Texas natives such as post oaks can endanger their health. Consult a certified arborist on ways to integrate these handsome, but sensitive, trees into your landscape and care for them properly.

Killing perennial weeds

Some common weeds that sprout back from perennial roots or runners are bindweed, Bermuda grass, Johnson grass, nutsedge, smilax, and Carolina snailseed. Garden plants that can become weedy include bamboo, Mexican petunia, mint, and *Liriope spicata*. Once they get established, perennial weeds are hard to eliminate. You can't just cut off the tops, because the plants keep sprouting back. You need to dig the weeds out, smother them, or kill them with an herbicide, and it's better to do this before you plant a bed.

Digging. You can often do a good job of removing a perennial weed if you dig carefully at the base of the stems, find the roots, and follow them as far as possible through the soil, pulling out every bit of root that you find. Some plant roots go deeper than you can dig. Most plants will resprout from the bits that you miss, but these leftover sprouts are easy to pull.

Smothering. This technique is easier than digging, particularly for eradicating large infestations, but much slower. First mow or cut the tops of the weeds as close to the ground as possible ❶. Then cover the area with sections from the newspaper, overlapped like shingles, or flattened-out cardboard boxes ❷. Top with a layer of mulch, such as straw, grass clippings, or wood chips, spread several inches deep ❸.

Smothering works by excluding light, which stops photosynthesis. If any shoots reach up through the covering and produce green leaves, pull them out immediately. Wait a few months, until you're sure the weeds are dead, before you dig into the smothered area and plant there.

In Texas, where summers are hot, you can also kill weeds through a process called solarization. Till the weeds into the soil and moisten the area. Then cover the soil with a thick sheet of clear plastic, sealing its edges by burying them in a shallow trench. The heat generated underneath the plastic kills the weeds.

Spraying. Herbicides are easy, fast, and effective weed killers when chosen and applied with care. Ask at the nursery for those that break down quickly into more benign substances, and make sure the weed you're trying to kill is listed on the product label. Apply all herbicides exactly as directed by the manufacturer. After spraying, you usually need to wait from one to four weeks for the weed to die completely, and some weeds need to be sprayed a second or third time before they give up.

Moving turf
❶ With a sharp spade, cut healthy turf into squares or strips of manageable size.
❷ Slice a few inches deep under each square and lift it out. Place the squares as soon as possible in a new spot.

Replacing turf

If you're planning to add a landscape feature where you now have lawn, you can "recycle" the turf to repair or extend the lawn elsewhere on your property.

The drawing above shows a technique for removing relatively small areas of strong healthy turf for replanting elsewhere. First, with a sharp spade, cut it into squares or strips about 1 to 2 ft. square (these small pieces are easy to lift) ❶. Then slice a few inches deep under each square and lift the squares, roots and all, like brownies from a pan ❷. Quickly transplant the squares to a previously prepared site. If necessary, level the turf with a water-filled roller from a rental business. Water well until the roots are established. You can rent a sod-cutting machine for larger areas.

If you don't need the turf anywhere else, or if it's straggly or weedy, leave it in place and kill the grass. One way to kill grass is to cover it with a tarp or a sheet of black plastic for about four weeks during the heat of summer. A single application of herbicide kills some grasses, but you may need to spray vigorous turf twice. After you've killed the grass, dig or till the bed, shredding the turf, roots and all, and mixing it into the soil. This is hard work if the soil is dry but less so if the ground has been softened by a recent rain or watering.

Removing large limbs

If there are large trees on your property now, you may want to remove some of the lower limbs so you can walk and see underneath them and so more light can reach plantings you're planning beneath them. Major pruning of large trees is a job for a professional arborist, but you can remove limbs smaller than 4 in. in diameter and less than 10 ft. above the ground yourself with a simple bow saw or pole saw.

Use the three-step procedure shown below to remove large limbs safely and without harming the tree. First, saw partway through the bottom of the limb, approximately 1 ft. out from the trunk ❶. This keeps the bark from tearing down the trunk when the limb falls. Then make a corresponding cut an inch or so farther out, down through the limb ❷. Finally, remove the stub ❸. Undercut it slightly or hold it as you finish the cut, so it doesn't fall away and peel bark off the trunk. Note that the cut is not flush with the trunk but is just outside the thick area at the limb's base, called the branch collar. Leaving the branch collar helps the wound heal quickly and naturally. Wound dressing is considered unnecessary today.

❷ Saw down to remove the limb.
Branch collar
❶ Saw up from the bottom.
❸ Remove the stub just outside the branch collar.

104 Guide to Installation

Clearing the Site 105

Sidebar
Detailed information on special topics, set within a ruled box.

Step-by-Step
Illustrations show process; steps are keyed by number to discussion in the main text.

Detailed Plant Information
Descriptions of each plant's noteworthy qualities and requirements for planting and care.

Plant Portraits
Photos of selected plants.

Plant Profiles

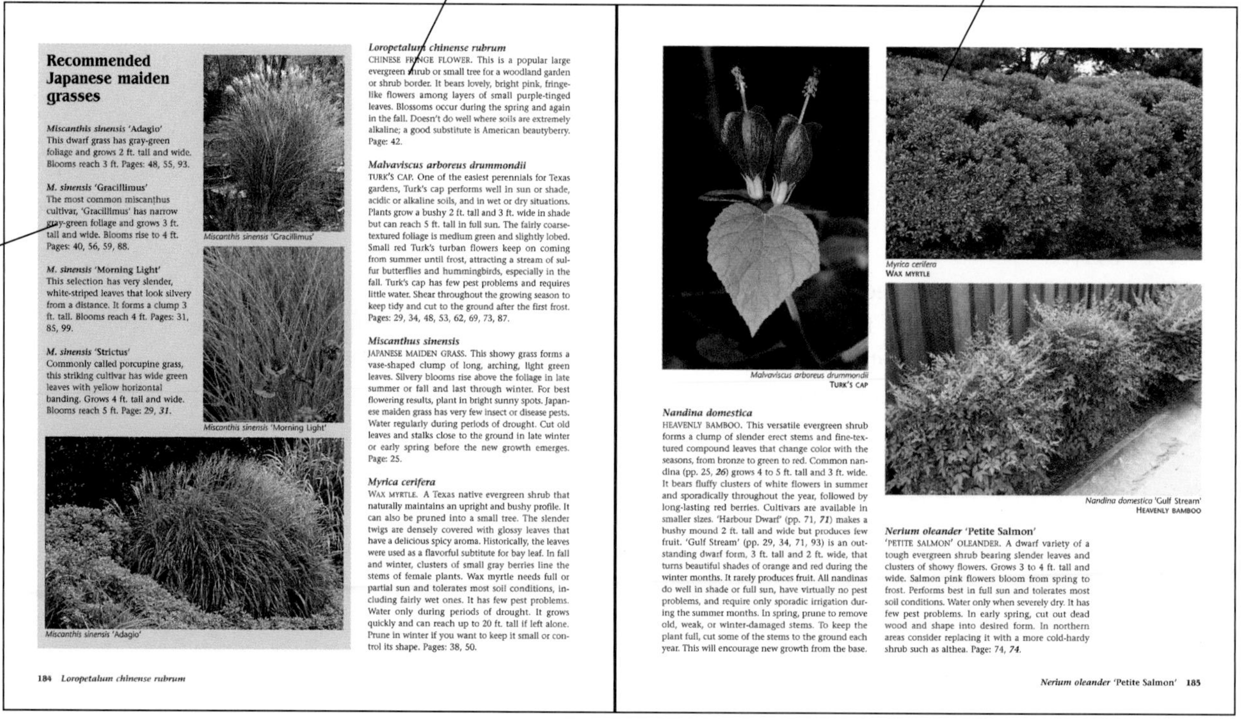

Recommended Japanese maiden grasses

***Miscanthis sinensis* 'Adagio'**
This dwarf grass has gray-green foliage and grows 2 ft. tall and wide. Blooms reach 3 ft. Pages: 48, 55, 93.

***M. sinensis* 'Gracillimus'**
The most common miscanthus cultivar, 'Gracillimus' has narrow gray-green foliage and grows 3 ft. tall and wide. Blooms rise to 4 ft. Pages: 40, 56, 59, 88.

***M. sinensis* 'Morning Light'**
This selection has very slender, white-striped leaves that look silvery from a distance. It forms a clump 3 ft. tall. Blooms reach 4 ft. Pages: 31, 85, 99.

***M. sinensis* 'Strictus'**
Commonly called porcupine grass, this striking cultivar has wide green leaves with yellow horizontal banding. Grows 4 ft. tall and wide. Blooms reach 5 ft. Page: 29, *31*.

Miscanthis sinensis 'Gracillimus'

Miscanthis sinensis 'Morning Light'

Miscanthis sinensis 'Adagio'

Loropetalum chinense rubrum
CHINESE FRINGE FLOWER. This is a popular large evergreen shrub or small tree for a woodland garden or shrub border. It bears lovely, bright pink, fringe-like flowers among layers of small purple-tinged leaves. Blossoms occur during the spring and again in the fall. Doesn't do well where soils are extremely alkaline; a good substitute is American beautyberry. Page: 42.

Malvaviscus arboreus drummondii
TURK'S CAP. One of the easiest perennials for Texas gardens, Turk's cap performs well in sun or shade, acidic or alkaline soils, and in wet or dry situations. Plants grow a bushy 2 ft. tall and 3 ft. wide in shade but can reach 5 ft. tall in full sun. The fairly coarse-textured foliage is medium green and slightly lobed. Small red Turk's turban flowers keep on coming from summer until frost, attracting a stream of sulfur butterflies and hummingbirds, especially in the fall. Turk's cap has few pest problems and requires little water. Shear throughout the growing season to keep tidy and cut to the ground after the first frost. Pages: 29, 34, 48, 53, 62, 69, 73, 87.

Miscanthus sinensis
JAPANESE MAIDEN GRASS. This showy grass forms a vase-shaped clump of long, arching, light green leaves. Silvery blooms rise above the foliage in late summer or fall and last through winter. For best flowering results, plant in bright sunny spots. Japanese maiden grass has very few insect or disease pests. Water regularly during periods of drought. Cut old leaves and stalks close to the ground in late winter or early spring before the new growth emerges. Page: 25.

Myrica cerifera
WAX MYRTLE. A Texas native evergreen shrub that naturally maintains an upright and bushy profile. It can also be pruned into a small tree. The slender twigs are densely covered with glossy leaves that have a delicious spicy aroma. Historically, the leaves were used as a flavorful subtitute for bay leaf. In fall and winter, clusters of small gray berries line the stems of female plants. Wax myrtle needs full or partial sun and tolerates most soil conditions, including fairly wet ones. It has few pest problems. Water only during periods of drought. It grows quickly and can reach up to 20 ft. tall if left alone. Prune in winter if you want to keep it small or control its shape. Pages: 38, 50.

Malvaviscus arboreus drummondii
TURK'S CAP

Myrica cerifera
WAX MYRTLE

Nandina domestica
HEAVENLY BAMBOO. This versatile evergreen shrub forms a clump of slender erect stems and fine-textured compound leaves that change color with the seasons, from bronze to green to red. Common nandina (pp. 25, *26*) grows 4 to 5 ft. tall and 3 ft. wide. It bears fluffy clusters of white flowers in summer and sporadically throughout the year, followed by long-lasting red berries. Cultivars are available in smaller sizes. 'Harbour Dwarf' (pp. 71, *71*) makes a bushy mound 2 ft. tall and wide but produces few fruit. 'Gulf Stream' (pp. 29, 34, 71, 93) is an outstanding dwarf form, 3 ft. tall and 2 ft. wide, that turns beautiful shades of orange and red during the winter months. It rarely produces fruit. All nandinas do well in shade or full sun, have virtually no pest problems, and require only sporadic irrigation during the summer months. In spring, prune to remove old, weak, or winter-damaged stems. To keep the plant full, cut some of the stems to the ground each year. This will encourage new growth from the base.

Nandina domestica 'Gulf Stream'
HEAVENLY BAMBOO

***Nerium oleander* 'Petite Salmon'**
'PETITE SALMON' OLEANDER. A dwarf variety of a tough evergreen shrub bearing slender leaves and clusters of showy flowers. Grows 3 to 4 ft. tall and wide. Salmon pink flowers bloom from spring to frost. Performs best in full sun and tolerates most soil conditions. Water only when severely dry. It has few pest problems. In early spring, cut out dead wood and shape into desired form. In northern areas consider replacing it with a more cold-hardy shrub such as althea. Page: 74, *74*.

184 *Loropetalum chinense rubrum*

Nerium oleander 'Petite Salmon' 185

Choices
Selections here help you choose from the many varieties of certain popular plants.

for planting; buying the recommended plants and putting them in place; and caring for the plants to keep them healthy and attractive year after year.

We've taken care to make installation of built elements simple and straightforward. The paths, trellises, and arbors all use basic, readily available materials, and they can be assembled by people who have no special skills or tools beyond those commonly used for home maintenance. The designs can be adapted easily to meet specific needs or to fit with the style of your house or other landscaping features.

Installing different designs requires different techniques. You can find the techniques that you need by following the cross-references in the Portfolio to pages in the Guide to Installation, or by skimming the Guide. You'll find that many basic techniques are reused from one project to the next. You might want to start with one of the smaller, simpler designs. Gradually you'll develop the skills and confidence to do any project you choose.

Most of the designs in this book can be installed in several weekends; some will take a little longer. Digging planting beds and erecting fences and arbors can be strenuous work. If you lack energy for such tasks, consider hiring a neighborhood teenager to help out; local landscaping services can provide more comprehensive help.

Plant Profiles

The final section of the book includes a description of each of the plants featured in the Portfolio. These profiles outline the plants' basic preferences for environmental conditions—such as soil, moisture, and sun or shade—and provide advice about planting and ongoing care.

Working with plant experts in Texas, we selected plants carefully, following a few simple guidelines: Every plant should be a proven performer in the state; once established, it should thrive without pampering. All plants should be available from a major local nursery or garden center. If they're not in stock, they could be ordered, or you could ask the nursery staff to recommend suitable substitutes.

In the Portfolio section, you'll note that plants are referred to by their common name but are cross-referenced to the Plant Profiles section by their latinized scientific name. While common names are familiar to many people, they can be confusing. Distinctly different plants can share the same common name, or one plant can have several different common names. Scientific names, therefore, ensure greater accuracy and are more appropriate for a reference section such as this. Although you can confidently purchase most of the plants in this book from local nurseries using the common name, knowing the scientific name allows you to ensure that the plant you're ordering is the same one shown in our design.

Texas and Surrounding Region: Hardiness Zones

This map is based on one developed by the U.S. Department of Agriculture. It divides Texas and its neighbors into "hardiness zones" based on minimum winter temperatures. While most of the plants in this book will survive the lowest temperatures in Zone 7, a few may not. These few are noted in the Plant Profiles descriptions, where we have usually suggested alternatives. When you buy plants, most will have "hardiness" designations corresponding to a USDA hardiness zone on the map. A Zone 7 plant, for example, can be expected to survive winter temperatures as low as 0°F, and it can be used with confidence in Zones 7 and 8 but not in the colder Zone 6. It is useful to know your zone and the zone designation of any plants that you wish to add to those in this book.

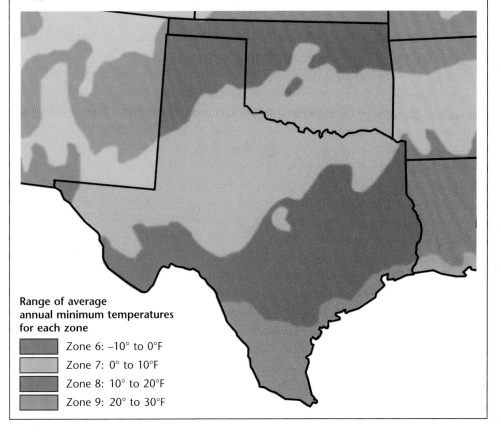

Range of average annual minimum temperatures for each zone

Zone 6: −10° to 0°F
Zone 7: 0° to 10°F
Zone 8: 10° to 20°F
Zone 9: 20° to 30°F

Seasons in Your Landscape

One of the rewards of landscaping is watching how plants change through the seasons. During the winter months, you look forward to the bright, fresh flowers of spring. Then the lush green foliage of summer is transformed into the blazing colors of fall. Perennials that rest underground in winter can grow chest-high by midsummer, and hence a flower bed that looks flat and bare in December becomes a jungle in July.

To illustrate typical seasonal changes, we've chosen one of the designs from this book (see pp. 64–65) and shown here how it would look in spring, summer, fall, and winter. As you can see, this planting looks different from one season to the next, but it always remains interesting. Try to remember this example of transformation as you look at the other designs in this book. There we show how the planting will appear in one season and call attention to any plants that will stand out at other times of year.

The task of tending a landscape also changes with the seasons. So we've noted the most important seasonal jobs in the annual work cycle.

Gaura

Dwarf pampas grass

Spring

Gaura

Dwarf pampas grass

Chaste tree

Soft-tip yucca

Trailing rosemary

Trailing rosemary

Summer

Chaste tree

Soft-tip yucca

Autumn sage

Gray santolina

Red yucca

Russian sage

Spring

The spring flower season begins in March in much of Texas and peaks in April when the lawns turn green and the trees leaf out. In this garden, spring offers a refreshing display of new growth. Grasses and perennials are greening up, and a thick profusion of new shoots sprout from the cut-back crown of the chaste tree. A sprinkling of miniature blue flowers on the rosemary and the gaura's pinkish white flower buds garnish the greenery. Do a thorough cleanup in early spring. Remove last year's perennial flower stalks and foliage, cut ornamental grasses to the ground, prune shrubs and trees, renew the mulch, lightly fertilize, and neaten the edges between flower beds and lawn.

Summer

The summer garden is an explosion of color. Nearly every plant is in bloom. The nodding lily-like flowers of the soft-tip yucca, the purple spikes of the chaste tree, and the coral red spikes of the red yucca make a big show. The diminutive blue, white, and yellow flowers of the Russian sage, gaura, and santolina shout less for attention but are no less pleasing. Despite its name, autumn sage produces a fine show of tubular red flowers. White plumes wave in the breeze above clumps of dwarf pampas grass. Water new plantings at least once a week during dry spells, and water older plants, too, if the soil gets so dry that they wilt. Pull any weeds that sprout up through the mulch; this is easiest when the soil is moist.

Fall

Fall brings changes in the garden as well as mercifully cooler temperatures. New for the season are the small lavender-purple flowers that almost smother the pale gray foliage of the fall aster. Deadheading has produced a full second bloom on the chaste tree, while distinctive seedpods have replaced bright flowers on the soft-tip and red yuccas. Gaura and autumn sage continue to bloom, and the plumes of the pampas grass reflect some weathering. The Russian sage has lost most of its tiny blossoms, but its foliage is an attractive, wispy presence. The santolina has been sheared to keep it tidy. You can leave grasses and perennial stalks standing all winter, if you choose, or clear them away whenever hard frosts turn them brown or knock them down. Toss the stems on the compost pile, along with any leaves that you rake up.

Fall

Gaura

Dwarf pampas grass

Autumn sage

Winter

Trailing rosemary

Chaste tree

Fall aster

Soft-tip yucca

Gray santolina

Red yucca

Russian sage

Trailing rosemary

Winter

In winter, when much of the landscape turns tan and brown, you appreciate evergreen plants such as the red and soft-tip yuccas, trailing rosemary, and santolina. After a hard frost, the Russian sage, fall aster, and gaura have been cut back to ground-hugging crowns. The narrow leaves and plumes of the dwarf pampas grass remain a pleasing sight throughout the winter, as do the branching forms of the chaste tree and autumn sage. In late winter, cut back these two plants in preparation for vigorous new growth in the spring.

As Your Landscape Grows

Landscapes change over the years. As plants grow, the overall look evolves from sparse to lush. Trees cast cool shade where the sun used to shine. Shrubs and hedges grow tall and dense enough to provide privacy. Perennials and ground covers spread to form colorful patches of foliage and flowers. Meanwhile, paths, arbors, fences, and other structures gain the comfortable patina of age.

Continuing change over the years—sometimes rapid and dramatic, sometimes slow and subtle—is one of the joys of landscaping. It is also one of the challenges. Anticipating how fast plants will grow and how big they will eventually become is difficult, even for professional designers, and it was a major concern in formulating the designs for this book.

To illustrate the kinds of changes to expect in a planting, these pages show one of the designs at three different "ages." Even though a new planting may look sparse at first, it will soon fill in. And because of careful spacing, the planting will look as good in ten to fifteen years as it does after three to five. It will, of course, look different, but that's part of the fun.

At Planting

'Spring Bouquet' viburnum

'Shi Shi Gashira' camellia

Wax myrtle

Polyantha rose

'Edward Goucher' glossy abelia

Three to Five Years

Tropical plumbago

'Shi Shi Gashira' camellia

'Edward Goucher' glossy abelia

'Bath's Pink' dianthus

'Blue Princess' verbena

'Indigo Spires' salvia

At Planting—Here's how the backyard hideaway (pp. 50–51) might appear immediately after a fall planting. The plants, of course, are small, though their size may vary from what we show here if you want to spend more for more mature trees and shrubs. The multitrunked wax myrtle looks like a bush rather than the small tree it will become. The viburnum, glossy abelia, and polyantha rose are several years from filling out their spaces or your expectations. With a good fall start and spring awakening, the perennials will make a creditable show next summer. The first year after planting, be sure to water during dry spells and to pull weeds that pop up through the mulch.

Three to Five Years—As shown here in fall, the planting has filled out nicely. Limbed up to about 5 ft., the wax myrtle provides shade for the bench, while the nearby shrubs have grown to make a comfy enclosure. The now well-established perennials join the shrubs in producing the blue and pink floral scene. Evergreen foliage of the wax myrtle, camellia, viburnum, and glossy abelia make this an attractive spot through the winter as well.

Ten to Fifteen Years—Shown again in fall, the planting has become even more of a hideaway with the passing years. The wax myrtle envelopes the site with its presence and its shade. The shrubs are fuller and larger, though kept in bounds by judicious pruning. The perennials have been divided several times since planting to keep them healthy and tidy looking. Their off-spring may feature in parts of the landscape elsewhere on the property.

Ten to Fifteen Years

Wax myrtle

'Spring Bouquet' viburnum

Tropical plumbago

'Shi Shi Gashira' camellia

Polyantha rose

'Blue Princess' verbena

'Indigo Spires' salvia

'Edward Goucher' glossy abelia

'Bath's Pink' dianthus

Portfolio
of Designs

This section presents designs for 20 situations common in home landscapes. You'll find designs to enhance entrances, decks, and patios. There are gardens of colorful perennials and shrubs, as well as structures and plantings that create shady hideaways, dress up nondescript walls, and even make a centerpiece of a lowly recycling area. Large color illustrations show what the designs will look like, and site plans delineate the layout and planting scheme. Texts explain the designs and describe the plants and projects appearing in them. Installed as shown or adapted to suit your site and personal preferences, these designs can make your property more attractive, more useful, and—most important—more enjoyable for you, your family, and your friends.

First Impressions

Make a pleasant passage to your front door

Site: Shady

Season: Spring

Concept: Easy-care plantings and a distinctive walkway enhance a home's main entrance.

Tropical plumbago **H**

'Yuletide' **C** sasanqua camellia

Dwarf **D** yaupon holly

Walkway **K**

Holly **G** fern

1 square = 1 ft.

Why wait until a visitor reaches the front door to extend a cordial greeting? An entryway landscape of well-chosen plants and a revamped walkway not only make the short journey a pleasant one, they can also enhance your home's most public face and help settle it comfortably in its surroundings.

In this design a flagstone walkway curves gracefully to the front door, creating a roomy planting bed near the house. Extending along the driveway, the paving makes it easier for passengers to get in and out of a car. Where the paving widens out at the front stoop, there's room for a welcoming bench sheltered by a small tree. Fragrant flowers and eye-catching foliage make the stroll to the door inviting, while providing interest to viewers inside the house and on the street.

The plants here are selected for a shady entry, one that gets less than six hours of sun a day. Flowers and foliage will keep the entry colorful and fragrant throughout the year. Redbud blossoms will join daffodils and dianthus in early spring, followed by columbine, plumbago, Mexican petunia, and gardenia. All but the gardenia continue to bloom well into fall. White daffodils and red camellias arrive in November and stay through the winter holidays.

Plants & Projects

Preparing the planting beds and laying the flagstone walkway are the main tasks in this design. Once plants are established, only seasonal cleanup and pruning are required.

A **Redbud** (use 1 plant)
Beginning with a splurge of tiny pink blossoms in early spring, this small deciduous tree is an eye-catching accent for many more months. Heart-shaped leaves are light green in summer and yellow in fall. See *Cercis canadensis*, p. 172.

B **'Daisy' gardenia** (use 2)
This desirable shrub will scent the entry with sweet white blossoms in May and June. Foliage stays fresh and glossy all year. See *Gardenia jasminoides* 'Daisy', p. 176.

C **'Yuletide' sasanqua camellia** (use 1)
This evergreen shrub or small tree grows 5 ft. tall and wears a thick coat of shimmering dark green leaves. Fragrant red flowers bloom in time for Christmas. See *Camellia sasanqua* 'Yuletide', p. 171.

D **Dwarf yaupon holly** (use 5)
These shrubs form neat low mounds of tiny, oval, evergreen leaves in front of the windows. Showy clusters of red berries decorate the foliage in winter. See *Ilex vomitoria* 'Nana', p. 179.

E **Dwarf Mexican petunia** (use 22)
The large lush leaves of this low-growing perennial emerge just in time to cover fading spring bulbs. Purple flowers bloom from the center of each plant all season. See *Ruellia brittoniana* 'Katie', p. 192.

F **Texas gold columbine** (use 3)
This perennial forms neat mounds of lacy foliage. Slender stalks bear delicate golden flowers in spring and summer. See *Aquilegia chrysantha hinckleyana*, p. 167.

G **Holly fern** (use 16)
An unusual evergreen fern with leathery, rather than lacy, fronds. The dark green glossy leaves add coarse-textured sheen under the redbud and along the walk. See Ferns: *Cyrtomium falcatum*, p. 176.

H **Tropical plumbago** (use 5)
Ideal as a ground cover beside the drive, this trouble-free perennial creates compact tufts of small, pointed, pale green leaves. Its clear blue flowers look cool and inviting next to the pavement, especially in summer heat. See *Plumbago auriculata*, p. 187.

I **'Bath's Pink' dianthus** (use 9)
This perennial creates a pretty border of fine-textured blue-green foliage topped in spring with masses of delicate and fragrant pink flowers. Leaves look fresh all year. See *Dianthus* 'Bath's Pink', p. 175.

J **'Ice Follies' daffodil** (use 27)
Scatter these bulbs on both sides of the walk for white flowers in spring. The spiky leaves are a nice blue-green. See Bulbs: *Narcissus pseudonarcissus* 'Ice Follies', p. 169.

K **Walkway**
Flagstones of random size and shape are perfect for the curved front walk and for the steppingstones into the front lawn. See p. 108.

L **Bench**
Extend your welcome beyond the front door with a comfortable bench next to the stoop.

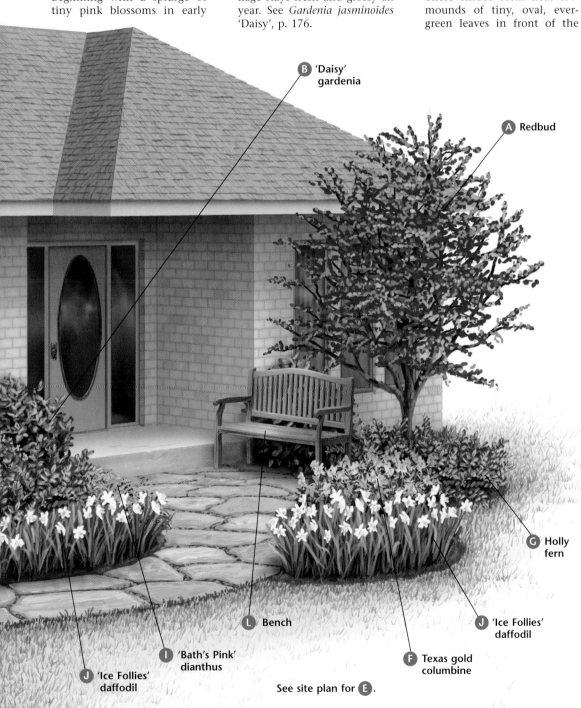

B 'Daisy' gardenia

A Redbud

G Holly fern

J 'Ice Follies' daffodil

L Bench

I 'Bath's Pink' dianthus

J 'Ice Follies' daffodil

F Texas gold columbine

See site plan for E.

Plant portraits

The attractive flowers and foliage of these shrubs and perennials will welcome visitors year-round.

● = First design, pp. 20–21
▲ = Second design, pp. 22–23

Althea (*Hibiscus syriacus*, p. 179) ▲

'Daisy' gardenia (*Gardenia jasminoides*, p. 176) ●

'Yuletide' sasanqua camellia (*Camellia sasanqua*, p. 171) ●

'Apple Blossom' yarrow (*Achillea millefolium*, p. 166) ▲

A sunny welcome

If your entrance is sunny, consider this design. Here, flagstone walkways invite visitors to stroll from the driveway to the front door along a choice of paths lined with eye-catching flowers and equally attractive foliage.

Many of these perennials bloom nonstop from spring to frost. Viburnum's fragrant white bouquets arrive early in March, and the lavender blossoms of aster appear in the fall, extending an already long season of bloom well into November. Handsome foliage, much of it evergreen, ensures interest all year. Like the planting in the previous design, this one needs only seasonal care.

Plants & Projects

Ⓐ Althea (use 1 plant)
A lavish floral display greets visitors when this deciduous shrub blooms in summer and fall. A cultivar with large lavender flowers suits this design well. Trim up about 3 ft. to make room for nearby plants. See *Hibiscus syriacus*, p. 179.

Ⓑ 'Spring Bouquet' viburnum (use 2)
This compact shrub has deep green foliage that stays attractive all year. Clusters of lightly scented white flowers open from pink buds in early spring. See *Viburnum tinus* 'Spring Bouquet', p. 198.

Ⓒ 'Belinda's Dream' rose (use 1)
This rose forms a lovely vase of glossy leaves and exquisite pink flowers. See *Rosa* × 'Belinda's Dream', p.189.

Ⓓ 'Edward Goucher' glossy abelia (use 3)
Small sparkling leaves line the arching branches of this evergreen shrub, turning from dark green to purple-bronze in winter. From spring to fall, clusters of honeysuckle-like pink blossoms dangle from all of the branches. See *Abelia* × *grandiflora*, 'Edward Goucher', p. 166.

Ⓔ Rosemary (use 3)
This low-growing evergreen shrub produces tiny pungent gray-green leaves. Whorls of equally aromatic blue flowers dot the shrub in late winter and early spring. See *Rosemarinus officinalis*, p. 191.

Ⓕ Daylily (use 16)
This mounding perennial trims the walk with slender grassy leaves and large trumpet-shaped flowers. There are many flower colors to choose from. We've shown a pale coral pink with a yellow throat. A soft yellow variety would work as well. See *Hemerocallis* hybrids, p. 177.

Ⓖ Fall aster (use 1)
Just one of these perennials will fill the space near the walkway with a dense stand of tiny gray-green leaves, blanketed all fall with small lavender daisylike flowers. See *Aster oblongifolius*, p. 168.

Ⓗ 'Apple Blossom' yarrow (use 7)
Fine feathery leaves and a lacework of tiny pink flowers that bloom for months makes this perennial an especially lovely companion for pink roses. See *Achillea millefolium* 'Apple Blossom', p. 166.

Ⓘ 'Homestead Purple' verbena (use 3)
This perennial forms a bright green mat of foliage that is covered from spring through fall with clusters of violet-purple flowers. See *Verbena* × *hybrida* 'Homestead Purple', p. 197.

Ⓙ 'Confetti' lantana (use 3)
A bushy perennial, it offers a festive mix of pink and yellow flowers throughout the growing season. Shear after bloom cycles. See *Lantana camara* 'Confetti', p. 181.

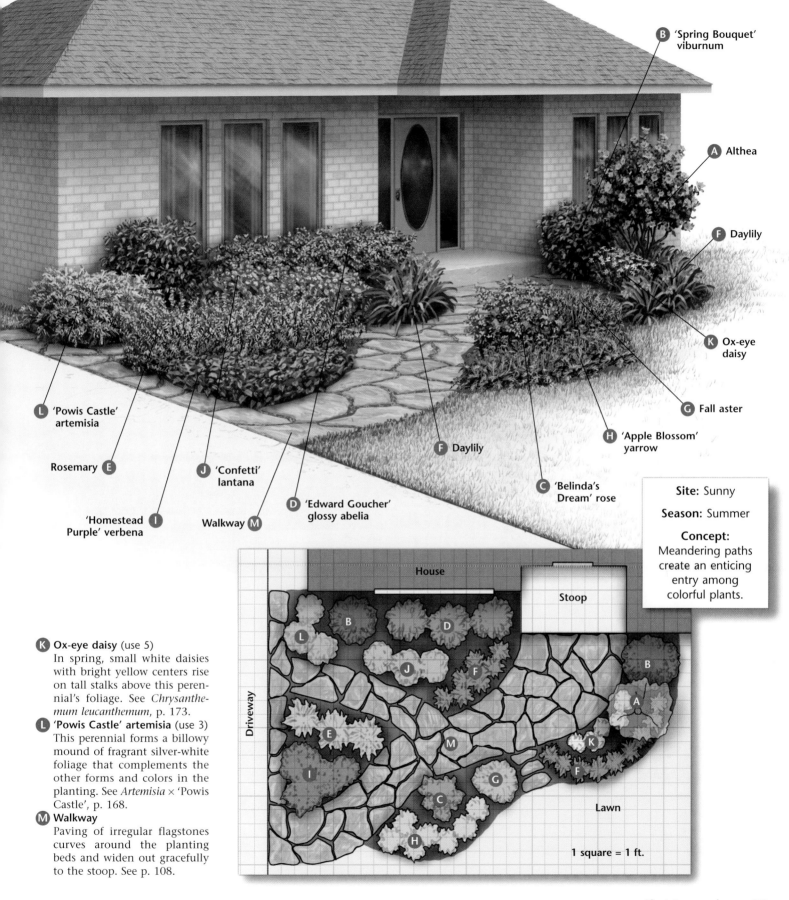

B 'Spring Bouquet' viburnum

A Althea

F Daylily

K Ox-eye daisy

G Fall aster

H 'Apple Blossom' yarrow

C 'Belinda's Dream' rose

F Daylily

M Walkway

D 'Edward Goucher' glossy abelia

J 'Confetti' lantana

I 'Homestead Purple' verbena

E Rosemary

L 'Powis Castle' artemisia

K **Ox-eye daisy** (use 5)
In spring, small white daisies with bright yellow centers rise on tall stalks above this perennial's foliage. See *Chrysanthemum leucanthemum*, p. 173.

L **'Powis Castle' artemisia** (use 3)
This perennial forms a billowy mound of fragrant silver-white foliage that complements the other forms and colors in the planting. See *Artemisia* × 'Powis Castle', p. 168.

M **Walkway**
Paving of irregular flagstones curves around the planting beds and widen out gracefully to the stoop. See p. 108.

Site: Sunny

Season: Summer

Concept: Meandering paths create an enticing entry among colorful plants.

House

Stoop

Driveway

Lawn

1 square = 1 ft.

First Impressions 23

A Foundation with Flair

Flowers and foliage create a front garden

Rare is the home without foundation plantings. These simple skirtings of greenery hide unattractive underpinnings and help integrate a house with its surroundings. Useful as these plantings are, they are too often monochromatic expanses of clipped evergreens, dull as dishwater. But, as this design shows, a low-maintenance foundation planting can be more varied, more colorful, and more fun.

By adding smaller plants in front of the taller shrubs near the house and including a small flowering tree, a mix of shrubs and perennials, and a flowering vine along the railing, the design transforms a foundation planting into a small garden. Here, there's something for everyone to enjoy, from porch sitters to passersby.

Starting in early spring with fragrant jasmine and rosemary and the eye-stopping flowers of the esperanza and

verbena, the garden reaches full exuberance in summer, with bright flowers in yellows, purples, blues, and oranges. Foliage in a mixture of greens and grays and a variety of textures showcases the flowers, several of which attract butterflies and hummingbirds. And the evergreen leaves of many plants extend the planting's appeal through the winter.

Site: Sunny

Season: Midsummer

Concept: Mixing small trees, vines, shrubs, and perennials makes a colorful foundation planting.

Carolina jasmine **J**

Firebush **C**

Japanese maiden grass **F**

'Blue Princess' verbena **H**

B Heavenly bamboo

D 'Gold Star' esperanza

I 'Goldsturm' black-eyed Susan

G 'Autumn Joy' sedum

A 'Catawba' crapemyrtle

C Firebush

H 'Blue Princess' verbena

B Heavenly bamboo

E Rosemary

F Japanese maiden grass

C Firebush

D 'Gold Star' esperanza

H 'Blue Princess' verbena

Plants & Projects

This is a low-care planting that offers a dazzling display of color in summer and fall. In addition to routine seasonal pruning, cut the firebush back in midsummer to keep it in check. If the verbena quits blooming, shear it back to about one-third to encourage new bloom. Train the jasmine up porch columns by attaching the vines to wires with twist ties. Add trellising if you want additional shade on the porch. For winter color in the beds, consider planting pansies or snapdragons when perennials fade.

A 'Catawba' crapemyrtle (use 1 plant)
Next to the steps, this small shrublike tree greets guests with showy purple flowers in summer and brilliant orange leaves in fall. See *Lagerstroemia indica* 'Catawba', p. 180.

B Heavenly bamboo (use 5)
The foliage of this evergreen shrub form lacy layers that take on burgundy tones in fall. Clusters of tiny white flowers in summer produce bright red berries that add interest in the winter. *See Nandina domestica*, p. 185.

C Firebush (use 6)
Small red-orange flowers light up this bushy tropical shrub in summer, attracting butterflies and hummingbirds as well as human admirers. See *Hamelia patens*, p. 177.

D 'Gold Star' esperanza (use 6)
Known also as Texas yellow bells, this shrub bears big bright clusters of yellow flowers from spring to fall, creating a colorful contrast with the crapemyrtle and firebush beside it. See *Tecoma stans* 'Gold Star', p. 196.

E Rosemary (use 2)
This shrubby perennial herb forms a tight bouquet of branches clad in small needlelike leaves and topped with small blue flowers in early spring. It makes a fragrant edging next to the steps, in easy reach to snip a few leaves for cooking. See *Rosmarinus officinalis*, p. 191.

F Japanese maiden grass (use 3)
A beautiful fine-textured grass that looks like a fountain. Flower plumes appear in late summer, and both leaves and flowers stay attractive through winter. See *Miscanthus sinensis*, p. 184.

G 'Autumn Joy' sedum (use 3)
This bold-textured perennial grows in neat mounds of grayish green succulent leaves. Dense clusters of tiny burnt orange flowers appear in fall, turn pink, and gradually fade to tan. See *Sedum* 'Autumn Joy', p. 194.

H 'Blue Princess' verbena (use 8)
Butterflies can't resist this perennial's lavender-blue flowers, which bloom continuously from spring to fall in clusters the size of silver dollars. See *Verbena × hybrida* 'Blue Princess', p. 197.

I 'Goldsturm' black-eyed Susan (use 4)
In early summer golden dark-eyed daisylike flowers rise above this perennial's deep green heart-shaped foliage. See *Rudbeckia fulgida* 'Goldsturm', p. 191.

J Carolina jasmine (use 3)
Shiny neat evergreen leaves and a show of fragrant yellow flowers in spring make this vigorous vine ideal for training up porch columns or along a railing. See *Gelsemium sempervirens*, p. 177.

Plant portraits

This mix of shrubs and perennials will dress up the most nondescript foundation, while requiring little care.

● = First design, pp. 24–25
▲ = Second design, pp. 26–27

Heavenly Bamboo
(*Nandina domestica*, p. 185) ●

'Catawba' crapemyrtle
(*Lagerstroemia indica*, p. 180) ●

Sasanqua camellia
(*Camellia sasanqua*, p. 171) ●

'Gumpo White' dwarf evergreen azalea
(*Rhododendron*, p. 189) ▲

'Wheeler's Dwarf' pittosporum
(*Pittosporum tobira*, p. 187) ▲

In a shady setting

This foundation planting graces a house with a shady entry. The mix of evergreen foliage and cool white flowers not only brightens up the shade, but also makes it even more welcome on a hot summer's day.

Foliage is the key here. The large jagged leaves of the fatsia and the more delicately cut fronds of the holly fern are striking accents. The less dramatic foliage of the camellia and evergreen azaleas is a highly effective backdrop for displaying the lovely flowers of these plants.

Lower-growing perennials and bulbs also contribute attractive foliage, and their flowers reinforce the planting's flowering color scheme of cool whites and pinks. With its mix of bold foliage and lovely flowers, this planting can be enjoyed from the windows as well as the street.

Plants & Projects

Ⓐ Sasanqua camellia (use 1 plant)
Lovely flowers and glossy leaves on this small evergreen tree will accent and soften the corner of the house. Camellias come in many sizes and flower colors. For this design, choose a late-blooming and tall-growing, white-flowered cultivar. See *Camellia sasanqua*, p. 171.

Ⓑ Fatsia (use 4)
This evergreen shrub hides its stems in layers of very large, shiny, bright green leaves. A handsome foundation plant, it also provides a bold contrast to the azaleas and ferns. See *Fatsia japonica*, p.175.

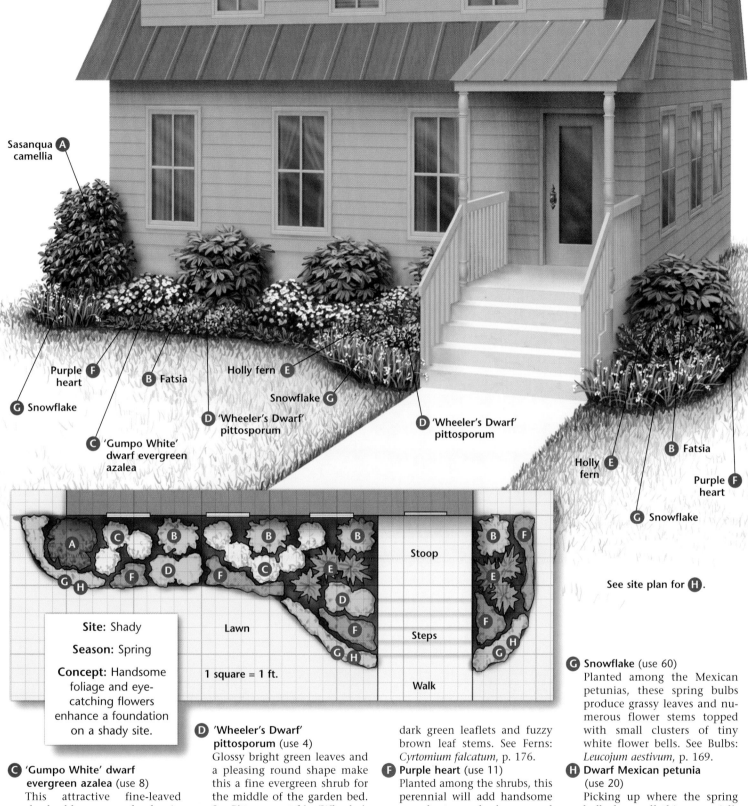

Sasanqua camellia **A**

Purple heart **F**

G Snowflake

B Fatsia

C 'Gumpo White' dwarf evergreen azalea

Holly fern **E**

Snowflake **G**

D 'Wheeler's Dwarf' pittosporum

D 'Wheeler's Dwarf' pittosporum

B Fatsia

Holly **E** fern

Purple **F** heart

G Snowflake

See site plan for **H**.

Site: Shady

Season: Spring

Concept: Handsome foliage and eye-catching flowers enhance a foundation on a shady site.

Stoop

Lawn

1 square = 1 ft.

Steps

Walk

C 'Gumpo White' dwarf evergreen azalea (use 8)
This attractive fine-leaved shrub blooms profusely in spring and is just the right size to tuck in under the windows. See *Rhododendron* × 'Gumpo White', p. 189.

D 'Wheeler's Dwarf' pittosporum (use 4)
Glossy bright green leaves and a pleasing round shape make this a fine evergreen shrub for the middle of the garden bed. See *Pittosporum tobira* 'Wheeler's Dwarf', p. 187.

E Holly fern (use 6)
This evergreen fern forms a dense patch of shiny, serrated, dark green leaflets and fuzzy brown leaf stems. See Ferns: *Cyrtomium falcatum*, p. 176.

F Purple heart (use 11)
Planted among the shrubs, this perennial will add handsome succulent purple leaves and showy pink flowers to the many greens of the summer garden. See *Setcreasea pallida* 'Purple Heart', p. 194.

G Snowflake (use 60)
Planted among the Mexican petunias, these spring bulbs produce grassy leaves and numerous flower stems topped with small clusters of tiny white flower bells. See Bulbs: *Leucojum aestivum*, p. 169.

H Dwarf Mexican petunia (use 20)
Picking up where the spring bulbs leave off, this perennial's elegant white blooms and dark leaves are on display from summer through fall. See *Ruellia brittoniana* 'Katie', p. 192.

Up Front Informal

Turn a small front yard into a welcoming garden

With a little imagination and a host of pleasing plants, front yards can be transformed into inviting front gardens. Replacing the existing lawn and concrete walkways with colorful plantings and decorative paving will not only reduce mowing and watering, it will also provide a pleasant setting for welcoming guests or watching the world go by.

The transformation from yard to garden begins here with an oversized front walk that widens into a space for sitting. The front walk and patio are tightly laid flagstone to accomodate heavy foot traffic and furniture. A more casual path to the drive is set with wide joints that are planted with a grasslike ground cover.

Bordering the seating area is an informal planting of trees and shrubs. The small red oak and two large hollies will create a cozy atmosphere around the entry, and the tree will provide shade as it matures. Beneath these taller plants are colorful shrubs, grasses, perennials, and a durable carpet of evergreen ground covers. While the ground covers won't stand up to much traffic, they will look good year-round with less water and maintenance than a turfgrass lawn.

The planting is illustrated here at its showiest—during the cooler months of fall—when the weather invites lingering outdoors. But each season holds attractions. An abundance of emerging foliage will give the garden a fresh look in spring, the Turk's cap blooms will invite hummingbirds in summer, and evergreen foliage and purple and red berries will keep color in the garden through winter.

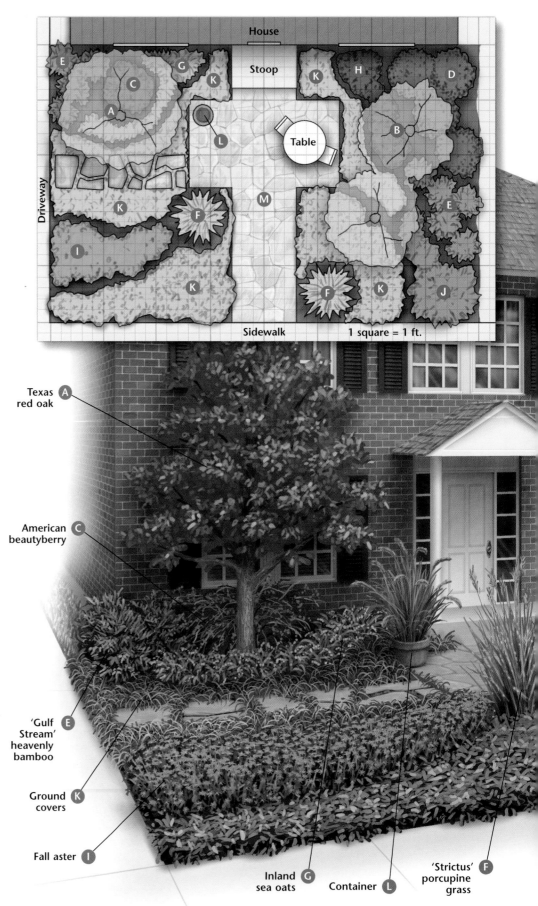

Texas red oak A

American beautyberry C

'Gulf Stream' heavenly bamboo E

Ground covers K

Fall aster I

Inland sea oats G

Container L

'Strictus' porcupine grass F

Plants & Projects

Once established, the plants in this design are not particularly demanding. Prune trees and shrubs as needed to maintain size and shape. Seasonal cleanup will keep the planting tidy.

Site: Sunny

Season: Fall

Concept: Well-chosen plants and paving create an entry garden of comfortable informality.

Ⓐ Texas red oak (use 1 plant)
Growing 30 ft. high and wide after many years, this red oak is a fitting shade tree for a small garden. It has silvery bark and lacy leaves that turn from green to red and orange in fall. See *Quercus buckleyi*, p. 188.

Ⓑ 'Warren's Red' possumhaw holly (use 2)
These multitrunked deciduous hollies have small lustrous dark green leaves. They bear countless showy red berries in fall that persist on bare silver-gray branches in the winter. See *Ilex decidua* 'Warren's Red', p. 179.

Ⓒ American beautyberry (use 1)
Prized for its bright clusters of violet berries that hang on through winter, this deciduous shrub spreads into a loose thicket of green leaves under the red oak. See *Callicarpa americana*, p. 171.

Ⓓ Dwarf Burford holly (use 4)
This durable shrub's glossy evergreen foliage and dense round shape create a handsome screen for the heavenly bamboo. Red berries peek through the foliage in winter. See *Ilex cornuta* 'Burfordii Nana', p. 179.

Ⓔ 'Gulf Stream' heavenly bamboo (use 9)
An outstanding evergreen shrub. Fine-textured foliage turns from bronze to green to red. See *Nandina domestica* 'Gulf Stream', p. 185.

Ⓕ 'Strictus' porcupine grass (use 2)
This ornamental grass forms a graceful vase of yellow-striped emerald green leaves. Silvery tan flower plumes wave above the plant in fall. The foliage and flowers stay showy even while the grass is dormant in winter. See *Miscanthus sinensis* 'Strictus', p. 184.

Ⓖ Inland sea oats (use 12)
A clump-forming grass grown for long, dangling, oatlike seedheads that dance above the foliage in late summer, turning from light green to bronze and then to tan. See *Chasmanthium latifolium*, p. 172.

Ⓗ Turk's cap (use 8)
Cousin to hibiscus, these bushy perennials make an attractive flowering hedge near the patio. Deep green foliage is speckled from late spring to fall with red blossoms resembling small Turkish turbans. See *Malvaviscus arboreus drummondii*, p. 184.

Ⓘ Fall aster (use 16)
These carefree perennials form a solid mass of fine-textured foliage completely covered in autumn with lavender-purple daisylike blossoms. See *Aster oblongifolius*, p. 168.

Ⓙ Mexican bush sage (use 7)
From late summer to frost, this grayish green bushy perennial bristles with long spikes of purple and white flowers. See *Salvia leucantha*, p. 193.

Ⓚ Ground covers (as needed)
Two low-growing evergreen perennials make durable "welcome mats" along the paths and around the patio. Asian jasmine (*Trachelospermum asiaticum*, p. 196) spreads to form a thick glossy carpet of small green leaves on both sides of the front walk. Mondo grass (*Ophiopogon japonicus*, p. 186) has fine dark green foliage that adds grassy texture around the patio and between the flagstones on the narrow walk to the driveway.

Ⓛ Container
Plant a patio pot with purple fountain grass for a fountain of foliage topped with foxtail-like flowers. See Annuals, p. 167.

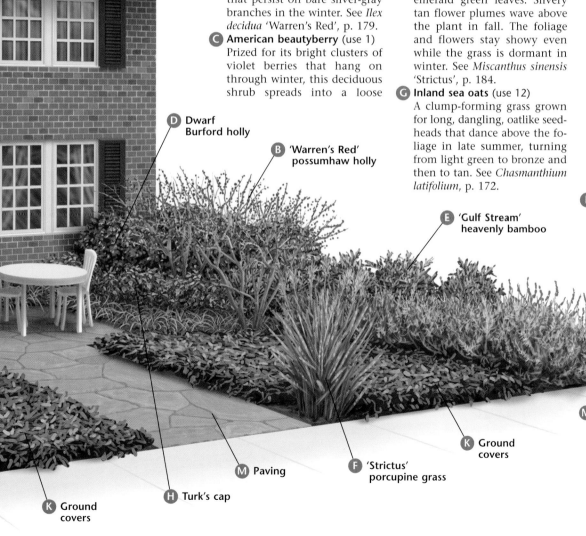

Ⓓ Dwarf Burford holly

Ⓑ 'Warren's Red' possumhaw holly

Ⓔ 'Gulf Stream' heavenly bamboo

Ⓙ Mexican bush sage

Ⓜ Paving

Ⓚ Ground covers

Ⓕ 'Strictus' porcupine grass

Ⓗ Turk's cap

Ⓚ Ground covers

Ⓜ Paving
A wide front walk of flagstone handles heavy foot traffic and outdoor furniture. A more casual flagstone path to the drive has wide joints filled with prepared soil and planted with mondo grass. See p. 108.

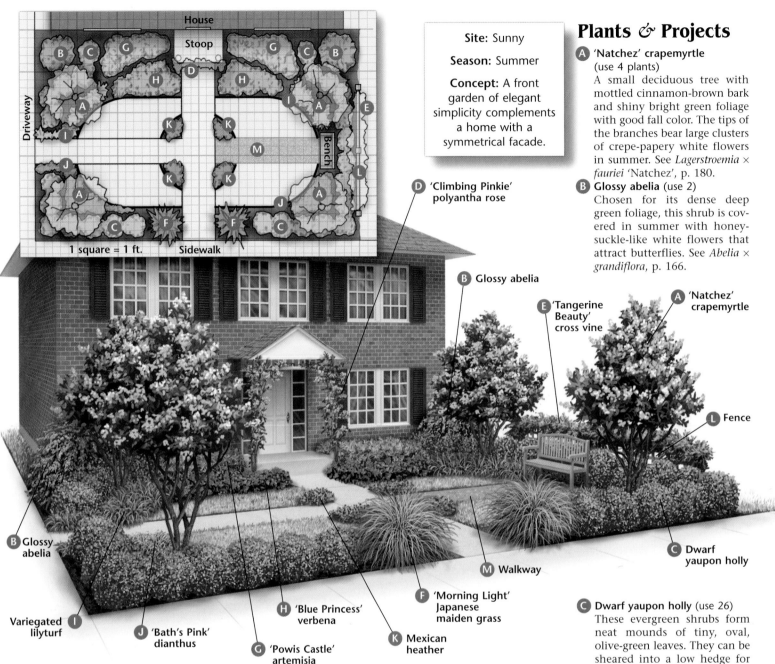

House

Stoop

Driveway

1 square = 1 ft.   Sidewalk

Site: Sunny

Season: Summer

Concept: A front garden of elegant simplicity complements a home with a symmetrical facade.

Plants & Projects

Ⓐ 'Natchez' crapemyrtle (use 4 plants)
A small deciduous tree with mottled cinnamon-brown bark and shiny bright green foliage with good fall color. The tips of the branches bear large clusters of crepe-papery white flowers in summer. See *Lagerstroemia × fauriei* 'Natchez', p. 180.

Ⓑ Glossy abelia (use 2)
Chosen for its dense deep green foliage, this shrub is covered in summer with honeysuckle-like white flowers that attract butterflies. See *Abelia × grandiflora*, p. 166.

Ⓓ 'Climbing Pinkie' polyantha rose

Ⓑ Glossy abelia

Ⓔ 'Tangerine Beauty' cross vine

Ⓐ 'Natchez' crapemyrtle

Ⓛ Fence

Ⓒ Dwarf yaupon holly

Ⓜ Walkway

Ⓕ 'Morning Light' Japanese maiden grass

Ⓚ Mexican heather

Ⓗ 'Blue Princess' verbena

Ⓖ 'Powis Castle' artemisia

Ⓙ 'Bath's Pink' dianthus

Ⓘ Variegated lilyturf

Ⓑ Glossy abelia

Ⓒ Dwarf yaupon holly (use 26)
These evergreen shrubs form neat mounds of tiny, oval, olive-green leaves. They can be sheared into a low hedge for an even more formal appearance. See *Ilex vomitoria* 'Nana', p. 179.

Ⓓ 'Climbing Pinkie' polyantha rose (use 2)
A mannerly, thornless, climbing rose that bears loose clusters of pink, semi-double flowers from April through November. See *Rosa × polyantha* 'Climbing Pinkie', p. 189.

Ⓔ 'Tangerine Beauty' cross vine (use 3)
This twining vine will cover the fence with lustrous, dark

Up front formal

Homes that have a symmetrical facade are especially suited for a formal garden makeover, one that complements and accents the geometry of the architecture. This design offers a simpler makeover than the first by retaining existing concrete walks. The symmetrical layout features a central oval of lawn flanked by almost mirror image plantings on each side of the main walk. A loose-surface path extends the cross walk to a garden bench, a perfect perch for enjoying the view.

Whether approaching from the street or the drive, visitors get an attractive welcome. Small flowering trees and a hedge of low-growing shrubs give the garden its structure. A variety of contrasting foliage textures and colors provide considerable interest year-round. And there are abundant roses and other flowers in spring and summer.

green leaves all year. Bears red-orange trumpet-shaped flowers in late spring and again in fall. See *Bignonia capreolata* 'Tangerine Beauty', p. 169.

F **'Morning Light' Japanese maiden grass** (use 2)
This lovely grass has slender foliage and a fountainlike shape. See *Miscanthus sinensis* 'Morning Light', p. 184.

G **'Powis Castle' artemisia** (use 14)
Silvery mounds of lacy foliage make this evergreen perennial an outstanding choice next to the lavender-blue verbena and the pink-blooming climbing rose. See *Artemisia* × 'Powis Castle', p. 168.

H **'Blue Princess' verbena** (use 16)
This perennial forms a fine mat of deep green leaves topped with masses of tiny lavender-blue flowers. Especially showy in spring. See *Verbena* × *hybrida* 'Blue Princess', p. 197.

I **Variegated lilyturf** (use 50)
This evergreen ground cover forms grassy clumps of slender leaves striped bright green and creamy yellow. Bears spikes of very small lavender flowers in June. See *Liriope muscari* 'Variegata', p. 183.

J **'Bath's Pink' dianthus** (use 44)
A fine-textured perennial that forms a mat of silver-gray foliage all year. Topped in spring with pretty pink flowers. See *Dianthus* 'Bath's Pink', p. 175.

K **Mexican heather** (use 12)
For texture as well as color, plant in the circular bed where the walks intersect. This tender perennial forms a low bush of tiny leaves in fernlike fans and delicate lavender-pink flowers. See *Cuphea hyssopifolia*, p. 174.

L **Fence**
Interlaced with flowering vines, the lattice-panel fence behind the bench creates a sense of privacy, as well as a focal point for the garden. See p. 131.

M **Walkway**
A loose surface of decomposed granite extends the existing walkway to the bench and provides a level surface beneath it. See p. 108.

Plant portraits

These well-behaved plants require little care while garnering lots of attention.

● = First design, pp. 28–29
▲ = Second design, pp. 30–31

Variegated lilyturf
(*Liriope muscari* 'Variegata', p. 183) ▲

'Strictus' porcupine grass
(*Miscanthus sinensis*, p. 184) ●

'Natchez' crapemyrtle
(*Lagerstroemia* × *fauriei*, p. 180) ▲

'Climbing Pinkie' polyantha rose
(*Rosa* × *polyantha*, p. 189) ▲

Dwarf Burford holly
(*Ilex cornuta* 'Burfordii Nana', p. 179) ●

'Warren's Red' possumhaw holly
(*Ilex decidua*, p. 179) ●

An Eye-Catching Corner

Beautify a boundary with easy-care plants

The corner where your property meets your neighbor's and the sidewalk is often a kind of grassy no-man's-land. This design defines that boundary with a planting that can be enjoyed by property owners, as well as passersby. Good gardens make good neighbors, so we've used well-behaved, low-maintenance plants that take the heat and won't make extra work for the person next door—or for you.

Because of its exposed location, remote from the house and close to the street, this is a less personal planting than those in more private and frequently used parts of your property. It is meant to be appreciated from a distance. Dramatic foliage and flowers are the key. At the center is the strikingly bold century plant. Playing off its coarse texture and gray tones are the gray-green foliage of the Mexican bush sage, gaura, and yucca. A patchwork blanket of blooms in yellow, orange, red, and purple offers cheery contrast to the foliage all season long.

Century plant **A**

'Radiation' lantana **E**

'Gold Star' esperanza **B**

Red yucca **D**

Edging **I**

'Homestead Purple' verbena **H**

Plants & Projects

As befits a planting that is some distance from the house, these durable, reliable plants are heat and drought tolerant, requiring little care beyond seasonal pruning and cleanup.

A **Century plant** (use 1 plant)
This regal perennial makes a striking centerpiece with its wide silvery blue leaves ending in single dark purple spines. See *Agave americana*, p. 167.

B **'Gold Star' esperanza** (use 1)
Clusters of yellow bell-shaped flowers adorn every branch of this bushy tropical shrub from summer to frost. Attractive bright green leaves. See *Tecoma stans* 'Gold Star', p. 196.

C **Mexican bush sage** (use 2)
This big bushy perennial fills the space behind the century plant with fine green-gray foliage. In fall the plant is topped with long spikes of lavender and white flowers. See *Salvia leucantha*, p. 193.

D **Red yucca** (use 3)
This evergreen perennial bears 3-ft. stalks of coral-red, trumpet-shaped flowers all season. They bloom above clumps of succulent gray-green foliage. See *Hesperaloe parviflora*, p. 178.

E **'Radiation' lantana** (use 1)
Round clusters of tiny bright orange and yellow flowers blanket this spreading perennial throughout the growing season. See *Lantana camara* 'Radiation', p. 181.

F **'New Gold' lantana** (use 3)
This lantana cultivar spreads even more cheer with masses of tiny golden yellow flowers covering dark green foliage. See *Lantana × hybrida* 'New Gold', p. 181.

G **Gaura** (use 3)
An outstanding Texas native, this fine-textured perennial softens the planting with airy masses of small pink and white flowers. They float above the countless stems like tiny butterflies. See *Gaura lindheimeri*, p. 176.

H **'Homestead Purple' verbena** (use 3)
Vibrant purple flowers top this perennial's clump of bright green foliage, forming a colorful mat in front of the century plant. See *Verbena × hybrida* 'Homestead Purple', p. 197.

I **Edging**
This decorative border of weathered-grey stones harmonizes with the colors of the foliage and flowers. See p. 110.

See site plan for **C**.

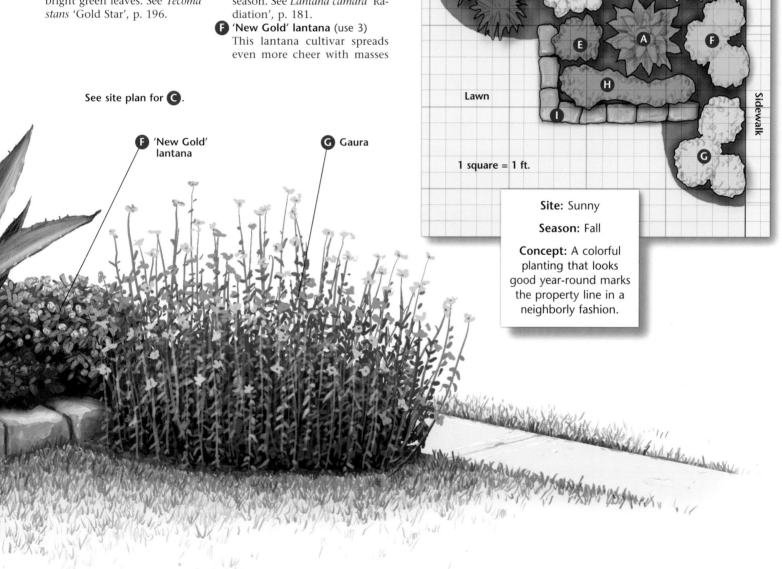

F 'New Gold' lantana

G Gaura

Lawn

Sidewalk

1 square = 1 ft.

Site: Sunny

Season: Fall

Concept: A colorful planting that looks good year-round marks the property line in a neighborly fashion.

A comfortable corner

Why not make the most of a shady corner with a welcoming garden bench under a small tree? Framed in by evergreen shrubs and perennials, the design offers a cosy corner for conversing with the neighbors, reading a book, or just sitting and relaxing. A small mound, or "berm," next to the walk helps nestle the bench into the garden setting. (Planted with sedum and daisies, this berm is about 12 in. above grade.) Two or three steppingstones edge the bench.

Viewed up close or from a distance, the planting offers color in every season: spring blossoms in a palette of pastels; vivid blue, gold, and red flowers in summer; fall foliage and flowers in yellows, pinks, and bronzes; and for winter, evergreens and plenty of cheerful red berries.

Plants & Projects

A Texas redbud (use 1 plant)
This lovely small tree provides a pleasant canopy for bench-sitters in every season. A profusion of small pink blossoms line bare branches in early spring, giving way to shiny heart-shaped green leaves scattered with light-green bean pods in summer, and bright yellow leaves in fall. Hints of violet-purple on the gray bark brighten up the branches in dull winter months. See *Cercis texensis*, p. 172.

B 'Gulf Stream' heavenly bamboo (use 3)
Prized for its lacy tiers of colorful foliage—emerald green and tipped with orange-bronze new growth in summer, taking on burgundy tones in fall and winter—these compact evergreen shrubs create a decorative fringe behind the bench and along the property line. They bear bright red berries in winter. See *Nandina domestica* 'Gulf Stream', p. 185.

C Turk's cap (use 1)
A Texas favorite, this perennial forms a low bush of large

Site: Afternoon shade

Season: Summer

Concept: A bench and pleasing plants provide a shady spot for catching up on neighborhood news.

1 square = 1 ft.

See site plan for **G**.

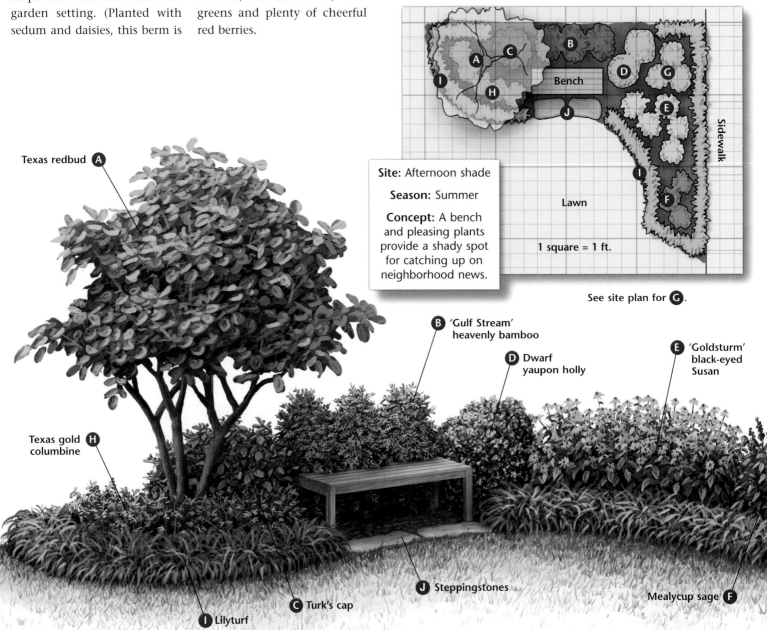

Texas redbud **A**

Texas gold columbine **H**

B 'Gulf Stream' heavenly bamboo

D Dwarf yaupon holly

E 'Goldsturm' black-eyed Susan

J Steppingstones

Mealycup sage **F**

C Turk's cap

I Lilyturf

heart-shaped leaves and red turban-like flowers in summer. Hummingbirds attracted to the flowers will hover near the bench. Other birds may stop by for the cherrylike berries. See *Malvaviscus arboreus drummondii*, p. 184.

D **Dwarf yaupon holly** (use 2)
This compact evergreen shrub forms a fine-textured globe of olive-green leaves that are free of spines. See *Ilex vomitoria* 'Nana', p. 179.

E **'Goldsturm' black-eyed Susan** (use 5)
Masses of golden "daisies" with dark eyes cover the coarse-leaves of this sturdy perennial in early summer. See *Rudbeckia fulgida* 'Goldsturm', p. 191.

F **Mealycup sage** (use 3)
An erect bushy perennial with narrow gray-green leaves. Its many flower spikes are lined with small deep blue blossoms from spring to fall. See *Salvia farinacea*, p. 192.

G **'Autumn Joy' sedum** (use 3)
A bold-textured perennial that grows in mounds of dull gray succulent leaves. Tight clusters of tiny buds open pink and fade to tan. See *Sedum* 'Autumn Joy', p. 194.

H **Texas gold columbine** (use 5)
This perennial's lacy, fernlike leaves form dainty mounds. Yellow-gold flowers nod above the foliage from late spring through summer. See *Aquilegia chrysantha hinckleyana*, p. 167.

I **Lilyturf** (use 46)
This evergreen perennial creates a lush low fringe around the border. See *Liriope muscari*, p. 183.

J **Steppingstones**
Gray flagstones provide a place to rest your feet. See p. 113.

I Lilyturf

Plant portraits

These tough plants provide a splash of color for many months in exchange for just a minimum of care.

● = First design, pp. 32–33
▲ = Second design, pp. 34–35

Century plant
(*Agave americana*, p. 167) ●

Dwarf yaupon holly
(*Ilex vomitoria* 'Nana', p. 179) ▲

Texas redbud
(*Cercis texensis*, p. 172) ▲

Mexican bush sage (*Salvia leucantha*, p. 193) ●

Lilyturf (*Liriope muscari*, p. 183) ▲

Streetwise and Stylish

Give your curbside strip a new look

Site: Sunny

Season: Fall

Concept: Plants with striking foliage and flowers transform an often neglected area and treat visitors and passersby to a colorful display.

Homeowners seldom give a thought to the part of their property adjacent to the street. Often bounded by a sidewalk, this area is at best a tidy patch of lawn and at worst a weed-choked eyesore. Yet this is one of the most public parts of many properties. Filling this strip with attractive plants and paths from street to sidewalk can give pleasure to passersby and visitors who park next to the curb, as well as enhancing the streetscape you view from the house. (Curbside strips are usually city-owned, so check local ordinances for restrictions before you start a remake.)

This can be a difficult site, subject to summer heat and drought, pedestrian and car traffic, and errant dogs. Plants need to be tough and drought-tolerant to perform well here. (Many towns and cities encourage water-conserving plantings in curbside areas.)

The plants in this design meet both criteria. And they look good, too. There are flowers from late winter to frost in the fall. Foliage in a variety of complementary shades and texture, much of it evergreen, keeps the curbside looking attractive through winter. The 4-ft.-wide path allows ample room for passengers getting in and out of a car.

If your curbside property doesn't include a sidewalk, you can extend the planting farther into the yard and connect the path to the walkway leading to your front door.

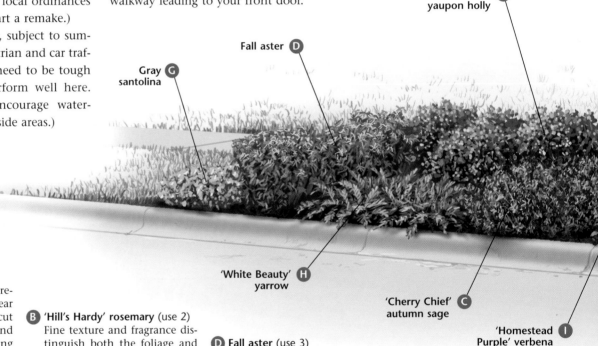

Dwarf yaupon holly A

Fall aster D

Gray santolina G

'White Beauty' yarrow H

'Cherry Chief' autumn sage C

'Homestead Purple' verbena I

Plants & Projects

Once established, these plants require very little care. You can shear off spent flowers, or, better yet, cut and dry the sage, santolina, and rosemary flowers for long-lasting arrangements. An occasional trim will keep the artemisia tidy. Prune the gaura to the ground after a freeze. Cut back the old stems of santolina in early spring.

A Dwarf yaupon holly
(use 5 plants)
This evergreen shrub forms a dense, rounded globe of tiny, spineless, oval leaves that never need shearing. See *Ilex vomitoria* 'Nana', p. 179.

B 'Hill's Hardy' rosemary (use 2)
Fine texture and fragrance distinguish both the foliage and flowers of this upright evergreen shrub. Blue flowers arrive in early spring. See *Rosmarinus officinalis*, p. 191.

C 'Cherry Chief' autumn sage (use 3)
This bushy perennial's small oval leaves echo the holly's foliage, but are softer and paler. Small red flowers bloom heavily in spring and lightly in summer and fall. See *Salvia greggii* 'Cherry Chief', p. 192.

D Fall aster (use 3)
Lavender-purple daisies literally blanket this carefree perennial's small dull green leaves in early summer. See *Aster oblongifolius*, p. 168.

E 'Dauphin' gaura (use 3)
With straight stems rising from a base of small pale green leaves and delicate pink and white flowers, this tall perennial adds an airy presence to the planting. See *Gaura lindheimeri* 'Dauphin', p. 176.

F 'Powis Castle' artemisia (use 4)
Prized for its foliage, this perennial forms a dense billowing mound of very fine silvery leaves. See *Artemisia* × 'Powis Castle', p. 168.

G Gray santolina (use 8)
This perennial spreads to form a low, dense cushion of fragrant gray leaves along the curb.

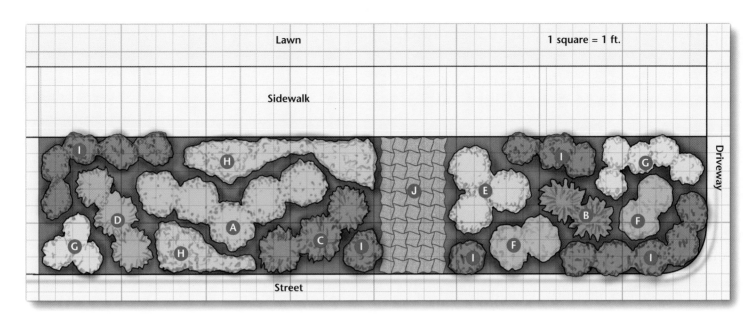

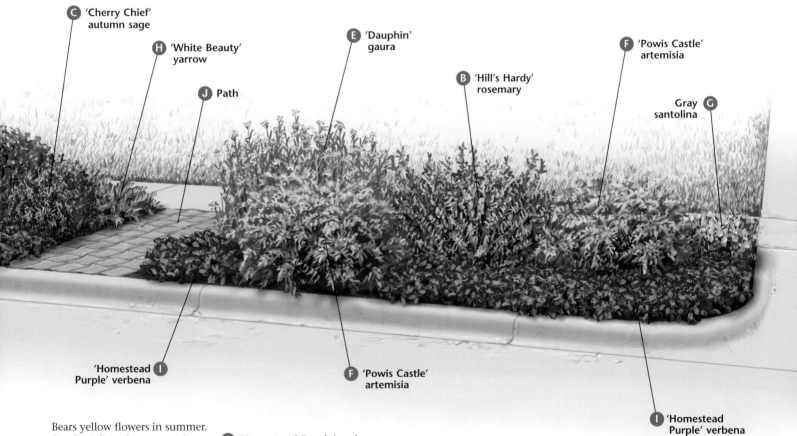

C 'Cherry Chief' autumn sage

H 'White Beauty' yarrow

J Path

E 'Dauphin' gaura

B 'Hill's Hardy' rosemary

F 'Powis Castle' artemisia

Gray santolina **G**

I 'Homestead Purple' verbena

F 'Powis Castle' artemisia

I 'Homestead Purple' verbena

Bears yellow flowers in summer. See *Santolina chamaecyparissus*, p. 193.

H **'White Beauty' yarrow** (use 13) The white flowers of this mat-forming perennial edge the walk in spring. Ferny leaves are green all year. See *Achillea mille-folium* 'White Beauty', p. 166.

I **'Homestead Purple' verbena** (use 15) This perennial's deeply cut bright green leaves and masses of purple flowers will enliven the curbside from spring to frost. See *Verbena × hybrida* 'Homestead Purple', p. 197.

J **Path** Interlocking pavers create an attractive, durable, and easily maintained surface. The gray paver shown here ties in with the sidewalk, street, and plant-ing. See p. 108.

Branching out

A small tree and a branching path distinguish this design and give it an informal appeal. The evergreen and long-lasting deciduous foliage of the shrubs and perennials is colorful year-round, mixing shades of green, gray, red, and purple. Flowers in white, pink, and yellow complement the foliage and are pretty in their own right.

Like the previous design, this one is a low-maintenance, low-water-use planting. It requires little more than shearing off spent flowers, trimming back the lantana after a freeze, and lightly pruning the spirea and barberry to maintain their size and shape.

Plants & Projects

A **Wax myrtle** (use 1 plant)
A graceful shrub that can be pruned into a shapely multi-trunked tree. In most parts of Texas, foliage stays green through the winter. See *Myrica cerifera*, p. 184.

B **'Anthony Waterer' Japanese spirea** (use 1)
Clusters of pink flowers top the fine-leaved branches of this attractive deciduous shrub in summer. Needs only light shearing to keep its rounded shape. See *Spirea × bumalda* 'Anthony Waterer', p. 194.

C **Dwarf Japanese barberry** (use 6)
This compact shrub has arching branches crowded with small oval maroon-red leaves.

See *Berberis thunbergii* 'Crimson Pygmy', p. 169.

D **Purple wintercreeper** (use 4)
This spreading evergreen ground cover fills in the space by the walk with handsome dark green leaves that turn red in winter. See *Euonymus fortunei* 'Coloratus', p. 175.

E **'Weeping White' trailing lantana** (use 13)
Clusters of pure white flowers cover this vigorous low-growing perennial from spring to fall. In mild-winter areas plant sometimes blooms all year. See

Lantana montevidensis 'Weeping White', p. 181.

F **St. John's wort** (use 13)
Under the wax myrtle, this evergreen shrub creates a dense, fine-textured carpet, dotted in summer with bright yellow periwinkle-like flowers. Small oval leaves turn reddish purple in winter. See *Hypericum calycinum*, p. 179.

G **'Bath's Pink' dianthus** (use 7)
Delightfully fragrant pink flowers greet visitors in spring. The rest of the year this perennial's fine blue-green foliage attracts all the attention. See *Dianthus* 'Bath's Pink', p. 175.

See p. 37 for the following:

H Path

Site: Sunny

Season: Summer

Concept: Two streetside paths join up with colorful plantings to welcome visitors.

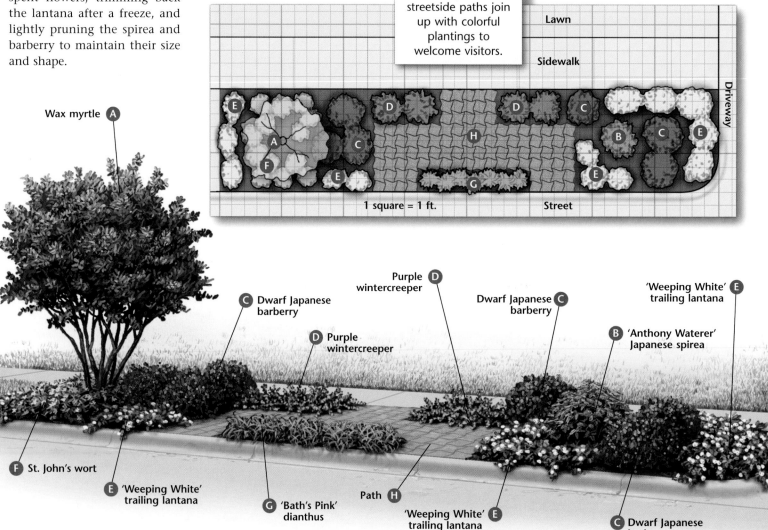

1 square = 1 ft.

Plant portraits

These low-maintenance plants will improve any curbside area, while withstanding the rigors of life by the street.

● = First design, pp. 36–37
▲ = Second design, p. 38

'Weeping White' trailing lantana
(*Lantana montevidensis*, p. 181) ▲

'Dauphin' gaura
(*Gaura lindheimeri*, p. 176) ●

Dwarf Japanese barberry
(*Berberis thunbergii*, p. 169) ▲

'Anthony Waterer' Japanese spirea
(*Spirea × bumalda*, p. 194) ▲

'Bath's Pink' dianthus
(*Dianthus*, p. 175) ▲

'Powis Castle' artemisia
(*Artemisia*, p. 168) ●

Fall aster
(*Aster oblongifolius*, p. 168) ●

Landscape a Low Wall

A two-tiered garden replaces a bland slope

Retaining wall and steps **J**

Some things may not love a wall, but plants and gardeners do. For plants, walls offer warmth for an early start in spring and good drainage for roots. Gardeners appreciate the rich visual potential of composing a garden on two levels, as well as the practical advantage of working on two relatively flat surfaces instead of a single sloping one.

This design places complementary plantings above and below a wall bounded at one end by a set of steps. While each bed is relatively narrow, when viewed from the lower level the two combine to form a border more than 10 ft. deep. Two other design features add depth to the display. A jog in the wall creates a niche for a splashy fountain grass, and the beds are rounded rather than linear. Together with a selection of billowy plants, these features soften the face of the wall and offer pleasing views from many vantage points.

Building the wall that makes this impressive sight possible doesn't require the time or skill it once did. Nor is it necessary to scour the countryside for tons of fieldstone or to hire an expensive contractor. Thanks to precast retaining-wall systems, anyone with a healthy back (or access to energetic teenagers) can install a knee-high do-it-yourself wall in as little as a weekend or two.

Plants & Projects

This planting showcases colorful flowers against curtains of soft silvery green foliage. All the plants tolerate heat and drought and need only a little care to keep them performing at their best. Trim the autumn and mealycup sages lightly through summer to encourage new bloom. The Mexican bush sage and mint marigold will benefit from pruning in late spring and again in midsummer to make them dense and full by showtime in fall.

A **'Gracillimus' Japanese maiden grass** (use 1 plant)
This perennial grass graces the steps with narrow arching leaves. Flowers rise another foot above the foliage in late summer. See *Miscanthus sinensis* 'Gracillimus', p. 184.

B **Compact Texas sage** (use 3)
A native evergreen shrub with small woolly leaves and a billowy shape. It bears masses of orchid pink flowers after summer rains. See *Leucophyllum frutescens* 'Compactum', p. 181.

C **Mexican bush sage** (use 1)
This big bushy perennial anchors the end of the border and echoes the arching habit of the fountain grass. Slender branches bear gray-green foliage. In autumn, long wands of small purple and white flowers bloom from branch tips. See *Salvia leucantha*, p. 193.

D **White autumn sage** (use 3)
This perennial forms a mat of small oval leaves that usually stay green all winter. A profusion of pure white flowers greets visitors at the steps from spring to fall. See *Salvia greggii* 'Alba', p. 192.

E **Mealycup sage** (use 6)
A fringe of blue flower spikes top the narrow grayish leaves of this compact bushy perennial throughout the growing season. Bumblebees will buzz among the blooms. See *Salvia farinacea*, p. 192.

F **Soft-tip yucca** (use 1)
This perennial forms an attractive rosette of succulent gray-blue leaves. It puts on a dazzling display of bloom in summer, when clusters of large creamy white bells rise from the center on sturdy stalks. See *Yucca gloriosa*, p. 199.

G **Mexican mint marigold** (use 1)
This compact perennial has narrow, emerald green leaves topped with a profusion of small gold flowers. See *Tagetes lucida*, p. 195.

H **Fall aster** (use 3)
In autumn, a solid mass of purple daisylike flowers makes this perennial a knockout in front of the gray foliage and white flowers of the sage. See *Aster oblongifolius*, p. 168.

I **'Blue Princess' verbena** (use 2)
Lavender-blue flowers blanket this low-growing perennial from spring through fall. It will spread wide enough to surround the yucca in a sea of bloom. See *Verbena* × *hybrida* 'Blue Princess', p. 197.

J **Retaining wall and steps**
Prefabricated wall systems make this project easy to install. See p. 120.

K **Path**
We've shown gravel here, but use any materials that complement the wall. See p. 108.

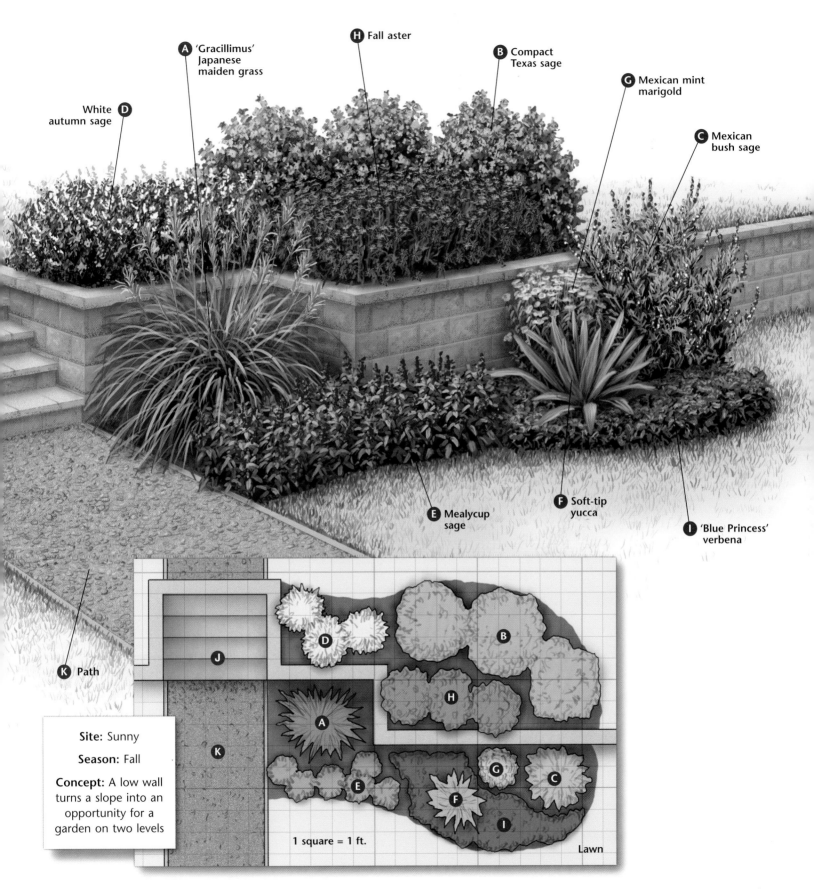

H Fall aster

A 'Gracillimus' Japanese maiden grass

B Compact Texas sage

G Mexican mint marigold

C Mexican bush sage

White **D** autumn sage

F Soft-tip yucca

E Mealycup sage

I 'Blue Princess' verbena

K Path

Site: Sunny

Season: Fall

Concept: A low wall turns a slope into an opportunity for a garden on two levels

1 square = 1 ft.

Lawn

Plant portraits

These plants double the pleasure of a retaining wall with eye-catching flowers and handsome foliage.

● = First design, pp. 40–41
▲ = Second design, pp. 42–43

Black mondo grass
(*Ophiopogon planiscapus* 'Ebony Knight', p. 186) ▲

'Gracillimus' Japanese maiden grass
(*Miscanthus sinensis*, p. 184) ●

Soft-tip yucca (*Yucca gloriosa*, p. 199) ●

White autumn sage (*Salvia greggii* 'Alba', p. 192) ●

Two tiers in the shade

A retaining-wall planting can be equally alluring in a shady yard. This design uses the same wall-and-step system but keeps the wall straight and nestles the steps into the lawn. Bold shrubs on both levels break up the retaining wall's horizontal plane while bringing the garden together as a whole. The shade-loving plants are chosen for their colorful foliage and flowers in a contrasting palette of rosy purples, cool blues, and cheerful yellows.

Plants & Projects

Ⓐ Chinese fringe flower (use 1 plant)
This evergreen shrub is valued for its luxuriant fringe of dainty pink flowers and its layers of small purple leaves. Where soils are alkaline, substitute American beautyberry. See *Loropetalum chinense rubrum*, p. 184.

Ⓑ Fatsia (use 1)
A bold and beautiful tropical-looking shrub. Glossy evergreen leaves will drape over the wall and nearby plants. See *Fatsia japonica*, p. 175.

Ⓒ American beautyberry (use 1)
This shrub wears a thick coat of pale green foliage most of the year. Clusters of eye-popping purple berries line the branches in late summer. See *Callicarpa americana*, p. 171.

Ⓓ Cast-iron plant (use 3)
An unusual and striking evergreen perennial, it has dark strappy leaves that jut directly from the ground like giant exclamation points. See *Aspidistra elatior*, p. 168.

Ⓔ Holly fern (use 9)
These glossy stands of evergreen fronds will keep the garden lit up through dull winter months. See Ferns: *Cyrtomium falcatum*, p. 176.

Ⓕ Carolina jasmine (use 1)
In no time at all this vine will twine under the redbud and trail over the wall. Tiny lance-like evergreen leaves are almost hidden in spring by sweet-scented yellow flower bells. See *Gelsemium sempervirens*, p. 177.

Ⓖ Louisiana iris (use 3)
This perennial forms an erect clump of narrow arching leaves. Large flowers rise above the foliage in spring. Choose a blue or lavender variety to complement the color scheme. See *Iris* × Louisiana hybrids, p. 180.

Ⓗ Texas gold columbine (use 3)
Plant this evergreen perennial at the front of the border to show off the neat mounds of attractive ferny foliage. Delicate yellow flowers with long spurs rise above the plant and bloom for a long time in spring. See *Aquilegia chrysantha hinckleyana*, p. 167.

Ⓘ St. John's wort (use 3)
This semi-evergreen perennial makes a thick mat of miniature leaves along the wall and cascading over it. Small yellow flowers decorate the plant in summer. Foliage is reddish purple in autumn. See *Hypericum calycinum*, p. 179.

Ⓙ Black mondo grass (use 15)
Slender purple-black leaves give this distinctive plant a bold look that also accents the other purples in the planting. See *Ophiopogon planiscapus* 'Ebony Knight', p. 186.

Ⓚ Dwarf Mexican petunia (use 6)
This low-growing perennial produces tufts of narrow, long, dark green leaves that are ideal for an informal edging. Slow to emerge in spring, this plant makes up time with a long season of purple bloom. The flowers are funnel-shaped and light purple. See *Ruellia brittoniana* 'Katie', p. 192.

Ⓛ Purple heart (use 1)
Given a chance, the succulent purple foliage of this mat-forming perennial will tumble decorously over the wall. See *Setcreasea pallida*, p. 194.

See p. 40 for the following:

Ⓜ Retaining wall and steps

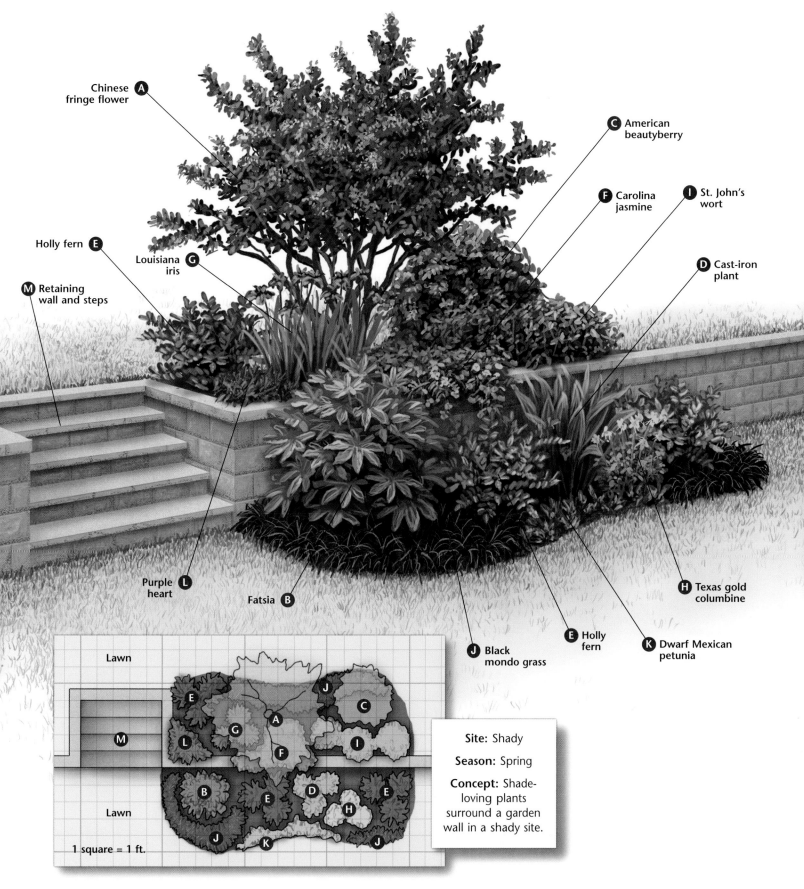

Chinese fringe flower **A**

C American beautyberry

F Carolina jasmine

I St. John's wort

Holly fern **E**

Louisiana iris **G**

D Cast-iron plant

M Retaining wall and steps

Purple heart **L**

Fatsia **B**

H Texas gold columbine

J Black mondo grass

E Holly fern

K Dwarf Mexican petunia

Lawn

E

M

L

G

A

F

J

C

I

B

E

D

H

E

J

K

Lawn

1 square = 1 ft.

Site: Shady

Season: Spring

Concept: Shade-loving plants surround a garden wall in a shady site.

Beautify a Blank Wall

A vertical garden makes the most of a narrow site

Just as a painting enhances a wall in your home, a blank wall outdoors can be decorated with plants. The design shown on these pages transforms a nondescript front entrance by showcasing perennials, vines, and a flowering shrub against an adjacent garage wall. Such entrances are common in suburban homes, but a vertical garden like this is ideal for other spots where yard space is limited.

Selected for a sunny site, these plants offer something in every season. Many are evergreen, with foliage that looks fresh year-round. From March to December flowers enhance the entrance with color and fragrance. In fall, the pomegranate will decorate the wall with large, cream-colored fruits.

The garden has two flowering peaks: spring and autumn. Fragrant white flowers of jasmine greet visitors to the front door early in spring. Chiming in later are the bold blossoms of the pomegranate, iris, and daylily and the more delicate blooms of dianthus and sage. Daylilies and sages continue to flower through the heat of summer, joined by santolina's bright yellow buttonlike blooms. Expect another round of bloom that covers much of the color wheel when the weather turns cool in fall.

> **Site:** Sunny
>
> **Season:** Spring
>
> **Concept:** Handsome plants arrayed against a blank wall make a picture that pleases year-round.

Plants & Projects

Training the pomegranate and the jasmine are the most demanding aspects of this planting. As the pomegranate grows, select horizontal branches that grow parallel to the wall and fasten them to wires attached to the wall. Prune to restrict growth to the wires. Train the jasmine vines by securing the runners to the trellises. The perennials are generally carefree.

A **'Wonderful' pomegranate** (use 1 plant)
This upright deciduous shrub is easily trained against a wall. It bears bright green glossy foliage and dazzling orange-red flowers in spring. A bounty of sweet, juicy pomegranates follows. Leaves are colorful in fall. See *Punica granatum* 'Wonderful', p. 188.

B **Star jasmine** (use 2)
This twining climber will cover the trellis year-round in small, shiny, dark green leaves. It bears abundant and fragrant pinwheel-shaped white flowers in spring. See *Trachelospermum jasminoides*, p. 196.

C **Mealycup sage** (use 5)
From spring to fall this upright perennial produces showy blue flower spikes that rise in clusters from clumps of slender gray-green leaves. See *Salvia farinacea*, p. 192.

D **Autumn sage** (use 3)
This bushy perennial has tiny oval leaves that contrast with the strappy foliage of the daylilies nearby. Colorful flower spikes surround the plant all season. We've shown a purple variety, but pink, white, or red are also available. See *Salvia greggii*, p. 192.

E **Gray santolina** (use 4)
This evergreen perennial forms a tight mound of narrow silver-gray foliage, just right for borders and tucked into corners. Small yellow flowers top the foliage in summer. See *Santolina chamaecyparissus*, p. 193.

F **Bearded iris** (use 3)
Prized for handsome swordlike foliage as well as large lavender blossoms, this perennial is a standout against the daintier dianthus. It often blooms again in autumn. See *Iris × germanica*, p. 180.

G **'Black-Eyed Stella' daylily** (use 5)
A popular perennial for hot sunny spots. Forms a clump of long, slender evergreen leaves crowned all summer with golden trumpet-shaped flowers tinged dark red in the centers. See *Hemerocallis* 'Black-Eyed Stella', p. 177.

H **'Bath's Pink' dianthus** (use 15)
Sprinkled with small pink flowers in spring, this perennial trims the walk the rest of the year with a fringe of fine silvery foliage. See *Dianthus* 'Bath's Pink', p. 175.

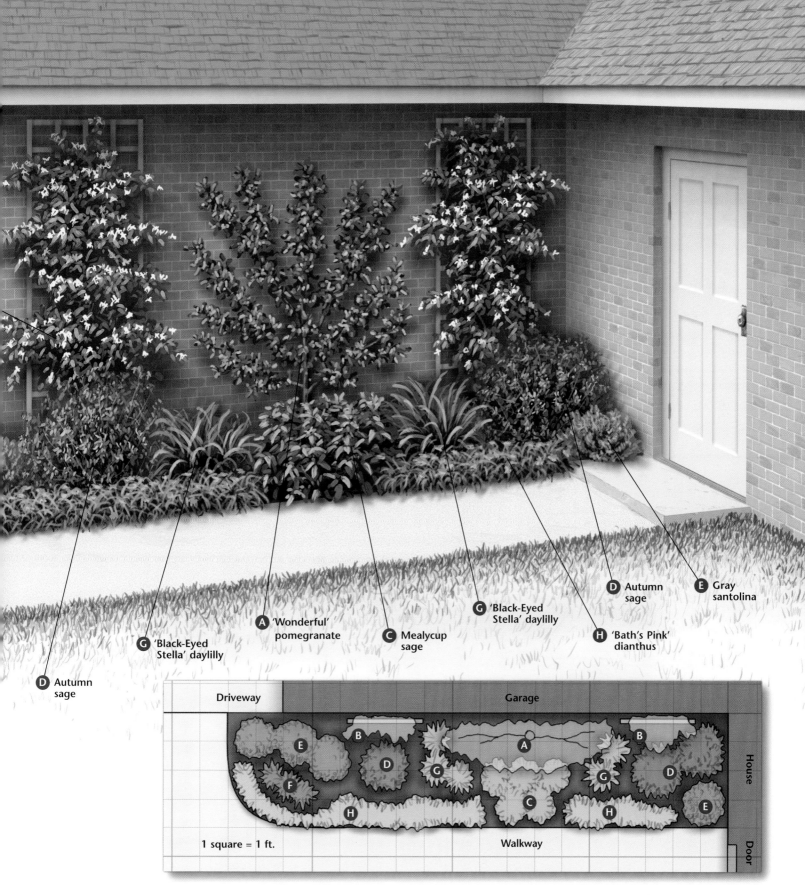

A 'Wonderful' pomegranate

C Mealycup sage

G 'Black-Eyed Stella' daylilly

H 'Bath's Pink' dianthus

D Autumn sage

E Gray santolina

G 'Black-Eyed Stella' daylilly

D Autumn sage

Driveway

Garage

1 square = 1 ft.

Walkway

House

Door

Plant portraits

These perennials and shrubs fill a blank wall with handsome foliage and pretty flowers for many months of the year.

● = First design, pp. 44–45
▲ = Second design, pp. 46–47

Golden bamboo (*Phyllostachys aurea*, p. 187) ▲

'Black-Eyed Stella' daylily (*Hemerocallis*, p. 177) ●

'Picturata' aucuba (*Aucuba japonica*, p. 168) ▲

English ivy (*Hedera helix*, p. 177) ▲

'Kyoto Dwarf' mondo grass (*Ophiopogon japonicus*, p. 186) ▲

Dressing up a shady wall

A shadier site calls for a different palette of plants. The basic idea of this design remains the same as the previous one—incorporate wall space to make the best use of a narrow plot.

Here the focus is on foliage. All the plants are evergreen or nearly so, and they offer a continuous array of colors, textures, and architectural qualities that brighten a dark space and deepen a narrow one. The result is a planting as bright and attractive in winter as it is the rest of the year.

Impressive canes of golden bamboo fill the corner with color, while dark-leaved ivy along a trellis provides a ruffled backdrop for two bold-leaved shrubs, the variegated aucuba and the tropical-looking fatsia. The border is trimmed in grassy ground covers of differing textures and colors. Summer flowers of the fatsia and lilyturf are seasonal treats.

Plants & Projects

Ⓐ Golden bamboo (use 1 plant)
This giant grass forms a striking clump of golden-yellow canes topped with straplike leaves. See *Phyllostachys aurea*, p. 187.

Ⓑ Fatsia (use 1)
Valued for its dressy foliage, this evergreen shrub also produces fuzzy white flower clusters in late summer and small black berries in fall. See *Fatsia japonica*, p. 175.

Ⓒ 'Picturata' aucuba (use 2)
A perfect complement for the bamboo, this durable evergreen shrub bears gold-splashed foliage edged in green. Red berries in winter. See *Aucuba japonica* 'Picturata', p. 168.

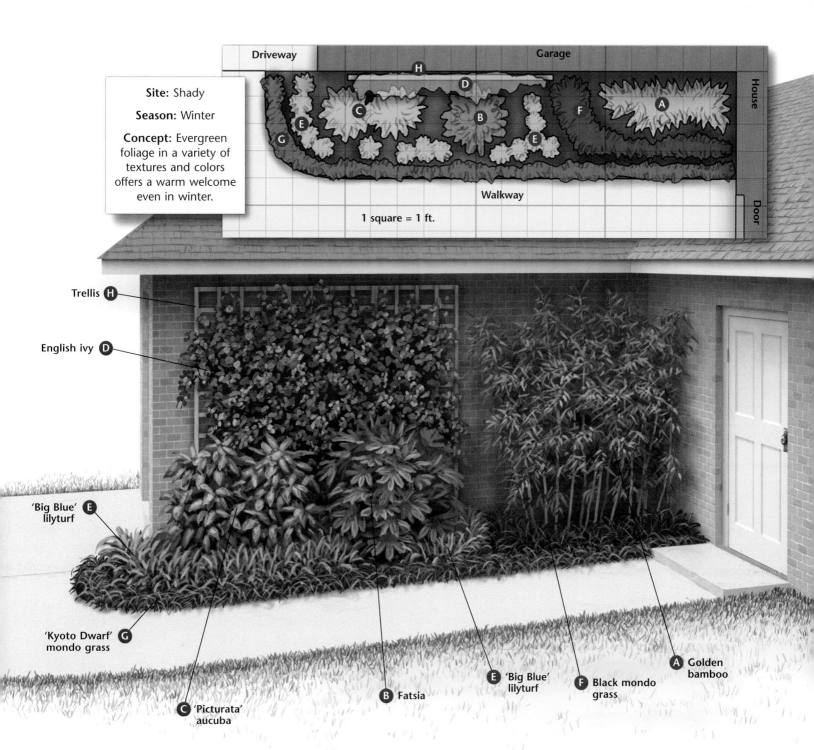

Site: Shady

Season: Winter

Concept: Evergreen foliage in a variety of textures and colors offers a warm welcome even in winter.

Driveway

Garage

House

H

D

C

B

F

A

E

G

E

Door

Walkway

1 square = 1 ft.

Trellis **H**

English ivy **D**

'Big Blue' **E** lilyturf

'Kyoto Dwarf' **G** mondo grass

C 'Picturata' aucuba

B Fatsia

E 'Big Blue' lilyturf

F Black mondo grass

A Golden bamboo

D English ivy (use 6)
This vigorous evergreen vine will cling tightly to the trellis and wall. Of the many cultivars available, we've chosen one with large dark green leaves that showcase the bright foliage of other evergreens, especially the aucuba and fatsia. See *Hedera helix*, p. 177.

E 'Big Blue' lilyturf (use 15)
Neat low mounds of fine-textured dark green foliage make this evergreen perennial an attractive year-round ground cover. Lavender flowers are a summer bonus. This cultivar has larger flowers than the species. See *Liriope muscari* 'Big Blue', p. 183.

F Black mondo grass (use 14)
The dark purple to black foliage of this ornamental evergreen plant makes a dramatic ground cover around the golden bamboo. See *Ophiopogon japonicus* 'Ebony Knight', p. 186.

G 'Kyoto Dwarf' mondo grass (use 50)
Dark green and very low grow-

ing, this evergreen plant adds a fine finish to the planting along the walk. See *Ophiopogon japonicus* 'Kyoto Dwarf', p. 186.

H Trellis
You can support the English ivy with the sturdy homemade trellis shown here, or buy one ready-made at a garden center. See p. 130.

Beautify a Blank Wall 47

A Shady Hideaway

Build a cozy retreat in a corner of your yard

One of life's pleasures is sitting in a shady spot reading or just looking out onto your garden. If your property is long on lawn and short on shade, a chair under an arbor can provide a cool respite from the heat or the cares of the day. Tucked into a corner of the yard and set among attractive shrubs, vines, and perennials, the arbor shown here is a desirable destination even when the day isn't sizzling.

A small tree and an overhead vine create a cozy enclosure, affording privacy as well as shade. Plantings in front of the arbor and extending along the property lines integrate the hideaway with the lawn and make a handsome scene when viewed from the house. The design is also effective in an open corner or backed by a property-line fence. The arbor is small; if you'd like more company beneath it, it's easy to make it wider and longer, extending the plantings.

Flowers contribute warm colors throughout the growing season. Festive yellows, pinks, and reds start the year off and continue until the first frost. Along with a canopy of honeysuckle blossoms, there will be showy hibiscus flowers and lantanas by the bench. Masses of black-eyed Susans and red pomegranate flowers join up in summer. And in fall, deciduous foliage adds to the colorful mix. This is primarily a warm-season planting, but pomegranate fruits and holly berries will make the hideaway well worth a winter visit.

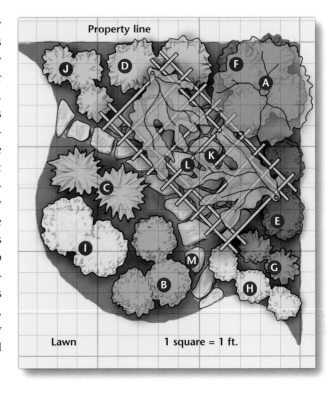

Property line

Lawn   1 square = 1 ft.

Plants & Projects

The arbor and plants can be installed in a few weekends. Once the plants are established, seasonal pruning and cleanup should keep this durable planting looking good.

A **Possumhaw holly** (use 1 plant)
This fast-growing deciduous tree makes a handsome screen for the hideaway. Smooth oval leaves turn yellow in fall. When they drop, they expose silvery branches with bright red, orange, or yellow berries, the color depending on the cultivar. See *Ilex decidua*, p. 179.

B **Compact pomegranate** (use 3)
A low-growing form of a popular deciduous shrub. Lustrous foliage showcases red carnation-like flowers in summer and small ornamental fruits in fall. See *Punica granatum* 'Nana', p. 188.

C **Dwarf Japanese maiden grass** (use 2)
One of the most compact fountain grasses. Abundant cream-colored flowers rise above long leaves in summer. Foliage turns tawny in winter. See *Miscanthus sinensis* 'Adagio', p. 184.

D **Texas star hibiscus** (use 2)
This perennial forms a large airy clump of slender, deeply divided, glossy leaves borne on red-tinged stems. Brilliant red five-petaled flowers open daily during the summer and fall. See *Hibiscus coccineus*, p. 179.

E **Firebush** (use 2)
Small slender flowers dangle at the ends of this perennial's many branches from summer to frost. Dull green leaves turn red in fall. See *Hamelia patens*, p. 177.

F **Turk's cap** (use 4)
This shrubby perennial will tolerate the eventual shade under the tree canopy, providing a lush screen of dark green leaves studded with small red turban-like flowers. *See Malvaviscus arboreus drummondii*, p. 184.

G **Cigar plant** (use 2)
Adding a vertical element to the planting, this perennial spreads to form a patch of upright stems topped with long narrow leaves. Thin orange and yellow flowers complement the firebush blossoms in summer. See *Cuphea micropetala*, p. 174.

H **'Goldstrum' black-eyed Susan** (use 3)
This popular perennial's abundant, golden, dark-eyed daisies bloom abundantly in summer, with plenty to spare for flower arrangements. See *Rudbeckia fulgida* 'Goldsturm', p. 191.

I **'New Gold' lantana** (use 2)
Tiny golden flowers in tight round clusters cover the foliage of this spreading perennial from late spring to frost. See *Lantana × hybrida* 'New Gold', p. 181.

J **Mexican mint marigold** (use 3)
Plant this perennial next to the bench for fragrant foliage and a fall display of rich yellow flowers. On your way into the house snip a few anise-flavored leaves for cooking and a handful of flowers for fall bouquets. See *Tagetes lucida*, p. 195.

K **Coral honeysuckle** (use 2)
Whorls of scarlet flowers decorate this popular vine from late spring to fall. Attractive blue-green foliage is evergreen. See *Lonicera sempervirens*, p. 183.

L **Arbor**
This simple structure can be built in a weekend or two. See p. 137.

M **Paving**
Flat fieldstones in tones of gray complement the arbor and the planting. See p. 108.

Site: Sunny

Season: Summer

Concept: Enjoy a colorful array of plants while you relax under a shady arbor.

Possumhaw holly **A**

Coral honeysuckle **K**

Arbor **L**

Texas star hibiscus **D**

See site plan for **F**.

Mexican mint marigold **J**

Dwarf Japanese maiden grass **C**

I 'New Gold' lantana

B Compact pomegranate

Firebush **E**

Paving **M**

Cigar plant **G**

H 'Goldsturm' black-eyed Susan

Plant portraits

Privacy, shade, flowers, foliage, and fragrance—these plants provide all the necessities for a relaxing backyard retreat.

● = First design, pp. 48–49
▲ = Second design, pp. 50–51

Compact pomegranate (*Punica granatum* 'Nana', p. 188) ●

Narcissus
(Bulbs: *Narcissus tazetta* 'Grand Primo', p. 169) ▲

Mexican mint marigold
(*Tagetes lucida*, p. 195) ●

Polyantha rose (*Rosa* × *polyantha* 'Marie Daly', p. 189) ▲

Homegrown hideaway

Instead of building your garden retreat, you can grow it. A small tree and midsize shrubs replace the arbor in the previous design. Their lush greenery provides a sense of enclosure and privacy year-round, and the cool flower colors (blues, pinks, and whites) will soothe the senses even as the temperature rises.

Reliably evergreen, the wax myrtle's deliciously scented leaves will cast dappled shade over the bench all year. The camellias, viburnums, and abelias are evergreen too, their dark glossy foliage a perfect foil for pink and white blossoms. There will be flowers in every season: sweet-scented viburnum in early spring, roses from May to October, camellias in November, and narcissus for snow-white blooms in winter.

Plants & Projects

Ⓐ Wax myrtle (use 1 plant)
This small evergreen tree offers a fragrant and shady canopy for bench-sitters. Leaves are smooth and slender. See *Myrica cerifera*, p. 184.

Ⓑ 'Shi Shi Gashira' camellia (use 3)
This low, compact, and lustrous evergreen shrub bears double rose-colored flowers in late fall. See *Camellia sasanqua* 'Shi Shi Gashira', p. 171.

Ⓒ 'Spring Bouquet' viburnum (use 1)
Pink buds open into scented white flowers when this evergreen shrub blooms in early spring. See *Viburnum tinus* 'Spring Bouquet', p. 198.

Ⓓ 'Edward Goucher' glossy abelia (use 3)
This evergreen shrub forms a low mound of small, pointed,

Plants & Projects

Once established, these plants will provide years of pleasure. Heat and drought tolerant in summer, they will do best if their roots are kept dry in winter.

A Desert willow (use 3 plants)
The fine leaves of this deciduous tree provide an airy canopy over the path without shading out the plants underneath. Showy white, pink, and lavender flowers bloom on and off all season. See *Chilopsis linearis*, p. 173.

B Spineless prickly pear (use 3)
A bold cactuslike accent with tiny hidden prickles. This evergreen shrub forms an interesting erect clump of succulent leaf pads, occasionally bearing yellow flowers in summer and showy purple fruit in fall. See *Opuntia lindheimeri*, p. 186.

C Compact Texas sage (use 4)
An evergreen shrub that forms a billowy mound of small fuzzy gray leaves on pale stems. This cultivar is a denser, bushier version of the popular Texas sage and has orchid pink flowers. See *Leucophyllum frutescens* 'Compactum', p. 181.

D 'Hill's Hardy' rosemary (use 2)
Both foliage and flowers of this handsome evergreen shrub are fragrant. Most cold tolerant of all the rosemary cultivars. See *Rosmarinus officinalis* 'Hill's Hardy', p. 191.

E Red yucca (use 15)
Slow-growing but worth it, these evergreen perennials create a low, striking hedge in front of the Texas sage. Spikes of coral pink flowers rise from the narrow succulent leaves and bloom from May to frost. See *Hesperaloe parviflora*, p. 178.

F 'Pink' autumn sage (use 7)
Massed on both sides of the entry, these fine-textured perennials help tie the planting together. 'Pink' is a large and dependable cultivar with bright pink blooms from spring to fall. Use this or any pink cultivar. Evergreen in warm winters. See *Salvia greggii* 'Pink', p. 192.

G Mexican bush sage (use 7)
These bushy perennials will fill the space under the tree with downy gray leaves and stems. The nectar of the white and purple flowers in autumn draws hummingbirds. See *Salvia leucantha*, p. 193.

H Mealycup sage (use 4)
For a touch of bright blue, plant this perennial among the pinks and yellows of autumn sage and lantana. See *Salvia farinacea*, p. 192.

I 'New Gold' lantana (use 7)
These vigorous perennials will spread to form a continuous border of gold flowers atop small green elliptical leaves. A butterfly favorite. See *Lantana × hybrida*, p. 181.

J 'Bath's Pink' dianthus (use 18)
This perennial is grown for its thick mat of tiny blue-green leaves and its fragrant pink flowers in early spring. See *Dianthus* 'Bath's Pink', p. 175.

K Jonquil (as needed)
Plant these bulbs for fresh grassy foliage and yellow trumpets that announce the arrival of early spring. Sprinkle them throughout, and particularly around plants that are dormant in winter, such as the salvias and lantana. See Bulbs: *Narcissus jonquilla*, p. 169.

L Steppingstones
Flagstones provide access from the slab through the planting to the side yard. See p. 113.

Desert willow **A**

E Red yucca

F 'Pink' autumn sage

H Mealycup sage

D 'Hill's Hardy' rosemary

I 'New Gold' lantana

J 'Bath's Pink' dianthus

F 'Pink' autumn sage

See site plan for **K** and **L**.

A touch of the tropics

Chosen for a niche in shade, these plants provide the look of a balmy Pacific island. Almost entirely evergreen, the planting will change little from season to season; the interest comes from the many contrasts in plant forms and in foliage texture and color.

Five windmill palms set a dramatic tone across the front of the planting. Their hairy trunks frame views of the plants behind. From front to back, the foliage progresses from fine-textured to coarse and alternates between light and dark colors, finishing with the very bold, very dark foliage of the fatsia. The pattern is repeated on a smaller scale and with some variation on the other side of the entry.

Attractive throughout the year, this planting is especially effective in late winter, the season shown here, when reminders of lush tropical islands are particularly welcome.

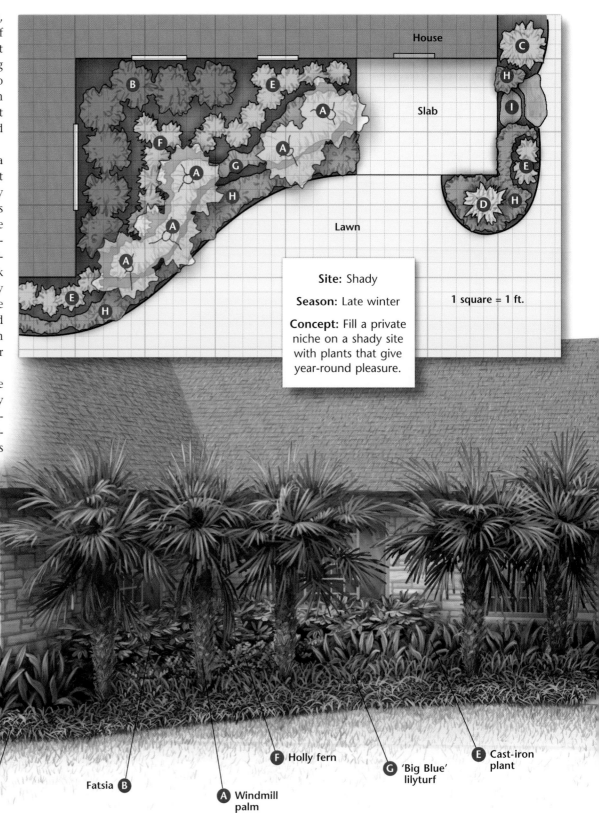

Site: Shady

Season: Late winter

1 square = 1 ft.

Concept: Fill a private niche on a shady site with plants that give year-round pleasure.

Cast-iron plant E

Mondo grass H

Fatsia B

Windmill palm A

Holly fern F

'Big Blue' lilyturf G

Cast-iron plant E

Plants & Projects

Ⓐ Windmill palm (use 5 plants)
A dwarf palm tree sporting dark green fronds and tan trunks matted on the surface with hairy fibers. Trunks provide an interesting contrast to the smooth, glossy foliage of this and the other plants. See *Trachycarpus fortunei*, p. 196.

Ⓑ Fatsia (use 7)
An evergreen shrub with big leaves that grow in attractive layers. Produces custers of white flowerballs in fall. See *Fatsia japonica*, p. 175.

Ⓒ Gold dust aucuba
(use 1 or more)
Year-round, this erect shrub wears a handsome coat of shiny green leaves dusted with yellow spots. Use one, or more if you'd like to extend the planting along the side of house. See *Aucuba japonica* 'Variegata', p. 168.

Ⓓ Umbrella sedge (use 1)
Often listed as a water plant, this grasslike perennial also thrives in a garden bed and in sun or shade. It makes an eye-catching clump of slender stalks, each one topped with circular spokes of ribbony foliage. See *Cyperus alternifolius*, p. 175.

Ⓔ Cast-iron plant (use 15)
The stiff leathery leaves of this perennial grow straight up from the ground, forming a dense stand of dark green. See *Aspidistra eliator*, p. 168.

Ⓕ Holly fern (use 6)
An evergreen fern with thick fronds divided into large glossy leaflets. The stems are fuzzy. See Ferns: *Cyrtomium falcatum*, p. 176.

Ⓖ 'Big Blue' lilyturf (use 40)
This curving band of grassy perennials links the windmill palms. For a greater color contrast, try one of the variegated cultivars. See *Liriope muscari* 'Big Blue', p. 183.

Ⓗ Mondo grass (use 60)
Another, darker band of grassy perennials for the front of the palms. See *Ophiopogon japonicus*, p. 186.

See p. 77 for the following:

Ⓘ Steppingstones

Plant portraits

Tropical or desertlike, these exotic looking plants provide interest all year.

● = First design, pp. 76–77
▲ = Second design, pp. 78–79

Jonquil (Bulbs: *Narcissus jonquilla*, p. 169) ●

Desert willow (*Chilopsis linearis*, p. 173) ●

Mondo grass (*Ophiopogon japonicus*, p. 186) ▲

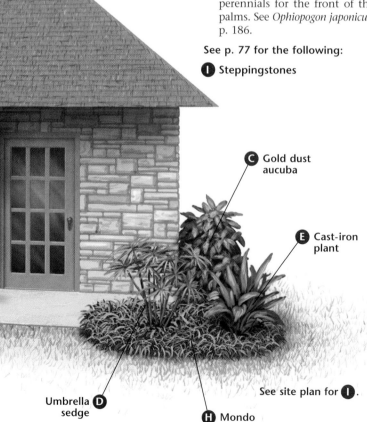

Ⓒ Gold dust aucuba

Ⓔ Cast-iron plant

Umbrella Ⓓ sedge

See site plan for Ⓘ.

Ⓗ Mondo grass

A Garden Path

Reclaim a narrow side yard for a stroll garden

Many residential lots include a slim strip of land between the house and a property line. Usually overlooked by everyone except children and dogs racing between the front yard and the back, this neglected passageway can become a valued addition to the landscape. In this design, a delightful little stroll garden invites adults, and even children, to linger as they move from one part of the property to another.

The wall of the house and a tall fence at the property line create a cozy "room," one that is enhanced by trees, vines, shrubs, and ground covers. Like furnishings in a room, the plantings make the small space seem bigger than it is. A gently curving flagstone path widens the passage visually and lengthens the stroll through it.

In spring, scented blossoms of daffodil, wisteria, and Texas mountain laurel will perfume the entire passage. As these flowers fade, the watermelon pink crapemyrtle will begin its long season of bloom, joined by purple verbena along the fence, bushy mounds of baby blue plumbago where the daffodils had been, and a continuous row of pretty pink salvia. As the trees grow, their boughs will arch over the path, creating a bower heavy with blossoms for much of the year.

1 square = 1 ft.

Plants & Projects

Install the fence and flagstone path. Then prepare and plant the beds. You'll need to add sturdy trellises or other strong supports for the vines. As the trees grow, prune them so they arch over the path yet provide headroom for strollers. Once established, the plants require seasonal care as well as pruning to maintain size and shape.

A **'Tonto' crapemyrtle** (use 2 plants)
A small deciduous tree deserving of its wide popularity. Attractive dark oval leaves showcase spectacular blossoms from summer to frost. This cultivar bears watermelon pink flowers. See *Lagerstroemia × fauriei* 'Tonto', p. 180.

B **Texas mountain laurel** (use 1)
Clusters of purple flowers hang from this small glossy evergreen tree in early spring. Passersby on both sides of the fence will appreciate the delightful perfume. Bean pods with bright red seeds follow the flowers. See *Sophora secundiflora*, p. 194.

C **Indian hawthorn** (use 4)
A mounding evergreen shrub that produces a dense covering of shiny oval leaves. It offers pink or white flowers in spring and purple-black berries in late summer. Choose a pink-flowering cultivar for this spot. See *Rhaphiolepis indica*, p. 188.

D **Tropical plumbago** (use 3)
After the daffodils fade, this perennial emerges apple green and bushy. In summer it spills over with big clusters of clear blue flowers. See *Plumbago auriculata*, p. 187.

E **'Pink' autumn sage** (use 6)
These low, bushy mounds of tiny oval leaves bristle with spires of bright pink flowers all season. Plant this or any pink cultivar. See *Salvia greggii* 'Pink', p. 192.

F **Chinese wisteria** (use 2)
In spring, this vine will virtually curtain the fence with fragrant violet flowers as large as clusters of grapes. A lacework of green foliage emerges after fragrant blossoms fade, turning yellowish in fall. See *Wisteria sinensis*, p. 199.

G **Purple verbena** (use 2)
Countless bright clusters of purple flowers rise airily from this perennial's base of dull green leaves. Blooms from midsummer to frost. See *Verbena bonariensis*, p. 197.

H **'Big Blue' lilyturf** (use 24)
This perennial makes an attractive edge of grassy dark green foliage. In summer, small lavender flowers float among the leaves. See *Liriope muscari*, p. 183.

I **'Ice Follies' daffodil** (as needed)
Fresh-looking white daffodil flowers with pale yellow centers line the path in early spring. See Bulbs: *Narcissus pseudonarcissus* 'Ice Follies', p. 169.

J **Fence**
Easy to build, this fence provides privacy and an attractive framework for plants. See p. 140.

K **Path**
Flagstones in random shapes and sizes trace a graceful curve through the planting. A neutral gray would complement any house. See p. 108.

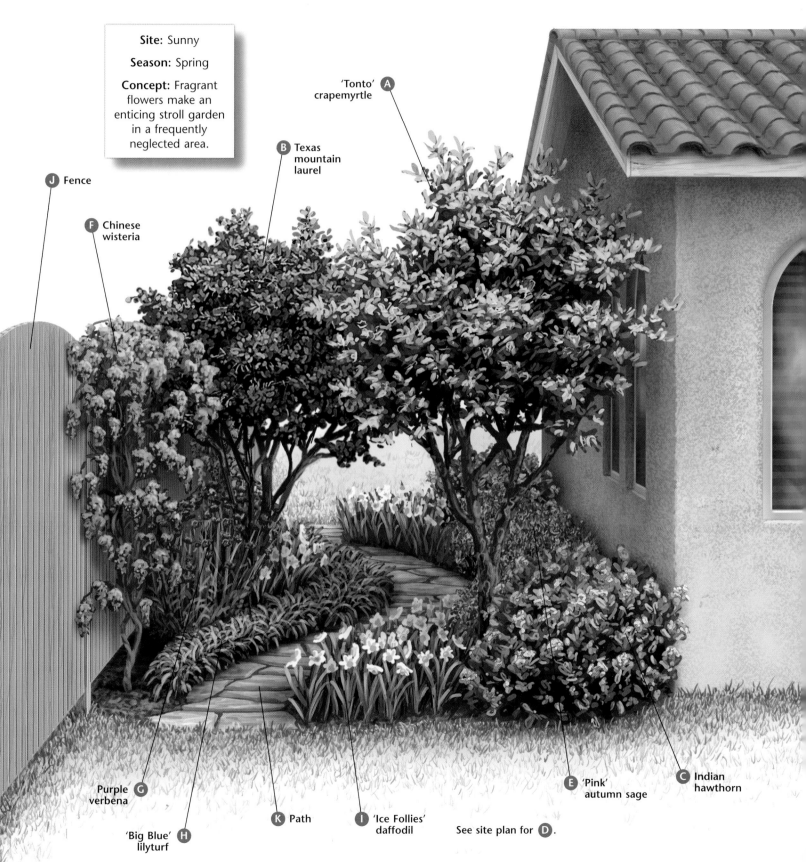

Site: Sunny

Season: Spring

Concept: Fragrant flowers make an enticing stroll garden in a frequently neglected area.

A 'Tonto' crapemyrtle

B Texas mountain laurel

J Fence

F Chinese wisteria

G Purple verbena

H 'Big Blue' lilyturf

K Path

I 'Ice Follies' daffodil

See site plan for D.

E 'Pink' autumn sage

C Indian hawthorn

Plant portraits

Eye-catching plants for an overlooked spot, here are flowers, foliage, and fragrance to make your side-yard stroll garden a favorite.

● = First design, pp. 80–81
▲ = Second design, pp. 82–83

Gold dust aucuba (*Aucuba japonica* 'Variegata', p. 168) ▲

'Ice Follies' daffodil
(Bulbs: *Narcissus pseudonarcissus*, p. 169) ●

'Pink' autumn sage
(*Salvia greggii*, p. 192) ●

Indian hawthorn
(*Rhaphiolepis indica*, p. 188) ●

'Tonto' crapemyrtle (*Lagerstroemia* × *fauriei*, p. 180) ●

Chinese wisteria (*Wisteria sinensis*, p. 199) ●

A shady corridor

If the side of your house has a shady exposure, try this design. Shade-loving shrubs and ground covers are arrayed in colorful layers along the passage. These "furnishings" are selected primarily for their foliage, ranging from light green to purple black, fine-textured to coarse, dull to glossy, and low-growing to large and bold. The big leaves of the fatsia and aucuba combine well with ground covers, soft fern fronds, and stiff, swordlike aspidistra. In this evergreen garden, flowers and berries are added enticements. Fragrant jasmine scents the air in spring and purple berries brighten a winter stroll.

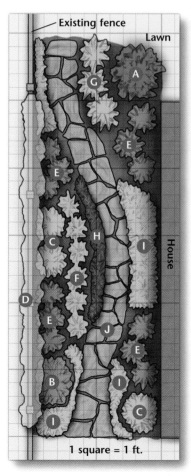

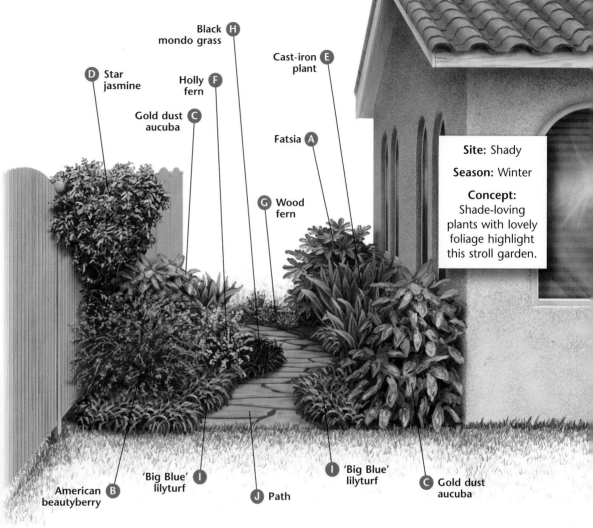

Site: Shady

Season: Winter

Concept: Shade-loving plants with lovely foliage highlight this stroll garden.

Plants & Projects

A Fatsia (use 1 plant)
A handsome evergreen shrub. Leaves like big hands look wonderful above feathery ferns and other fine-textured plants. See *Fatsia japonica*, p. 175.

B American beautyberry (use 1)
This shrub has an open, slightly sprawling habit. Purple berries are showy on bare branches in fall and winter. See *Callicarpa americana*, p. 171.

C Gold dust aucuba (use 3)
Speckled and shiny, this evergreen shrub is a striking accent plant, made more so by borders of dark green lilyturf and purple-black mondo grass. See *Aucuba japonica* 'Variegata', p. 168.

D Star jasmine (use 3)
This vine's stiff oval foliage will "wallpaper" the fence with year-round color and texture. Clouds of tiny white flowers cover the vine in spring. They'll fill the passage with fragrance. See *Trachelospermum jasminoides*, p. 196.

E Cast-iron plant (use 12)
This unusual evergreen plant forms a patch of long leathery leaves that jut from the ground like fence pickets. See *Aspidistra eliator*, p. 168.

F Holly fern (use 6)
An evergreen fern distinguished by leathery fronds. It contrasts nicely with the mondo grass and other evergreens. See Ferns: *Cyrtomium falcatum*, p. 176.

G Wood fern (use 3)
This is a deciduous fern with a soft shaggy look. Cut back after frost for an attractive brown flat-top. See Ferns: *Thelypteris kunthii*, p. 176.

H Black mondo grass (use 12)
Plant this perennial along the path for its unusual color and neat habit. Shear off tops in early spring for new growth. See *Ophiopogon planiscapus* 'Ebony Knight,' p. 186.

See p. 80 for the following:

I 'Big Blue' lilyturf (use 24)

J Path

Down to Earth

Harmonize your deck with its surroundings

'Morning Light' Japanese maiden grass — **E**

Texas mountain laurel — **A**

Russian sage — **F**

Mexican mint marigold — **H**

'Pink' autumn sage — **K**

'Powis Castle' artemisia — **J**

Gaura — **G**

Yarrow — **L**

'John Fanick' garden phlox — **I**

Carolina jasmine — **D**

'Hill's Hardy' rosemary — **C**

A backyard deck is a perfect spot for enjoying the garden or a distant view. Too often, however, the deck offers little connection to its surroundings. Perched on bare posts above a patch of lawn, it is a lonely outpost rather than an inviting gateway to the outdoors.

This design nestles the deck into its immediate surroundings while preserving the vista from the deck and the windows. The one exception to the low landscape of shrubs, vines, and groundcovers is a small tree, whose fragrant spring flowers and attractive foliage will improve rather than screen the view.

Decreasing in height from the deck to the ground, the planting makes it easier for the eye to move between levels. Japanese maiden grasses and rosemary rise railing-high on one side of the deck, and glossy abelias fill in the other. Around the grasses is an airy border of Russian sage. A lower edging of fine-leaved yarrow frames the front of the deck.

Striking to look at, this deckside planting appeals to other senses as well. In March and April the large flower clusters of Texas mountain laurel will give off their distinctive fragrance (some liken it to grape soda). The spring air will also carry the heady perfume of Carolina jasmine. Many of the plants also have fragrant leaves, releasing their pungence to the touch, or on their own when days are hot. A few are flavorful too, adding zest to culinary dishes.

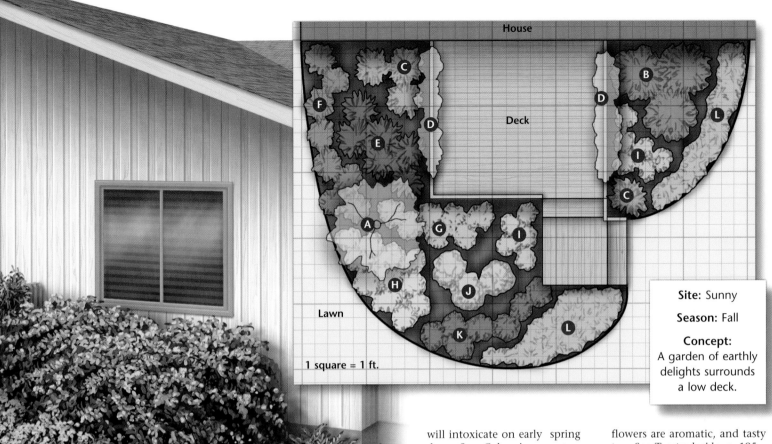

House

Deck

C
F
D
E
A
G
H
I
J
K
L

B
D
L
I
C

Lawn

1 square = 1 ft.

Site: Sunny

Season: Fall

Concept:
A garden of earthly delights surrounds a low deck.

Ⓘ 'John Fanick' garden phlox

Ⓛ Yarrow

Ⓑ Glossy abelia

Plants & Projects

You'll need to water young plants to get them established. But after a year or two, these durable perennials and shrubs will require infrequent supplemental watering and little care beyond routine seasonal pruning and clean up.

Ⓐ **Texas mountain laurel** (use 1 plant)
Deliciously fragrant purple flowers will entice you outdoors in early spring. This native shrub or tree has interesting gnarled branches and shiny evergreen foliage. See *Sophora secundiflora*, p. 194.

Ⓑ **Glossy abelia** (use 3)
Another shrub with scented blossoms and luxuriant semi-evergreen foliage. Honeysuckle-like flowers are pinkish white and bloom from spring to fall. See *Abelia × grandiflora*, p. 166.

Ⓒ **'Hill's Hardy' rosemary** (use 4)
This attractive evergreen shrub deserves a spot by the steps. Crush a few leaves in your hand as you go by to release their pungent aroma. The piney branches are dotted with fragrant lavender-blue flowers in late winter and spring. See *Rosmarinus officinalis* 'Hills Hardy', p. 191.

Ⓓ **Carolina jasmine** (use 2)
A popular evergreen vine bearing small, medium green, lance-shaped leaves. The perfume of its small yellow flowers will intoxicate on early spring days. See *Gelsemium sempervirens*, p. 177.

Ⓔ **'Morning Light' Japanese maiden grass** (use 6)
A variegated (gray to medium green) ornamental grass that grows into a fountain-shaped mound. In fall large buff-colored tassels may rise above a porch railing. The dried flowers are showy into late winter. See *Miscanthus sinensis*, p. 184.

Ⓕ **Russian sage** (use 8)
This erect perennial forms a vase of silvery see-through stems and small aromatic gray leaves. Tiny pale blue flowers bloom along stem tips from spring through summer. See *Perovskia atriplicifolia*, p. 186.

Ⓖ **Gaura** (use 7)
Masses of delicate white to pink flowers float above low clumps of pale green foliage from spring through summer. A favorite perennial of butterflies. See *Gaura lindheimeri*, p. 176.

Ⓗ **Mexican mint marigold** (use 13)
Golden daisylike blossoms smother these upright perennials in autumn. Leaves and flowers are aromatic, and tasty too. See *Tagetes lucida*, p. 195.

Ⓘ **'John Fanick' garden phlox** (use 11)
Big fragrant clusters of long-blooming flowers make this perennial a great one to plant near patios and decks. This mildew-resistant cultivar bears pink flowers from spring to July. See *Phlox paniculata* 'John Fanick', p. 187.

Ⓙ **'Powis Castle' artemisia** (use 3)
This perennial's silvery foliage makes a beautiful foil for the pale pink gaura flowers and the deeper pink of the autumn sage. See *Artemisia ×* 'Powis Castle', p. 168.

Ⓚ **'Pink' autumn sage** (use 7)
Fine-textured bushy perennial with small oval medium-green leaves and spikes of bright pink flowers. Blooms nonstop from March to October. See *Salvia greggii* 'Pink', p. 192.

Ⓛ **Yarrow** (use 36)
The dense ferny foliage of this mounding perennial makes a fine edging. You can choose among many flower colors. Blooms in spring. See *Achillea millefolium*, p. 166.

Skirting a shady deck

This design also integrates the deck with its surroundings but does so in a shadier environment produced perhaps by large trees nearby. The layout is similar to the previous one, but the plants are shade-lovers from the forest understory.

Mostly deciduous, this woodland garden offers a changing landscape throughout the year. A native redbud by the deck marks each of the seasons as it flowers, leafs out, turns gold, and bares its branches. For balance on the other side of the deck, a cherry laurel provides an evergreen presence. The railings are draped with cross vine and autumn clematis, two vines that bloom beautifully in shade.

Wrapping around the deck is a collection of shrubs and ground covers for a woodland setting. Inland sea oats is one of the best ornamental grasses for shade. And what woodland would be complete without ferns? A leafy ground cover of Virginia creeper grows at their feet, underplanted with a host of narcissus for early spring color and fragrance.

Plants & Projects

A **Redbud** (use 1 plant)
This small native deciduous tree brings pink flowers to the deck in spring and a canopy of heart-shaped leaves in summer. Foliage turns yellow in fall. See *Cercis canadensis,* p. 172.

B **Compact Carolina cherry laurel** (use 1)
A glossy-leaved evergreen shrub with enough stature to balance the redbud. Trim to enhance the plant's natural conical shape. Inconspicuous but fragrant spring flowers are followed by black berries. See *Prunus caroliniana* 'Compacta', p. 188.

C **American beautyberry** (use 1)
This deciduous shrub creates a loose thicket of arching branches lined in fall with

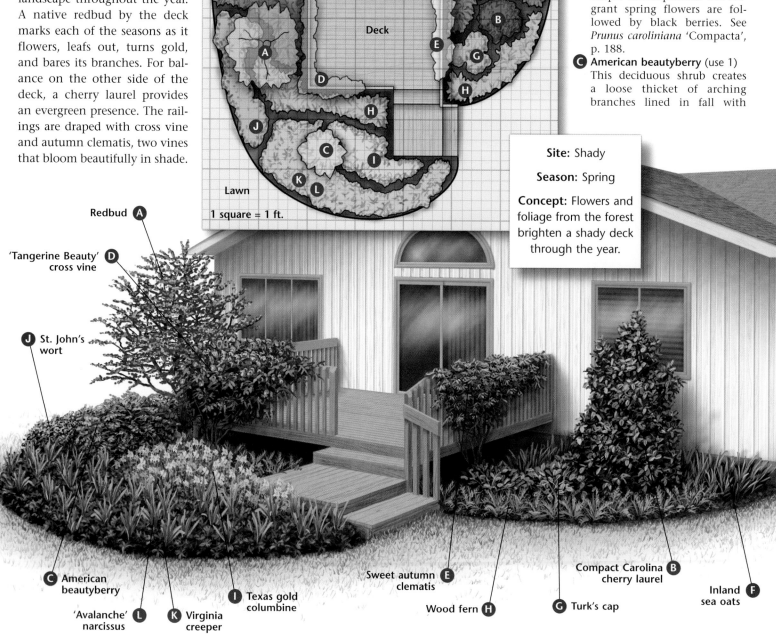

House

Deck

Lawn

1 square = 1 ft.

Site: Shady

Season: Spring

Concept: Flowers and foliage from the forest brighten a shady deck through the year.

Redbud **A**

'Tangerine Beauty' cross vine **D**

J St. John's wort

C American beautyberry

'Avalanche' **L** narcissus

K Virginia creeper

I Texas gold columbine

Sweet autumn clematis **E**

Wood fern **H**

G Turk's cap

Compact Carolina **B** cherry laurel

Inland **F** sea oats

long-lasting purple berries. See *Callicarpa americana*, p. 171.

D **'Tangerine Beauty' cross vine** (use 1)
An evergreen climber with lustrous deep green foliage. It produces showy clusters of orange trumpet flowers in spring and occasionally afterwards. See *Bignonia capreolata*, p. 169.

E **Sweet autumn clematis** (use 1)
In fall, this vine's leaves are hidden in a fragrant cloud of tiny white flowers. Seed heads form a delicate tracery among bare vines in winter. See *Clematis terniflora*, p. 173.

F **Inland sea oats** (use 30)
This grass grows in a dense upright clump that reaches knee high. In late summer, decorative seed heads unfurl among the leaves. See *Chasmanthium latifolium*, p. 172.

G **Turk's cap** (use 3)
After emerging from dormancy, this perennial will grow 2 ft. tall and 3 ft. wide by summer. It bears lobed leaves and curious red flowers. See *Malvaviscus arboreus drummondii*, p. 184.

H **Wood fern** (use 44)
Lacy, bright green fronds distinguish this woodland fern. See Ferns: *Thelypteris kunthii*, p. 176.

I **Texas gold columbine** (use 23)
A decorative screen for the space under the deck, this native perennial forms a lacy clump of fernlike foliage topped with gold flowers in spring. See *Aquilegia chrysantha hinckleyana*, p. 167.

J **St. John's wort** (use18)
A low-growing semi-evergreen shrub that forms a fine-textured mound of small oval leaves, turning red and purple in fall. Bears five-petaled yellow flowers in summer. See *Hypericum calycinum*, p. 179.

K **Virginia creeper** (use 3)
Usually grown as a climber, this native deciduous vine is also useful as a ground cover. Compound leaves turn colorful in the autumn. See *Parthenocissus quinquefolia*, p. 186.

L **'Avalanche' narcissus** (use 35)
This bulb produces small white-and-yellow flowers in early spring. See Bulbs: *Narcissus tazetta* 'Avalanche', p. 169.

Plant portraits

These plants can enhance a deck with lovely foliage textures and colors as well as pretty flowers.

● = First design, pp. 84–85
▲ = Second design, pp. 86–87

'Tangerine Beauty' cross vine
(*Bignonia capreolata*, p. 169) ▲

'Avalanche' narcissus (Bulbs: *Narcissus tazetta*, p. 169) ▲

Virginia creeper
(*Parthenocissus quinquefolia*, p. 186) ▲

Glossy abelia (*Abelia* × *grandiflora*, p. 166) ●

Gateway Garden

Arbor, fence, and plantings make an inviting entry

Entrances are an important part of any landscape. They can welcome visitors onto your property; highlight a special feature, such as a rose garden; or mark the passage between two areas with different character or function. The design shown here can serve in any of these situations.

A picket fence set amid shrubs and perennials creates a friendly and attractive barrier, just enough to signal the boundary of the front yard. The simple vine-covered arbor provides welcoming access.

Uncomplicated elements are combined imaginatively in this design, creating interesting details to catch the eye and an informal, happy-to-see-you overall effect. The arbor will be covered with cheerful yellow flowers in spring, and the fence with fragrant honeysuckle blossoms in summer. For winter color, both offer evergreen foliage. A multilayered planting in front of the fence offers contrasts in foliage texture as well as pretty flowers, and enough structure to be inviting after the blossoms fade.

Coral honeysuckle **E**

Russian sage **F**

'Gracillimus' Japanese maiden grass **C**

'Goldsturm' black-eyed Susan **G**

'Stella d'Oro' daylily **I**

J Mealycup sage

Plants & Projects

For many people, a picket fence and vine-covered arbor represent old-fashioned neighborly virtues. The structures and plantings are easy to install. You can extend the fence and plantings as needed.

A **Carolina jasmine** (use 2 plants)
A lovely evergreen vine for the arbor. Sweetly fragrant clear yellow flowers bloom among the masses of shiny leaves in early spring. See *Gelsemium sempervirens*, p. 177.

B **Firebush** (use 1)
Summers set this perennial ablaze with orange-red flowers. New clusters keep coming until frost. It is planted near the arbor so you can catch a

glimpse of hummingbirds as you come and go. See *Hamelia patens*, p. 177.

C **'Gracillimus' Japanese maiden grass** (use 1)
This fine-textured grass makes an attractive anchor at one end of the planting. Stalks of creamy white flower plumes rise above the foliage in fall. See *Miscanthus sinensis* 'Gracillimus', p. 184.

D **'Radiation' lantana** (use 1)
This perennial spreads to form a 3-ft. mound of coarse green leaves topped with many small, round clusters of orange

and yellow flowers. Blooms prolifically all season. See *Lantana camara* 'Radiation', p. 181.

E **Coral honeysuckle** (use 4)
Unlike the more invasive honeysuckles, this native vine is mannerly, climbing up the fence in neat tiers of rounded blue-green leaves. Clusters of coral-colored flowers radiate from the foliage in summer and sometimes fall. See *Lonicera sempervirens* p. 183.

F **Russian sage** (use 4)
These perennials make a big splash when planted together. They offer silvery foliage and

blue flowers to cool down the border's many hot colors. See *Perovskia atriplicifolia*, p. 186.

G **'Goldsturm' black-eyed Susan** (use 1)
A popular perennial companion of ornamental grasses. It forms a robust stand of dark leaves that are blanketed in summertime with bright gold flowers. See *Rudbeckia fulgida* 'Goldsturm', p. 191.

H **Cigar plant** (use 2)
An upright perennial with the look of a dwarf oleander. It forms a dense bush bearing multiple branches of narrow

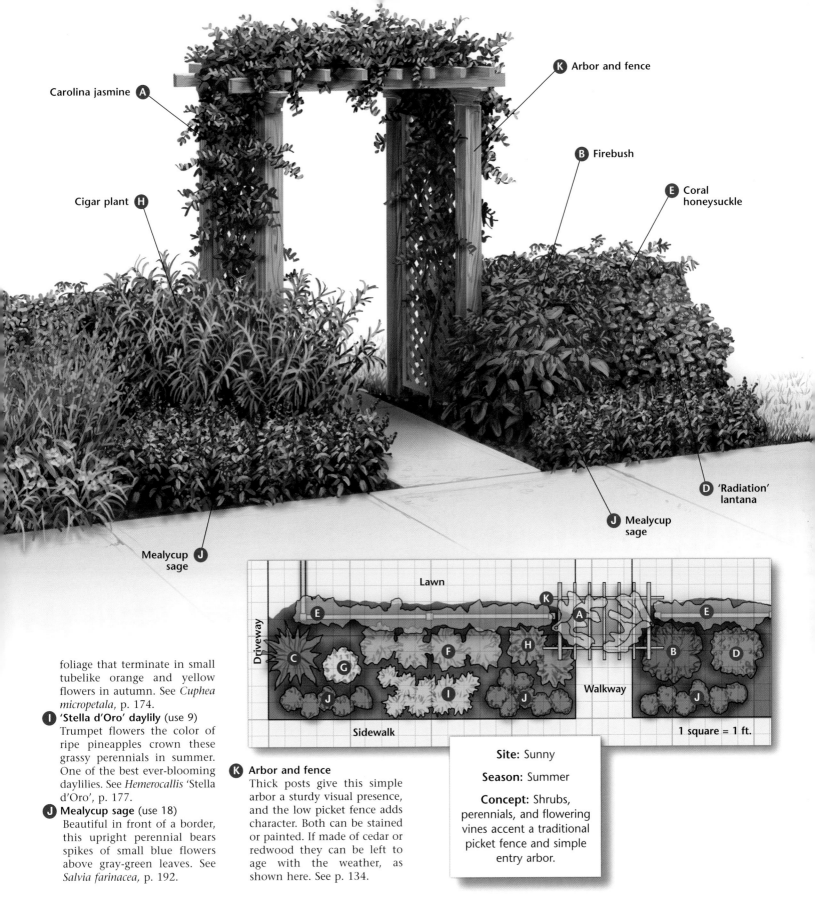

Carolina jasmine **A**

K Arbor and fence

B Firebush

E Coral honeysuckle

Cigar plant **H**

D 'Radiation' lantana

J Mealycup sage

Mealycup sage **J**

foliage that terminate in small tubelike orange and yellow flowers in autumn. See *Cuphea micropetala*, p. 174.

I 'Stella d'Oro' daylily (use 9)
Trumpet flowers the color of ripe pineapples crown these grassy perennials in summer. One of the best ever-blooming daylilies. See *Hemerocallis* 'Stella d'Oro', p. 177.

J Mealycup sage (use 18)
Beautiful in front of a border, this upright perennial bears spikes of small blue flowers above gray-green leaves. See *Salvia farinacea*, p. 192.

K Arbor and fence
Thick posts give this simple arbor a sturdy visual presence, and the low picket fence adds character. Both can be stained or painted. If made of cedar or redwood they can be left to age with the weather, as shown here. See p. 134.

Lawn

Driveway

Walkway

Sidewalk

1 square = 1 ft.

Site: Sunny

Season: Summer

Concept: Shrubs, perennials, and flowering vines accent a traditional picket fence and simple entry arbor.

Say hello with roses

Not every entry calls for a fence. This design offers a traditional welcome with a rose garden. A border of tea roses and other flowering shrubs and perennials serves as a fragrant and colorful barrier on each side of a rose-covered entry arbor. The formal symmetry (an element often associated with rose gardens) is enhanced by boxwoods trimmed into pyramids at the foot of the arbor. The roses will bloom for many months. In spring they're joined by pink dianthus and blue iris, and in late summer and fall by purple asters and sage. The boxwood's evergreen foliage provides green in winter.

Tea roses are less difficult than many people fear, but they do require regular attention.

Site: Sunny

Season: Fall

Concept: Fragrant roses and other flowers provide a sweet welcome.

Plants & Projects

A **'Climbing Old Blush' China rose** (use 2 plants)
This delicate-looking rose is nonetheless a vigorous climber. It bears apple green foliage and a steady bloom of baby pink semi-double flowers, especially in spring. See *Rosa chinensis* 'Climbing Old Blush', p. 189.

B **'Gilbert Nabonnand' tea rose** (use 2)
The silky flowers of this bushy rose are pale pink and very fragrant all season. Petals are semi-double. See *Rosa × odorata* 'Gilbert Nabonnand', p. 189.

C **'Martha Gonzales' rose** (use 6)
Wine red flowers cover this reliable dwarf rose in spring and fall. New shoots and leaves are

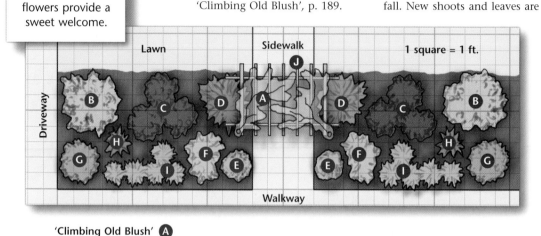

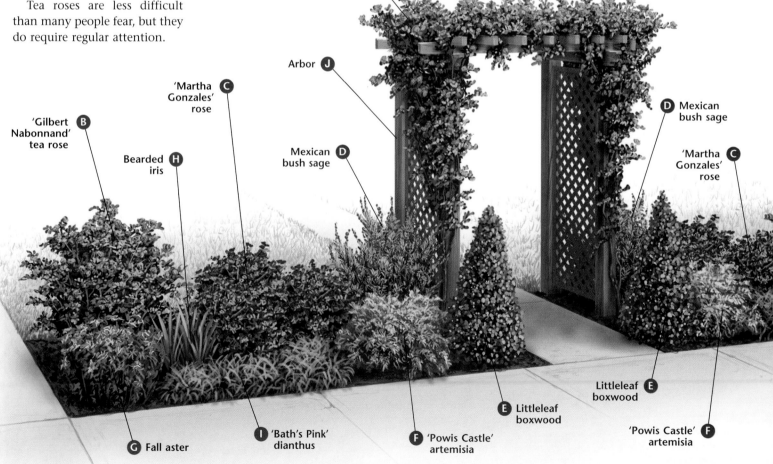

'Climbing Old Blush' China rose **A**

'Martha Gonzales' rose **C**

Arbor **J**

'Gilbert Nabonnand' tea rose **B**

Bearded iris **H**

Mexican bush sage **D**

Mexican bush sage **D**

'Martha Gonzales' rose **C**

Littleleaf boxwood **E**

'Powis Castle' artemisia **F**

G Fall aster

I 'Bath's Pink' dianthus

F 'Powis Castle' artemisia

E Littleleaf boxwood

also red. See *Rosa chinensis* 'Martha Gonzales', p. 189.

D Mexican bush sage (use 2)
This tall perennial adds height at the trellis. Bears spikes of purple and white flowers in fall. See *Salvia leucantha*, p. 193.

E Littleleaf boxwood (use 2)
Plant these dense, glossy evergreen shrubs in front of the arbor and trim them into pyramids to enhance the formal look of this arbor entry. See *Buxus microphylla*, p. 169.

F 'Powis Castle' artemisia (use 2)
Prized for its foliage texture and color, this perennial forms silvery pillows beside the boxwoods. See *Artemisia* × 'Powis Castle', p. 168.

G Fall aster (use 2)
Another fine-textured gray-green perennial to complement the boxwoods. For many weeks in fall it bursts into eye-catching lavender-purple bloom. See *Aster oblongifolius*, p. 168.

H Bearded iris (use 2)
This perennial's foliage adds a spiky presence to the planting as well as showy blue flowers in spring. *Iris* × *germanica*, p. 180.

I 'Bath's Pink' dianthus (use 10)
This perennial spreads to form low, wide tufts of very fine-textured foliage. Delicate pink flowers blanket the gray-green leaves in spring. See *Dianthus* 'Bath's Pink', p. 175.

See p. 89 for the following:

J Arbor

B 'Gilbert Nabonnand' tea rose

G Fall aster

H Bearded iris

I 'Bath's Pink' dianthus

Plant portraits

Combining compelling fragrance, lovely flowers, and handsome foliage, these plants create a distinctive entry.

● = First design, pp. 88–89
▲ = Second design, pp. 90–91

'Martha Gonzales' rose
(*Rosa chinensis*, p. 189) ▲

'Gilbert Nabonnand' tea rose
(*Rosa* × *odorata*, p. 189) ▲

'Climbing Old Blush' China rose
(*Rosa chinensis*, p. 189) ▲

Littleleaf boxwood
(*Buxus microphylla*, p. 169) ▲

A Green Screen

Hide bins for refuse and recycling with a fence, foliage, and flowers

Sometimes the simplest landscaping project packs a surprisingly big punch. This design creates a multipurpose space for storing waste and recycling bins, bags of compost, or other items that don't quite fit in the garage, keeping them out of sight but easily accessible. The paving, screen, and plantings can be installed in a weekend. With this small investment of time and money you can turn a frequently visited part of your property into a more inviting feature.

A wooden screen angles around a paved area that is roomy enough to hold recycling bins, yard-waste containers, and even a lawnmower. Made of thin vertical slats, the screen obscures the area from view yet allows ventilation. It opens at the driveway, where the bins or the mower are most likely to be wheeled out. Against the screen, a simple planting of shrubs, vines, and perennials makes a bold year-round display.

Flowers, foliage, and fruit offer warm colors throughout the year. The planting stays cheery even in the winter months. Then, the nandinas will be bright red; dormant grasses will wave their plumes; and the rosemary will begin to offer blue flowers, while continuing to recycle fresh and fragrant greenery.

Site: Sunny

Season: Late summer

Concept: Flowers, foliage, and screen integrate a refuse and recycling area into the backyard.

House

1 square = 1 ft.

Lawn

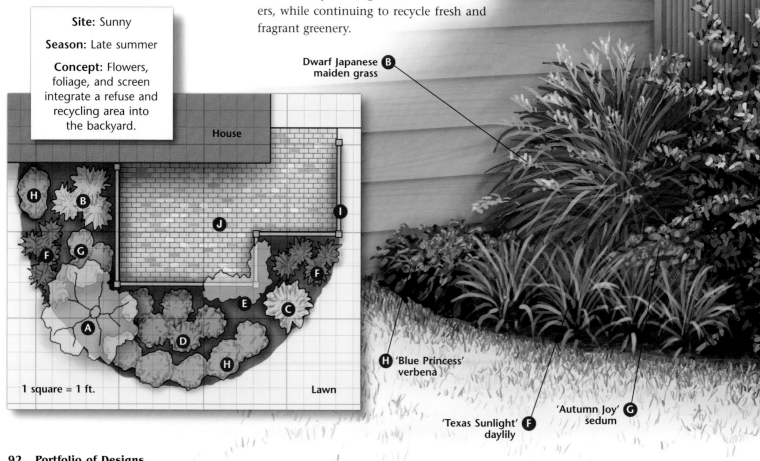

Dwarf Japanese maiden grass **B**

H 'Blue Princess' verbena

'Texas Sunlight' **F** daylily

'Autumn Joy' **G** sedum

Plants & Projects

Spend a weekend installing this project. Then keep it looking good with no more than seasonal care.

Ⓐ 'Wonderful' pomegranate (use 1 plant)

A very ornamental deciduous shrub. It decorates the space with graceful branches, glossy leaves, large orange flowers, and bright fruits as big and sweet as apples. See *Punica granatum* 'Wonderful', p. 188.

Ⓑ Dwarf Japanese maiden grass (use 3)

Planted together, these grasses form small fountains of slender foliage topped with creamy white flower heads in fall. Foliage and seed heads last through winter. See *Miscanthus sinensis* 'Adagio', p. 184.

Ⓒ 'Hill's Hardy' rosemary (use 1)

This Mediterranean shrub is prized in the garden and the kitchen for its fine-textured fragrant evergeen foliage. Small blue flowers make a welcome appearance in late winter. See *Rosmarinus officinalis* 'Hill's Hardy', p. 191.

Ⓓ 'Gulf Stream' heavenly bamboo (use 5)

The fine-textured foliage of this tidy evergreen shrub changes color with the seasons. In winter it puts on a bright red coat. See *Nandina domestica* 'Gulf Stream', p. 185.

Ⓔ Sweet autumn clematis (use 1)

This leafy vine covers the fence in fall with a fine cloud of fragrant starlike flowers. After the bloom an attractive filligree of silvery seed heads persists through winter. Vine can be left alone or pruned to concentrate the foliage and flowers along the top. See *Clematis terniflora*, p. 173.

Ⓕ 'Texas Sunlight' daylily (use 9)

This perennial forms a neat mound of grassy foliage crowned with large, gold, bell-shaped flowers. It blooms happily in the midsummer heat. See *Hemerocallis* 'Texas Sunlight', p. 177.

Ⓖ 'Autumn Joy' sedum (use 3)

A great perennial partner for maiden grass. Large succulent leaves and flat-topped flower heads create bold contrast. Blooms turn from pink to tan from late summer to fall. See *Sedum* 'Autumn Joy', p. 194.

Ⓗ 'Blue Princess' verbena (use 6)

This perennial spreads to form a fine mat of leaves topped with lavender-blue flowers. Continuous bloom from spring to autumn if regularly deadheaded. See *Verbena × hybrida* 'Blue Princess', p. 197.

Ⓘ Screen

A simple structure of louvered slats screens bins from sight while allowing air to circulate. See p. 136.

Ⓙ Paving

Simple to install, precast pavers make a durable surface that is easy to sweep up when bags break or bins overflow. See p. 108.

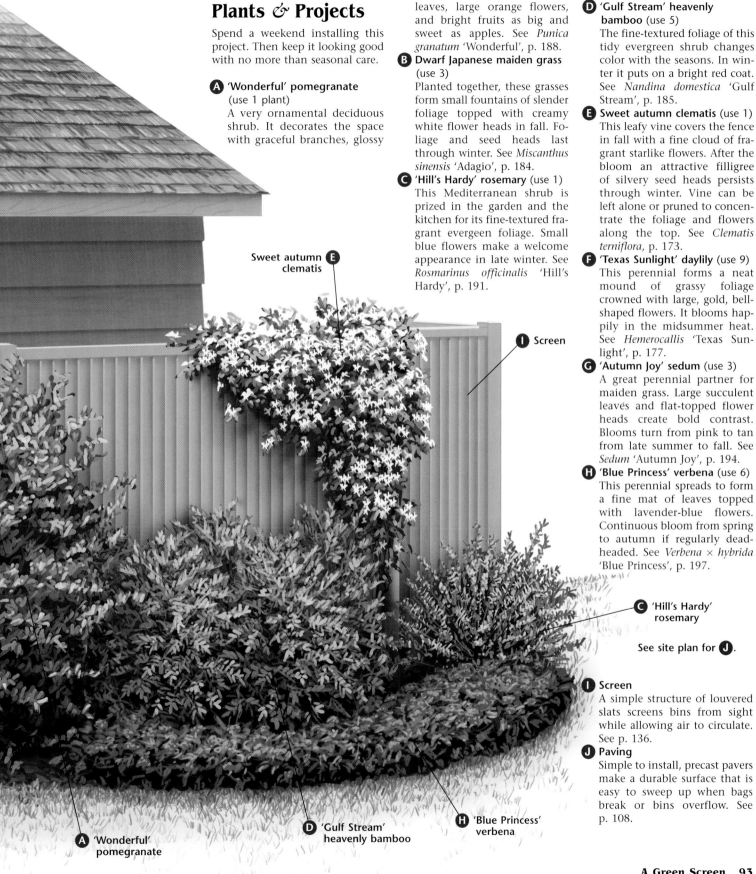

Sweet autumn clematis **Ⓔ**

Ⓘ Screen

Ⓒ 'Hill's Hardy' rosemary

See site plan for **Ⓙ**.

Ⓐ 'Wonderful' pomegranate

Ⓓ 'Gulf Stream' heavenly bamboo

Ⓗ 'Blue Princess' verbena

Screen for a shady site

The concept here is similar to that in the preceding design—create a storage area and screen it from view with just a weekend's work. The difference is that the plants in this design will do all the screening and thrive in dappled shade.

On the side facing the house, evergreen shrubs make an effective and attractive screen throughout the year. A small flowering tree and perennials taper off the screen around the back, creating a more open view from the backyard.

The tones and textures of the evergreen foliage will look cool and refreshing in the heat of summer. And the purples and greens will brighten up fall and winter months. Flowers add to the seasonal display, starting with redbud and columbine in early spring. Mexican petunia and purple heart follow in summer, and pink camellias arrive in the autumn.

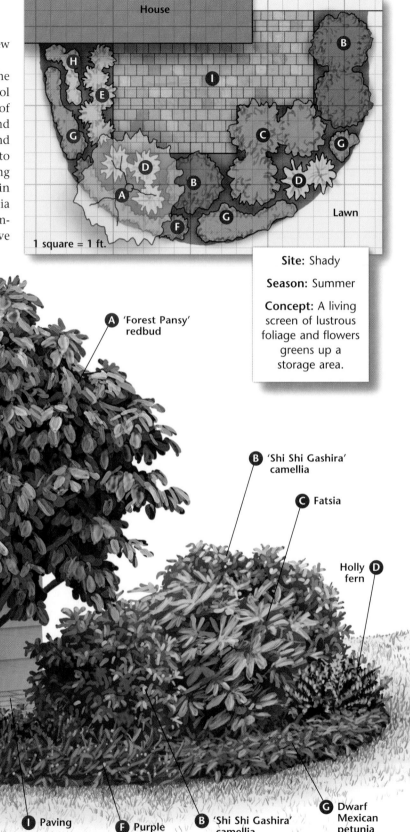

Site: Shady

Season: Summer

Concept: A living screen of lustrous foliage and flowers greens up a storage area.

1 square = 1 ft.

A 'Forest Pansy' redbud

B 'Shi Shi Gashira' camellia

C Fatsia

D Holly fern

H Texas gold columbine

G Dwarf Mexican petunia

E Inland sea oats

D Holly fern

I Paving

F Purple heart

B 'Shi Shi Gashira' camellia

G Dwarf Mexican petunia

Plants & Projects

Ⓐ 'Forest Pansy' redbud
(use 1 plant)
This small deciduous tree dazzles in spring, first producing pink flowers and then red-purple leaves that gradually turn green. See *Cercis canadensis* 'Forest Pansy', p. 172.

Ⓑ 'Shi Shi Gashira' camellia
(use 3)
Shimmering dark green leaves and neat growth habit make this evergreen shrub a beautiful and an effective year-round screen. Rose-colored flowers bloom for many weeks in fall. See *Camellia sasanqua* 'Shi Shi Gashira', p. 171.

Ⓒ Fatsia (use 3)
A bold tropical-looking shrub with layers of very large, deeply-lobed leaves that keep their shine all year. See *Fatsia japonica*, p. 175.

Ⓓ Holly fern (use 5)
This evergreen fern forms a patch of fuzzy brown stems and leathery fronds. See Ferns: *Cyrtomium falcatum*, p. 176.

Ⓔ Inland sea oats (use 5)
This perennial grass creates an informal knee-high hedge; green in summer, russet in winter. In midsummer distinctive seed heads dangle among the foliage. See *Chasmanthium latifolium*, p. 172.

Ⓕ Purple heart (use 3)
An old-fashioned perennial favorite. The lavender-purple foliage heightens the purple undertones of the redbud leaves. See *Setcreasea pallida* 'Purple Heart', p. 194.

Ⓖ Dwarf Mexican petunia
(use 19)
With its dark green foliage and lavender purple flowers this perennial makes an attractive informal border. See *Ruellia brittoniana* 'Katie', p. 192.

Ⓗ Texas gold columbine (use 4)
Native to Texas, this perennial forms a neat mound behind the coarser ruellia. In spring it sends up slender stalks of golden flowers as bright and airy as butterflies. See *Aquilegia chrysantha hinckleyana*, p. 167.

See p. 93 for the following:

Ⓘ Paving

Plant portraits

A mix of carefree plants creates or complements a colorful screen in all seasons.

● = First design, pp. 92–93
▲ = Second design, pp. 94–95

'Shi Shi Gashira' camellia
(*Camellia sasanqua*, p. 171) ▲

Purple heart
(*Setcreasea pallida*, p. 194) ▲

Sweet autumn clematis
(*Clematis terniflora*, p. 173) ●

'Forest Pansy' redbud (*Cercis canadensis*, p. 172) ▲

Elegant Symmetry
Make a formal garden for your backyard

Formal landscaping often lends dignity to the public areas around a home (see pp. 30–31). Formality can also be rewarding in a more private setting. There, the groomed plants, geometric lines, and symmetrical layout of a formal garden can help to organize the surrounding landscaping, provide an elegant area for entertaining, or simply be enjoyed for their own sake.

"Formal" need not mean elaborate. This elegant design is no more than a circle inside a square. Concentric low hedges of clipped boxwood define the circle; a gravel path around the perimeter defines the square. The path continues through the center, opening into a small square decorated with a terra cotta planter set on a grassy carpet.

The tallest elements in the design are four white-flowering trees interplanted with pyramidal evergreens. Enclosed in semicircular hedges and surrounded by grassy ground covers, white roses, and stately purple and gold perennials, these trees and shrubs create the effect of an enchanted *bosque*, a French word for a small, formal wood.

Even more than other types of landscaping, formal gardens work well only when carefully correlated with other elements in the landscape, including structures and plants. A round garden can be difficult to integrate. Relate it to rectilinear elements, such as a fence or hedges. And repeat plants used in the design elsewhere in your landscape to tie things together.

Plants & Projects

Of all gardens, a formal garden most obviously reflects the efforts of its makers. After the hedge has filled in, this garden requires attention mostly to keep it looking neat—shearing the hedges, pruning, deadheading the perennials, and seasonal cleanup.

A **'Diana' althea** (use 4 plants)
Pruned here as small trees, they wear a healthy coat of green leaves. In summer and fall they bear beautiful white hibiscus blossoms. See *Hibiscus syriacus* 'Diana', p. 179.

B **Compact Carolina cherry laurel** (use 4)
A native evergreen shrub, it offers shiny dark green leaves and spikes of scented white flowers in spring. Shear to maintain a formal shape. See *Prunus caroliniana* 'Compacta', p. 188.

Site: Sunny

Season: Early summer

Concept: This self-contained planting could fill a small backyard or join other features on a larger property.

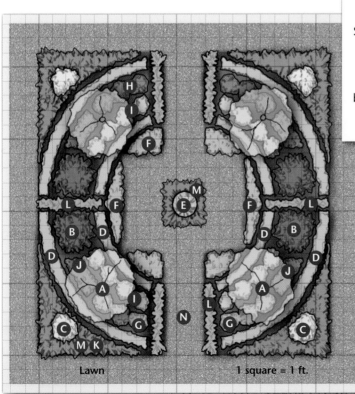

'Diana' althea **A**

Dwarf Mexican petunia **J**

'Green Beauty' littleleaf boxwood **D**

'Marie Pavie' polyantha rose **C**

Lawn

1 square = 1 ft.

See site plan for **K**.   **M** Mondo grass

C 'Marie Pavie' polyantha rose (use 4)
Clusters of small white roses cover this shrub rose from spring to frost. Buds have a pink cast. If this cultivar isn't available, consider 'White Pet' or 'Marie Daly'. See *Rosa × polyantha* 'Marie Pavie', p. 189.

D 'Green Beauty' littleleaf boxwood (use 68)
A dense habit and fine texture make this evergreen shrub ideal for shearing into clipped hedges. See *Buxus microphylla* 'Green Beauty', p. 169.

E Yellow variegated agave (use 1)
Similar to yucca but shorter, this shrub creates a bold centerpiece above a planting of fine-leafed grass. See *Agave americana* 'Marginata', p. 167.

F 'Trailing Lavender' lantana (use 6)
Lantanas are prized for their continuous and lavish bloom. This cultivar frames the central walkway with lacy clusters of lavender-purple flowers from spring to frost. See *Lantana montevidensis* 'Trailing Lavender', p. 181.

G Texas gold columbine (use 6)
This perennial's bright yellow flowers float above soft mounds of fernlike foliage in spring.

Blooms are abundant and long-lasting. See *Aquilegia chrysantha hinckleyana*, p. 167.

H Purple verbena (use 6)
Masses of wispy purple flowers wave above low clumps of foliage. This perennial complements the gold columbine. See *Verbena bonariensis,* p. 197.

I St. John's wort (use 16)
This mounding semi-evergreen shrub forms a dense mass of medium-green foliage that turns colorful in fall. Yellow flowers appear in summer. See *Hypericum calycinum*, p. 179.

J Dwarf Mexican petunia (use 20)
A beautiful and durable perennial ground cover. Clusters of purple petunia-like blooms appear at the center of neat leafy mounds. See *Ruellia brittoniana* 'Katie', p. 192.

K White rainlily (use 48)
Planted among the lilyturf, this bulb makes white flowers after late summer rains. See Bulbs: *Zephyranthes candida,* p. 169.

L 'Big Blue' lilyturf (use 30)
This grasslike perennial makes a neat edging along the path. Bears spikes of small lavender flowers. See *Liriope muscari* 'Big Blue', p. 183.

M Mondo grass (use 100)
This perennial will gradually grow into a continuous mat of very fine leaves. See *Ophiopogon japonicus*, p. 186.

N Walkway
Crushed stone is easy to install and suits the simple lines of this design. The pink granite we've shown here weathers to a terracotta pink. See p. 108.

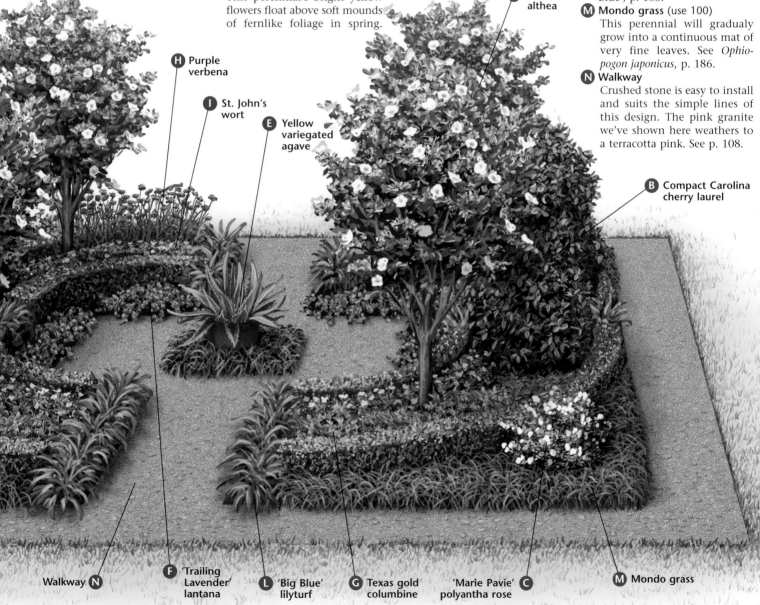

H Purple verbena

I St. John's wort

E Yellow variegated agave

A 'Diana' althea

B Compact Carolina cherry laurel

Walkway **N**   **F** 'Trailing Lavender' lantana   **L** 'Big Blue' lilyturf   **G** Texas gold columbine   'Marie Pavie' polyantha rose **C**   **M** Mondo grass

Garden oasis

Palms and a pool give this garden a tropical look. The layout takes its inspiration from a compass or sundial. Four columnar palm trees planted outside the perimeter path mark the four directions of the compass. Interior paths lead from the "living" columns to a small lily pond at the center.

The planting beds are designed with the sun's path in mind. Two beds on the side of the afternoon sun are planted with bold shrubs and perennials that look cool even in the heat. The beds receiving morning light feature delicate roses and fine-textured grasses. All are chosen for their drought and heat tolerance, but as in any oasis, added water will produce more foliage and flowers.

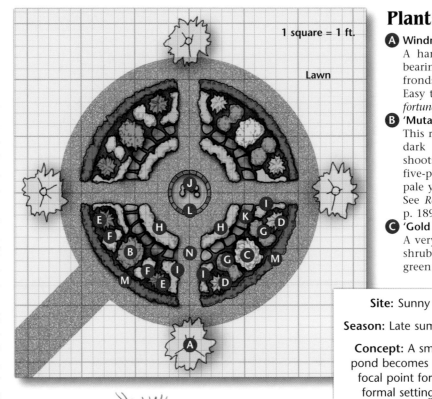

1 square = 1 ft.

Lawn

Plants & Projects

A **Windmill palm** (use 4 plants)
A handsome little palm tree bearing a crown of dark green fronds and a shaggy trunk. Easy to grow. See *Trachycarpus fortunei*, p. 196.

B **'Mutabilis' China rose** (use 2)
This rose forms a 4 ft. bush of dark green leaves and red shoots. The flowers are single, five-petaled, and change from pale yellow to orange to pink. See *Rosa chinensis* 'Mutabilis', p. 189.

C **'Gold Star' esperanza** (use 2)
A very showy tropical-looking shrub. The foliage is bright green and has a crisp look.

Site: Sunny

Season: Late summer

Concept: A small pond becomes the focal point for a formal setting.

A Windmill palm

See site plan for **K**.

Gray **H** santolina

'Mutabilis' **B** China rose

'Gold Star' **C** esperanza

Path **N**

Tropical **F** plumbago

'Morning Light' **E** Japanese maiden grass

'Bath's Pink' **I** dianthus

Pond **L**

J Dauben water lily

D Soft-tip yucca

G Purple heart

M 'Big Blue' lilyturf

Golden bell-like flowers bloom in clusters from May to November. Deciduous in most parts of Texas. See *Tecoma stans* 'Gold Star', p. 196.

D Soft-tip yucca (use 4)
A bold accent plant, this perennial bears long pointed sword-like leaves with bent tips. It sends up branched stalks of large white flowers in summer. See *Yucca gloriosa,* p. 199.

E 'Morning Light' Japanese maiden grass (use 4)
A must for a cool oasis, this grass forms a fountain of arching light green foliage. See *Miscanthus sinensis* 'Morning Light,' p. 184.

F Tropical plumbago (use 8)
This perennial will fill the space with small, oval, bright green leaves. Bears tight clusters of cool blue flowers in the heat of summer. See *Plumbago auriculata,* p. 187.

G Purple heart (use 8)
This perennial ground cover creates a thick mat of colorful, interesting foliage. Pale pink flowers bloom throughout the season. See *Setcreasea pallida* 'Purple Heart', p. 194.

H Gray santolina (use 20)
A handsome low-growing shrub. Thick gray foliage looks like lavender. Yellow flowers in the summer. See *Santolina chamaecyparissus,* p. 193.

I 'Bath's Pink' dianthus (use 32)
Another excellent edging, this perennial forms a year-round mat of short, very narrow silver foliage. Spring flowers are pink and fragrant. See *Dianthus* 'Bath's Pink', p. 175.

J Dauben water lily (use 1)
A small plant for a small-scale pond. Lavender flowers bloom among floating leaves nonstop in summer heat. See p. 198.

K Steppingstones
Gray limestone makes a decorative edging around the santolina. See p. 113.

L Pond
Use a round fiberglass shell for this small pool. See p. 116.

See p. 97 for the following:

M 'Big Blue' lilyturf (use 48)

N Path

Plant portraits

These well-behaved, low-care shrubs, bulbs, and perennials bring form, texture, flowers, and scent to a formal garden.

● = First design, pp. 96–97
▲ = Second design, pp. 98–99

Dauben water lily
(Water plants: *Nymphaea,* p. 198) ▲

'Green Beauty' littleleaf boxwood
(*Buxus microphylla,* p. 169) ●

'Diana' althea (*Hibiscus syriacus,* p. 179) ●

'Marie Pavie' polyantha rose (*Rosa × polyantha,* p. 189) ●

Yellow variegated agave
(*Agave americana* 'Marginata', p. 167) ●

White rainlily
(Bulbs: *Zephyranthes candida,* p. 169) ●

Guide to Installation

In this section, we introduce the hard but rewarding work of landscaping. Here you'll find the information you need about all the tasks required to install any of the designs in this book, organized in the order in which you'd most likely tackle them. Clearly written text and numerous illustrations help you learn how to plan the job; clear the site; construct paths, patios, ponds, fences, arbors, and trellises; prepare the planting beds; and install and maintain the plantings. Roll up your sleeves and dig in. In just a few weekends you can create a landscape feature that will provide years of enjoyment.

Organizing Your Project

If your gardening experience is limited to mowing the lawn, pruning the bushes, and growing some flowers and vegetables, the thought of starting from scratch and installing a whole new landscape feature might be intimidating. But in fact, adding one of the designs in this book to your property is completely within reach, if you approach the job the right way. The key is to divide the project into a series of steps and take them one at a time. This is how professional landscapers work. It's efficient and orderly, and it makes even big jobs seem manageable.

On this and the facing page, we explain how to think your way through a landscaping project and anticipate the various steps. Subsequent topics in this section describe how to do each part of the job. Detailed instructions and illustrations cover all the techniques you'll need to install any design from start to finish.

The step-by-step approach

Choose a design and adapt it to your site. The designs in this book address parts of the home landscape. In the most attractive and effective home landscapes, all the various parts work together. Don't be afraid to change the shape of beds; alter the number, kinds, and positions of plants; or revise paths and structures to bring them into harmony with their surroundings.

To see the relationships with your existing landscape, you can draw the design on a scaled plan of your property. Or you can work on the site itself, placing wooden stakes, pots, or whatever is handy to represent plants and structures.

Lay out the design on site. Once you've decided what you want to do, you'll need to lay out the paths and structures and outline the beds. Some people are comfortable pacing off distances and relying on their eye to judge sizes and relative positions. Others prefer to transfer the grid from the plan full size onto the site, using garden lime (a white powder available at nurseries) like chalk on a blackboard to "draw" a grid or outlines of planting beds.

Digging postholes

Amending soil

16-16-16

COMPOST

Clear the site. (See pp. 104–105.) Sometimes you have to work around existing features—a nice big tree, a building or fence, a sidewalk—but it's usually easiest to start a new landscaping project by removing unwanted structures or pavement and killing, cutting down, or uprooting all the plants. This can generate a lot of debris to dispose of, but it's often worth the trouble to make a fresh start.

Make provisions for water. (See pp. 106–107.) In Texas, most landscape plants require more water than nature provides. A well-thought-out irrigation strategy and system can help you make the most of this increasingly precious natural resource. You'll need to plan its installation carefully. Some permanent parts of most watering systems need to be installed before the other landscape features. Additional parts are installed after the soil is prepared. And the final components are normally placed after planting.

Build the "hardscape." (See pp. 108–141.) Hardscape includes landscape structures such as fences, trellises, arbors, retaining walls, walkways, edging, and outdoor lighting. Install these elements before you start any planting.

Prepare the soil. (See pp. 142–145.) On most properties, it's uncommon to find soil that's as good as it should be for growing plants. Typically, the soil around a new house is shallow, compacted, and infertile. Some plants tolerate such poor conditions, but they don't thrive. To grow healthy, attractive plants, you need to improve the quality of the soil throughout the entire area that you're planning to plant.

Do the planting and add mulch. (See pp. 146–151.) Putting plants in the ground usually goes quite quickly and gives instant gratification. Mulching the soil makes the area look neat even while the plants are still small.

Maintain the planting. (See pp. 151–163.) Most plantings need regular watering and occasional weeding for the first year or two. After that, depending on the design you've chosen, you'll have to do some routine maintenance—watering, pruning, shaping, cutting back, and cleaning up—to keep the plants looking their best. This may take as little as a few hours a year or as much as an hour or two every week throughout the growing season.

Planting

Setting flagstones

Clearing the Site

The site you've chosen for a landscaping project may or may not need to be cleared of fences, old pavement, construction debris, and other objects. Unless your house is newly built, the site will almost certainly be covered with plants.

Before you start cutting plants down, try to find someone to identify them for you. As you walk around together, make a sketch that shows which plants are where, and attach labels to the plants, too. Determine if there are any desirable plants worth saving—mature shade trees that you should work around, shapely shrubs that aren't too big to dig up and relocate or give away, worthwhile perennials and ground covers that you could divide and replant, healthy sod that you could lay elsewhere. Likewise, decide which plants need to go—diseased or crooked trees, straggly or overgrown shrubs, weedy brush, invasive ground covers, tattered lawn.

You can clear small areas yourself, bundling the brush for pickup and tossing soft-stemmed plants on the compost pile, but if you have lots of woody brush or any trees to remove, you might want to hire someone else to do the job. A crew armed with power tools can turn a thicket into a pile of wood chips in just a few hours. Have them pull out the roots and grind the stumps, too. Save the chips; they're good for surfacing paths, or you can use them as mulch.

Working around a tree

If there are any large, healthy trees on your site, be careful as you work around them. It's okay to prune off some of a tree's limbs, as shown on the facing page, but respect its trunk and its roots. Keep heavy equipment from beneath the tree's canopy, and don't raise or lower the level of the soil there. Try never to cut or wound the bark on the trunk (don't nail things to a tree), because that exposes the tree to disease organisms. Planting beneath existing Texas natives such as post oaks can endanger their health. Consult a certified arborist on ways to integrate these handsome, but sensitive, trees into your landscape and care for them properly.

Killing perennial weeds

Some common weeds that sprout back from perennial roots or runners are bindweed, Bermuda grass, Johnson grass, nutsedge, smilax, and Carolina snailseed. Garden plants that can become weedy include bamboo, Mexican petunia, mint, and *Liriope spicata*. Once they get established, perennial weeds are hard to eliminate. You can't just cut off the tops, because the plants keep sprouting back. You need to dig the weeds out, smother them, or kill them with an herbicide, and it's better to do this before you plant a bed.

Digging. You can often do a good job of removing a perennial weed if you dig carefully at the base of the stems, find the roots, and follow them as far as possible through the soil, pulling out every bit of root that you find. Some plant roots go deeper than you can dig. Most plants will resprout from the bits that you miss, but these leftover sprouts are easy to pull.

Smothering. This technique is easier than digging, particularly for eradicating large infestations, but much slower. First mow or cut the tops of the weeds as close to the ground as possible ❶. Then cover the area with sections from the newspaper, over-

Smothering weeds

❶ Smothering kills weeds by depriving them of light. Cut the tops off close to the ground.

❷ Cover with thick newspaper or cardboard.

❸ Top with several inches of mulch. Wait a few months to be sure weeds are dead; then till rotted newspaper and mulch into the soil.

Moving turf

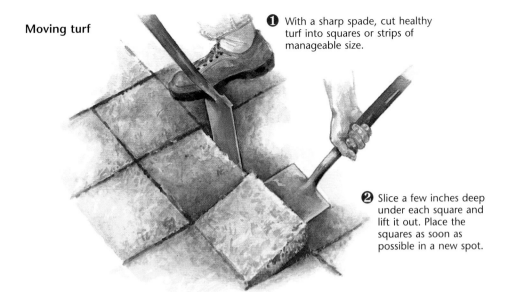

❶ With a sharp spade, cut healthy turf into squares or strips of manageable size.

❷ Slice a few inches deep under each square and lift it out. Place the squares as soon as possible in a new spot.

lapped like shingles, or flattened-out cardboard boxes ❷. Top with a layer of mulch, such as straw, grass clippings, or wood chips, spread several inches deep ❸.

Smothering works by excluding light, which stops photosynthesis. If any shoots reach up through the covering and produce green leaves, pull them out immediately. Wait a few months, until you're sure the weeds are dead, before you dig into the smothered area and plant there.

In Texas, where summers are hot, you can also kill weeds through a process called solarization. Till the weeds into the soil and moisten the area. Then cover the soil with a thick sheet of clear plastic, sealing its edges by burying them in a shallow trench. The heat generated underneath the plastic kills the weeds.

Spraying. Herbicides are easy, fast, and effective weed killers when chosen and applied with care. Ask at the nursery for those that break down quickly into more benign substances, and make sure the weed you're trying to kill is listed on the product label. Apply all herbicides exactly as directed by the manufacturer. After spraying, you usually need to wait from one to four weeks for the weed to die completely, and some weeds need to be sprayed a second or third time before they give up.

Replacing turf

If you're planning to add a landscape feature where you now have lawn, you can "recycle" the turf to repair or extend the lawn elsewhere on your property.

The drawing above shows a technique for removing relatively small areas of strong healthy turf for replanting elsewhere. First, with a sharp spade, cut it into squares or strips about 1 to 2 ft. square (these small pieces are easy to lift) ❶. Then slice a few inches deep under each square and lift the squares, roots and all, like brownies from a pan ❷. Quickly transplant the squares to a previously prepared site. If necessary, level the turf with a water-filled roller from a rental business. Water well until the roots are established. You can rent a sod-cutting machine for larger areas.

If you don't need the turf anywhere else, or if it's straggly or weedy, leave it in place and kill the grass. One way to kill grass is to cover it with a tarp or a sheet of black plastic for about four weeks during the heat of summer. A single application of herbicide kills some grasses, but you may need to spray vigorous turf twice. After you've killed the grass, dig or till the bed, shredding the turf, roots and all, and mixing it into the soil. This is hard work if the soil is dry but less so if the ground has been softened by a recent rain or watering.

Removing large limbs

If there are large trees on your property now, you may want to remove some of the lower limbs so you can walk and see underneath them and so more light can reach plantings you're planning beneath them. Major pruning of large trees is a job for a professional arborist, but you can remove limbs smaller than 4 in. in diameter and less than 10 ft. above the ground yourself with a simple bow saw or pole saw.

Use the three-step procedure shown below to remove large limbs safely and without harming the tree. First, saw partway through the bottom of the limb, approximately 1 ft. out from the trunk ❶. This keeps the bark from tearing down the trunk when the limb falls. Then make a corresponding cut an inch or so farther out, down through the limb ❷. Finally, remove the stub ❸. Undercut it slightly or hold it as you finish the cut, so it doesn't fall away and peel bark off the trunk. Note that the cut is not flush with the trunk but is just outside the thick area at the limb's base, called the branch collar. Leaving the branch collar helps the wound heal quickly and naturally. Wound dressing is considered unnecessary today.

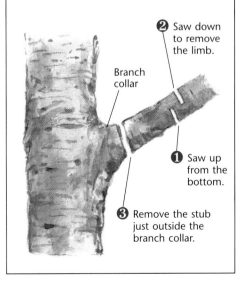

❷ Saw down to remove the limb.

Branch collar

❶ Saw up from the bottom.

❸ Remove the stub just outside the branch collar.

Water for Your Plants

Texas's long, dry summers and frequent droughts make watering a critical concern of gardeners here. Though some plants will survive long dry periods once established, almost all plants will need regular watering the first few years after planting. And most will need summer watering their entire life to look their best.

But there is more at stake than just the survival of plants. Water conservation is a daily obligation in Texas, where water is a valuable and limited resource. Outdoor landscapes use a large portion of urban water, so nothing should be wasted. During periods of drought, mandatory conservation is often strictly enforced.

So for the health of your plants and for the preservation of a valuable resource, make water conservation part of your landscape planning from the beginning.

The box below outlines effective water-saving practices for home landscapes. (See pp. 154–155 for more on when and how much to water.) You can also consult your local water department for advice about watering gardens and lawns.

Watering systems

One of the best ways to conserve water is to use an efficient delivery system. The simplest watering systems—watering cans and hand-held hoses—are also the most limited and inefficient. They can be adequate for watering new transplants or widely separated individual plants. But sprinkling plants in an entire bed with a hose and nozzle for even as long as an hour may provide less water than half an inch of rainfall. And wetting just the top few inches of soil this way encourages shallow root growth, making it necessary to water more frequently. To provide enough water to soak the soil to a depth of a foot or more, you need a system that can run untended for extended periods.

Hose-end sprinklers are easy to set up and leave to soak an area. But they're also inefficient: Water is blown away by wind. It runs off sloped or paved areas. It is applied unevenly, or it falls too far away from individual plants to be of use to them. And because sprinklers soak leaves as well as soil, the damp foliage may breed fungal diseases.

Low-volume irrigation. For garden beds and landscape plantings like those in this book, low-volume irrigation systems are the most efficient and offer the most flexibility and control. Frequently called "drip" irrigation systems, they deliver water at low pressure through a network of plastic pipes, hoses, and tubing and a variety of emitters and microsprinklers. Such systems are designed to apply water slowly and directly to the roots of targeted plants, so very little water is lost to runoff and evaporation or wasted on plants that don't need it. Because water is usually applied at soil level, the risk of foliar diseases is reduced. And because less soil is watered, weeds are also reduced.

Simple low-volume systems can be attached to ordinary outdoor faucets or garden hoses and controlled manually, just like a sprinkler. You can set such a system up in less than an hour. Sophisticated systems include (1) their own attachment to your main water supply, (2) a network of valves and buried pipes that allow you to divide your property into zones, and (3) an electronic control device that can automatically water each zone at preset times for preset durations. Such systems often incorporate sprinkler systems for lawns.

A person with modest mechanical skills and basic tools can plan and install a low-volume irrigation system. Extensive multi-zoned systems (particularly those with

Water-Wise Practices

Choose plants carefully. Many plants that require little water, including Texas natives, thrive in the state's dry summer climate and are increasingly available from local nurseries and garden centers.

Group plants with similar water needs. Position plants that require the most water near the house, where they can be more easily tended and served by watering systems. Use drought-tolerant plants farther from the house.

Mulch plantings. A 2- to 3-in. layer of mulch reduces evaporation by keeping the soil cool and sheltering it from wind.

Create water-retaining basins. Use these to direct irrigation water to large plants. Make a low soil mound around the plant's perimeter, at its drip line. (Basins aren't necessary in drip-irrigated beds.)

Plant in fall. This way, new plants will have the cooler, wetter winter and spring seasons to become established before facing the heat of summer.

Limit lawn size. Lawns demand lots of water. Reduce the size of your lawn by planting beds, borders, and less thirsty ground covers.

Water in the morning. Lower morning temperatures and less wind mean less water is lost to evaporation.

Adjust watering to conditions. Water less during cool weather in the spring and fall. Turn off automatic timers during rainy periods.

Install, monitor, and maintain an irrigation system. Even a simple drip system conserves water. Once it's installed, check and adjust the equipment regularly.

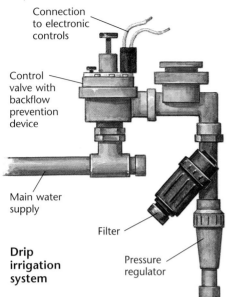

Connection to electronic controls

Control valve with backflow prevention device

Main water supply

Filter

Pressure regulator

Drip irrigation system

Basic components of a drip irrigation system are shown here. Individual systems will vary. Several common types of emitters are shown; systems can incorporate others.

their own attachment to the main water supply) are more difficult to design and install. If you tackle one, have a professional review your plans before you start. You can buy kits or individual components from garden centers, nurseries, or specialty suppliers. (The main components of low-volume systems are outlined below.) Good criteria for choosing among different local suppliers are their knowledge of system design and installation and their ability to help you with both. A supplier may charge for this service, but good advice is worth the money.

Low-volume-system components. Any irrigation system connected to a domestic water supply needs a **backflow prevention device** (also called an antisiphon device) at the point of connection to the water supply to protect drinking water from contamination. Backflow devices are often mandated by city building codes, so check with local health or building officials to determine if a specific type of backflow prevention device is required.

Install a **filter** to prevent minerals and flakes that slough off metal water pipes from clogging the emitters. You'll need to clean the filter regularly. Between the filter and emitters, all hoses and tubing should be plastic, not metal.

Pressure regulators reduce the mains' water pressure to levels required by the system's low-volume emitters.

Supply lines deliver water from the source to the emitters. Some systems incorporate buried lines of rigid plastic pipe to carry water to plantings anywhere on the property. For aboveground use, you'll need flexible tubing designed specifically for low-volume irrigation.

Emitters and **soaker hoses** deliver the water to the plants. A wide range of emitters are available for different kinds of plants and garden situations. Various drip fittings, bubblers, and microsprinklers can be plugged into the flexible plastic tubing. A single emitter or a group of emitters might serve individual or groups of plants.

Soaker hoses and "ooze" tubes seep or drip water along their length. Consult with your supplier about which delivery systems best meet your plants' needs. (The high calcium and salt content of many water sources in Texas can clog drip emitters, so check emitters regularly to make sure they are watering properly.)

A **timer** or **electronic controller** helps ensure efficient water use. Unlike you, a controller won't forget and leave the water on too long. (It may also water during a rainstorm, however.) Used in conjunction with zoned plantings, these devices provide control and flexibility to deal with the specific water needs of groups of plants or even individual specimens. They also allow you to go on vacation confident that your plants will get enough water.

Installation. Permanent irrigation equipment should be installed early in any landscaping project. Lay underground piping that crosses paths, patios, or similar landscape features after the site is cleared but before installing any of these permanent features. It is best to lay pipes in planting areas, including lawns, after you have prepared the soil. That way, you won't damage the piping when digging or rototilling. Install underground pipe in trenches dug to the appropriate depth. Then temporarily cap the ends. Hook up the aboveground tubing and position emitters after planting.

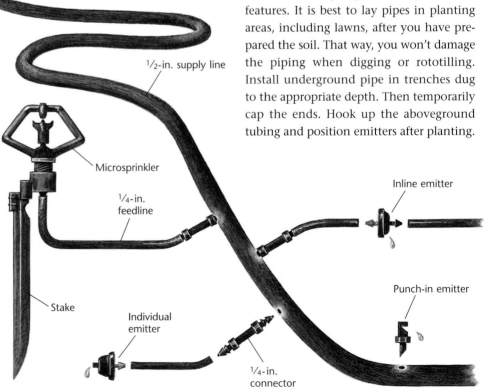

½-in. supply line

Microsprinkler

¼-in. feedline

Stake

Individual emitter

¼-in. connector

Inline emitter

Punch-in emitter

Making Paths and Walkways

Every landscape needs paths and walkways if for no other reason than to keep your feet dry as you move from one place to another. A path can also divide and define the spaces in the landscape, orchestrate the way the landscape is viewed, and even be a key element enhancing its beauty.

Whether it is a graceful curving garden path or a utilitarian slab leading to the garage, a walk has two main functional requirements: durability and safety. It should hold up through seasonal changes. It should provide a well-drained surface that is easy to walk on and to maintain.

A path's function helps determine its surface and its character. In general, heavily trafficked walkways leading to a door, garage, or shed need hard, smooth (but not slick) surfaces and should take you where you want to go fairly directly. A path to a backyard play area could be a strip of soft wood bark, easy on the knees of impatient children. A relaxed stroll in the garden might require only a hopscotch collection of flat stones meandering from one prized plant to another.

Before laying out a walk or path, spend some time observing existing traffic patterns. If your path makes use of a route people already take (particularly children), they'll be more likely to stay on the path and off the lawn or flowers. Avoid areas that are slow to drain. When determining path width, consider whether the path must accommodate rototillers and wheelbarrows or two strollers walking abreast, or just provide steppingstone access for maintaining the plants.

Dry-laid paths

You can make a path simply by laying bricks or spreading wood chips on top of bare earth. While quick and easy, this method has serious drawbacks. Laid on the surface, with no edging to contain them, loose materials are soon scattered, and solid materials are easily jostled out of place. If the earth base doesn't drain very well, the path will be a swamp after a rainstorm. In cold-winter areas of Texas, repeated freezing and thawing expands and contracts the soil, moving path and

walkway materials laid on it. The effect of this "frost heaving" is minimal on loose materials such as wood chips or gravel, but it can shift brick and stone significantly out of line, making the path unsightly and potentially dangerous.

The method we recommend—laying surface material on an excavated base of sand or gravel, or both—minimizes these problems. Water moves through sand and gravel quickly, and such a base "cushions" the surface materials from any freeze-thaw movement of the underlying soil. Excavation can place the path surface at ground level, where the surrounding soil or an edging can contain loose materials and keep hard materials from shifting.

All styles, from a wood-bark path to a cut-stone entry walk, and all the materials discussed in this section can be laid on an excavated base of sand or gravel, alone or in combination.

Drainage

Few things are worse than a path dotted with puddles or icy patches. To prevent these from forming, the soil around and

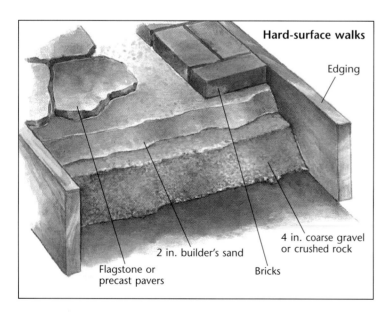

Hard-surface walks

Edging

4 in. coarse gravel or crushed rock

2 in. builder's sand

Flagstone or precast pavers

Bricks

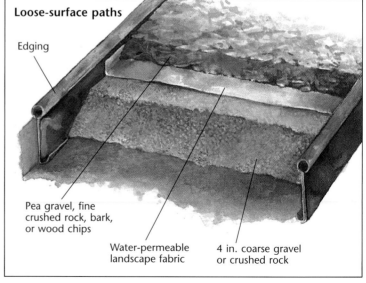

Loose-surface paths

Edging

Pea gravel, fine crushed rock, bark, or wood chips

Water-permeable landscape fabric

4 in. coarse gravel or crushed rock

Choosing a surface

Walkways and paths can be made of either hard or soft material. Your choice of material will depend on the walkway's function, your budget, and your personal preferences.

Soft materials, including bark, wood chips, pine needles, and loose gravel, are best for informal and low-traffic areas. Inexpensive and simple to install, they settle, scatter, or decompose and must be replenished or replaced every few years.

Hard materials, such as brick, flagstone, and concrete pavers, are more expensive and time-consuming to install, but they are permanent, requiring only occasional maintenance. (Compacted crushed stone can also make a hard-surface walk.) Durable and handsome, they're ideal for high-traffic, "high-profile" areas.

Bark, wood chips, and pine needles

Perfect for a "natural" look or a quick temporary path, these loose materials can be laid directly on the soil or, if drainage is poor, on a gravel bed. Bagged materials from a nursery or garden center will be cleaner, more uniform, and considerably more expensive than bulk supplies bought by the cubic yard. Check with local suppliers to find the best prices on bulk material.

Gravel and crushed rock

Loose rounded gravel gives a bit underfoot, creating a "soft" but somewhat messy path. The angular facets of crushed stone and decomposed granite eventually compact into a "hard" and tidier path that can, if the surrounding soil is firm enough, be laid without an edging or base. Gravel and stone vary from area to area. Buy these materials by the ton or cubic yard.

Concrete pavers

Precast concrete pavers are versatile, readily available, and often the least expensive hard-surface material. They come in a range of colors and shapes, including interlocking patterns. Precast edgings are also available. Most home and garden centers carry a variety of precast pavers, which are sold by the piece.

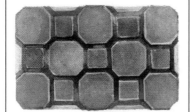

Precast pavers

Brick

Widely available in a range of sizes, colors, and textures, brick complements many design styles, both formal and informal. When carefully laid on a well-prepared sand-and-gravel base, brick provides an even, safe, and long-lasting surface. If you buy used brick, pick the densest and hardest. Avoid brick with glazed faces; the glaze traps moisture and salts, which eventually damage the brick. If you live where it regularly freezes and thaws, buy bricks rated to withstand the weather conditions.

Running bond

Two-brick basket weave

Herringbone

Diagonal herringbone

Flagstone

"Flagstone" is a generic term for stratified stone that can be split to form pavers. Limestone and sandstone are common paving materials. The surfaces of marble and slate are typically too smooth to make safe paving because they are slippery when wet. Cut into squares or rectangles, flagstone can be laid as individual steppingstones or in interesting patterns. Flags with irregular outlines present other patterning opportunities. Flagstones come in a range of colors, textures, and sizes. Flags for walks should be at least 2 in. thick; thinner stones fracture easily. Purchased by weight, surface area, or pallet load, flagstones are usually the most expensive paving choice.

Cut flagstone

Cut and irregular flagstone

Irregular flagstone

(Continued from p. 108)

Edgings

All walk surfaces need to be contained in some fashion along their edges. Where soil is firm or tightly knit by turf, neatly cut walls of the excavation can serve as edging. An installed edging often provides more effective containment, particularly if the walk surface is above grade. It also prevents damage to bricks or stones on the edges of paths. Walkway edgings are commonly made of 1- or 2-in.-thick lumber, thicker landscaping timbers, brick, or stone.

Wood edging

Wood should be rot-resistant redwood or cedar, or some other wood pressure-treated for ground-contact use. If you're working in loose soils, fix a deep wooden edging to support stakes with double-headed nails. When the path is laid, pull the nails, and fill and tamp behind the edging. Then drive the stakes below grade. In firmer soils, or if the edging material is not wide enough, install it on top of the gravel base. Position the top of the edging at the height of the path. Dimension lumber that is 1 in. thick is pliable enough to bend around gradual curves.

Treated dimensional lumber
with support stakes

Landscape timbers with
crossties laid on gravel base

Brick and stone edging

In firm soil, a row of bricks laid on edge and perpendicular to the length of the path adds stability. For a more substantial edging, stand bricks on end on the excavated soil surface, add the gravel base, and tamp earth around the base of the bricks on the outside of the excavation. Stone edgings laid on end can be set in the same way. "End-up" brick or stone edgings are easy to install on curved walks.

Bricks on edge, laid on gravel base

Bricks on end, laid on soil

beneath the path should drain well. The path's location and construction should ensure that rainwater does not collect on the surface. Before you locate a path, observe runoff and drainage on your property during and after heavy rains. Avoid routing a path through areas where water courses, collects, or is slow to drain.

While both loose and hard paving can sometimes be successfully laid directly on well-drained compacted soil, laying surface materials on a base of sand or gravel will help improve drainage and minimize frost heaving. Where rainfall is scant or drainage is good, a 4-in. base of either sand or gravel is usually sufficient. For most other situations, a 4-in. gravel bed topped with 2 in. of sand will work well. Very poorly drained soils may require more gravel, an additional layer of coarse rock beneath the gravel, or even drain tiles. If you suspect your site has serious drainage problems, consult a landscape architect or contractor.

Finally, keep water from pooling on a walk by making its surface higher in the center than at the edges. The center of a 4-ft.-wide walk should be at least $1/2$ in. higher than its edges. If you're using a drag board to level the sand base, make its lower edge curved to create this "crown." Otherwise crown the surface by eye.

Preparing the base

Having decided on location and materials, you can get down to business. The initial steps of layout and base preparation are much the same for all surface materials. Before you construct paths or walkways, check your irrigation plans. If underground water lines will cross any paths, be sure to lay the lines first.

Layout

Lay out straight sections with stakes and string ❶. You can plot curves with stakes and "fair" the curve with a garden hose, or you can outline the curve with the hose alone, marking it with lime or sand.

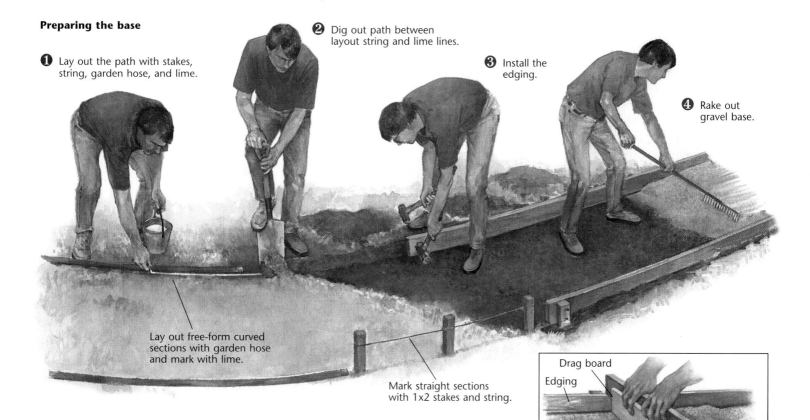

Preparing the base

❶ Lay out the path with stakes, string, garden hose, and lime.

❷ Dig out path between layout string and lime lines.

❸ Install the edging.

❹ Rake out gravel base.

Lay out free-form curved sections with garden hose and mark with lime.

Mark straight sections with 1x2 stakes and string.

Drag board

Edging

❺ Level sand base with a drag board.

Excavation

The excavation depth depends on how much sand-and-gravel base your soil's drainage calls for, the thickness of the surface material, and its position above or below grade ❷. Mark the depth on a stake or stick and use this to check depth as you dig. Walking surfaces are most comfortable if they are reasonably level across their width. Check the bottom of the excavation with a level as you dig. If the walk cuts across a slope, you'll need to remove soil from the high side and use it to fill the low side to produce a level surface. If you've added soil or if the subsoil is loose, compact it by tamping.

Edging installion

Some edgings can be installed immediately after excavation; others are placed on top of the gravel portion of the base ❸. (See the sidebar "Edgings" on the facing page.) If the soil's drainage permits, you can lay soft materials, loose gravel, or crushed stone now on the excavated, tamped, and edged soil base. To control weeds, and to keep bark, chips, or pine needles from mixing with the subsoil, you can spread water-permeable landscape fabric over the excavated soil base.

Laying the base

Now add gravel (if required), rake it level, and compact it ❹. Use gravel up to 1 in. in diameter or $1/4$- to $3/4$-in. crushed stone, which drains and compacts well. You can rent a hand tamper (a heavy metal plate on the end of a pole) or a machine compactor if you have a large area to compact.

If you're making a loose-gravel or crushed-stone walk, add the surface material on top of the base gravel. (See "Loose materials" at right.) For walks of brick, stone, or pavers, add a 2-in. layer of builder's sand, not the finer sand masons use for mixing mortar.

Rake the sand smooth with the back of a level-head rake. You can level the sand with a wooden drag board, also called a screed ❺. Nail together two 1x4s or notch a 1x6 to place the lower edge at the desired height of the sand, and run the board along the path edging. To settle the sand, dampen it thoroughly with a hose set on fine spray. Fill any low spots, rake or drag the surface level, and then dampen it again.

Laying the surface

Whether you're laying a loose or hard material, take time to plan your work. Provide access so delivery trucks can place material close to the work site.

Loose materials

Install water-permeable landscape fabric over the gravel base to prevent gravel from mixing with the surface material. Spread bark or wood chips 2 to 4 in. deep. For a pine-needle surface, spread 2 in. of needles on top of several inches of bark or chips. Spread loose pea gravel about 2 in. deep. For a harder, more uniform surface, add 1/2 in. of fine crushed stone on top of the gravel. You can let traffic compact crushed-rock surfaces, or compact them by hand or with a machine.

Bricks and precast pavers

Take time to figure out the pattern and spacing of the bricks or pavers by laying them out on the lawn or driveway, rather than disturbing your carefully prepared sand base. When you're satisfied, begin in a corner, laying the bricks or pavers gently on the sand so the base remains even ❶. Lay full bricks first; then cut bricks to fit as needed at the edges. To produce uniform joints, space bricks with a piece of wood cut to the joint width. You can also maintain alignment with a straightedge or with a string stretched across the path between nails or stakes. Move the string as the work proceeds.

As you complete a row or section, bed the bricks or pavers into the sand base with several firm raps of a rubber mallet or a hammer on a scrap 2x4. Check with a level or straightedge to make sure the surface is even ❷. (You'll need to do this by feel or eye across the width of a crowned path.) Lift low bricks or pavers carefully and fill beneath them with sand; then reset them. Don't stand on the walk until you've filled the joints.

When you've finished a section, sweep fine dry mason's sand into the joints, working across the surface of the path in all directions ❸. Wet thoroughly with a fine spray and let dry; then sweep in more sand if necessary. If you want a "living" walk, sweep a loam-sand mixture into the joints and plant small, tough, ground-hugging plants, such as dwarf mondo grass.

Rare is the brick walk that can be laid without cutting something to fit. To cut

Loose materials

Cover gravel base with water-permeable landscape fabric and add 2 to 3 in. of bark or wood chips.

Bricks and precast pavers

To turn square corners, align the edging board with a carpenter's square.

❶ Begin laying in a corner.

❷ Check the surface with a level or straightedge. Fill under low bricks; tamp down high ones. Use a plank to distribute your weight if you must work on the path.

❸ Sweep fine, dry sand into the joints to fix the bricks or pavers in place.

Cutting bricks

Wear safety glasses.

Scored line

Brickset chisel

brick, mark the line of the cut with a dark pencil all around the brick. With the brick resting firmly on sand or soil, score the entire line by rapping a wide mason's chisel called a "brickset" with a heavy wooden mallet or a soft-headed steel hammer as shown on the facing page. Place the brickset in the scored line across one face and give it a sharp blow with the hammer to cut the brick.

If you have many bricks to cut, or if you want greater accuracy, consider renting a masonry saw. Whether you work by hand or by machine, always wear safety glasses.

Flagstones

Install cut stones of uniform thickness as described for bricks and pavers. Working out patterns beforehand is particularly important—stones are too heavy to move around more than necessary. To produce a level surface with cut or irregular stones of varying thickness, you'll need to add or remove sand for each stone. Set the stone carefully on sand; then move it back and forth to work it into place ❶. Lay a level or straightedge over three or four stones to check the surface's evenness ❷. When a section is complete, fill the joints with sand or with sand and loam as described for bricks and pavers.

You can cut flagstone with a technique similar to that used for bricks. Score the line of the cut on the top surface with a brickset and hammer. Prop the stone on a piece of scrap wood, positioning the line of cut slightly beyond the edge of the wood. Securing the bottom edge of the stone with your foot, place the brickset on the scored line and strike sharply to make the cut.

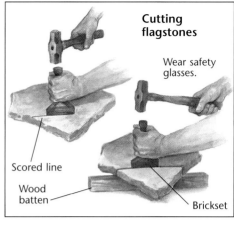

❶ Set flagstones in place carefully to avoid disturbing the sand base.

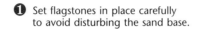

Flagstones

❷ Extend a straightedge over several stones to check the surface for evenness. Tap high spots to level.

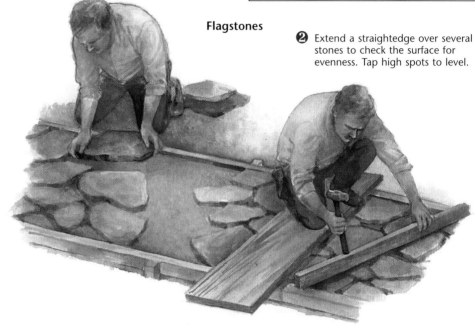

Steppingstones

A steppingstone walk set in turf creates a charming effect and is very simple to lay. You can use cut or irregular flagstones or fieldstone, which is irregular in thickness as well as in outline. Arrange the stones on the turf; then set them one by one. Cut into the turf around the stone with a sharp flat spade or trowel, and remove the stone; then dig out the sod with the spade. Placing stones at or below grade will keep them away from mower blades. Fill low spots beneath the stone with earth or sand so the stone doesn't move when stepped on.

Cut around steppingstone with spade or trowel.

Remove sod and soil.

Set in place, filling with sand or soil to bed stone firmly.

Laying a Patio

You can make a simple patio using the same techniques and materials we have discussed for paths. To ensure good drainage, an even surface, and durability, lay hard surfaces such as brick, flagstone, and pavers on a well-prepared base of gravel, sand, and compacted soil. (Crushed-rock and gravel surfaces likewise benefit from a sound base.) Make sure the surface drains away from any adjacent structure (house or garage); a drop-off of ¼ in. per foot is usu-ally adequate. If the patio isn't near a struc-ture, make it higher in the center to avoid puddles forming on the surface.

Establish the outline of the patio as described for paths; then excavate the area roughly to accommodate 4 in. of gravel, 2 in. of sand, and the thickness of the paving surface. (Check with your paver supplier or a landscape contractor to find out if local conditions require alterations in the type or amounts of base material.) Now grade the rough excavation to provide drainage, using a simple 4-ft. grid of wooden stakes as shown in the drawings.

Drive the first row of stakes next to the house (or in the center of a freestanding patio), leveling them with a 4-ft. builder's level or a smaller level resting on a straight 2x4. The tops of these stakes should be at the height of the eventual sand base (fin-ish grade of the patio less the thickness of the surface material) ❶. Working from this row of stakes, establish another row about 4 to 5 ft. from the first. Make the tops of these stakes 1 in. lower than those of the first row, using a level and spacer

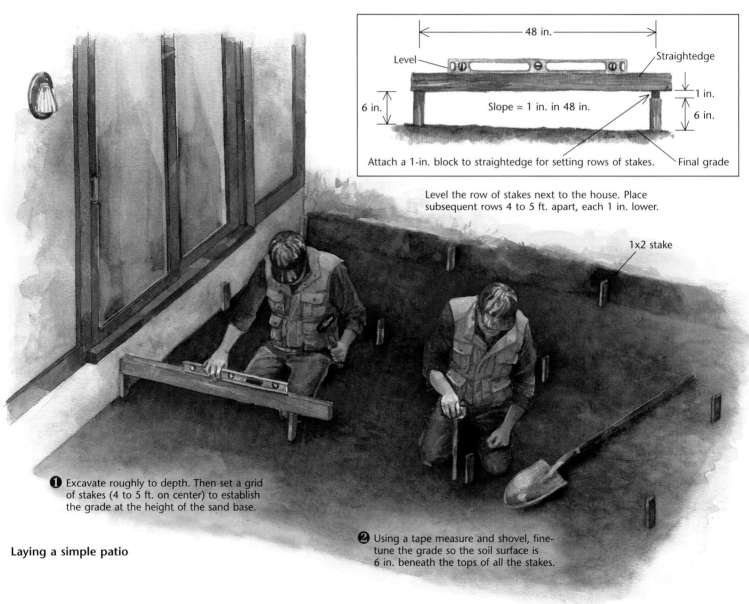

48 in.

Level — Straightedge

6 in.

Slope = 1 in. in 48 in.

1 in.

6 in.

Attach a 1-in. block to straightedge for setting rows of stakes. — Final grade

Level the row of stakes next to the house. Place subsequent rows 4 to 5 ft. apart, each 1 in. lower.

1x2 stake

❶ Excavate roughly to depth. Then set a grid of stakes (4 to 5 ft. on center) to establish the grade at the height of the sand base.

Laying a simple patio

❷ Using a tape measure and shovel, fine-tune the grade so the soil surface is 6 in. beneath the tops of all the stakes.

block, as shown on the facing page. Continue adding rows of stakes, each 1 in. lower than the previous row, until the entire area is staked. Then, with a tape measure or ruler and a shovel, fine-tune the grading by removing or adding soil until the excavated surface is 6 in. (the thickness of the gravel-sand base) below the tops of all the stakes ❷.

When installing the sand-and-gravel base, you'll want to maintain the drainage grade you've just established and produce an even surface for the paving material. If you have a good eye or a very small patio, you can do this by sight. Otherwise, you can use the stakes to install a series of 1x3 or 1x4 "leveling boards," as shown in the drawing below. (Before adding gravel, you may want to cover the soil with water-permeable landscape fabric to keep perennial weeds from growing; just cut slits to accommodate the stakes.)

Add a few inches of gravel ❸. Then set leveling boards along each row of stakes, with the boards' top edges even with the top of the stakes ❹. Drive additional stakes to sandwich the boards in place (don't use nails). Distribute the remaining inch or so of gravel and compact it by hand or machine; then add the 2 in. of sand. Drag-ging a straight 2x4 across two adjacent rows of leveling boards will produce a precise grade and an even surface ❺. Wet the sand and fill low spots that settle.

You can install the patio surface as previously described for paths, removing the leveling boards as the bricks or pavers reach them ❻. Disturbing the sand surface as little as possible, slide the boards out from between the stakes and drive the stakes an inch or so beneath the level of the sand. Cover the stakes and fill the gaps left by the boards with sand, tamped down carefully; then continue laying the paving. Finally, sweep fine sand into the joints.

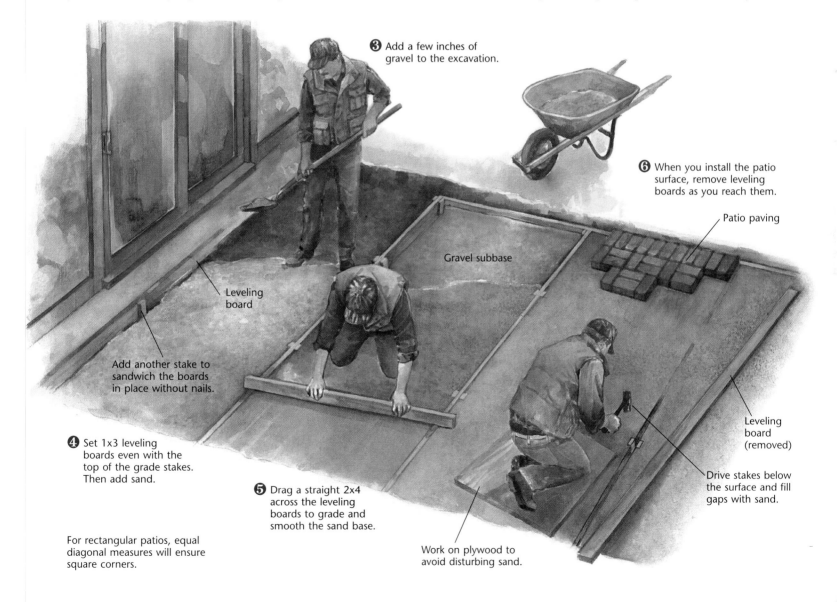

❸ Add a few inches of gravel to the excavation.

❻ When you install the patio surface, remove leveling boards as you reach them.

Patio paving

Gravel subbase

Leveling board

Add another stake to sandwich the boards in place without nails.

❹ Set 1x3 leveling boards even with the top of the grade stakes. Then add sand.

❺ Drag a straight 2x4 across the leveling boards to grade and smooth the sand base.

Leveling board (removed)

Drive stakes below the surface and fill gaps with sand.

Work on plywood to avoid disturbing sand.

For rectangular patios, equal diagonal measures will ensure square corners.

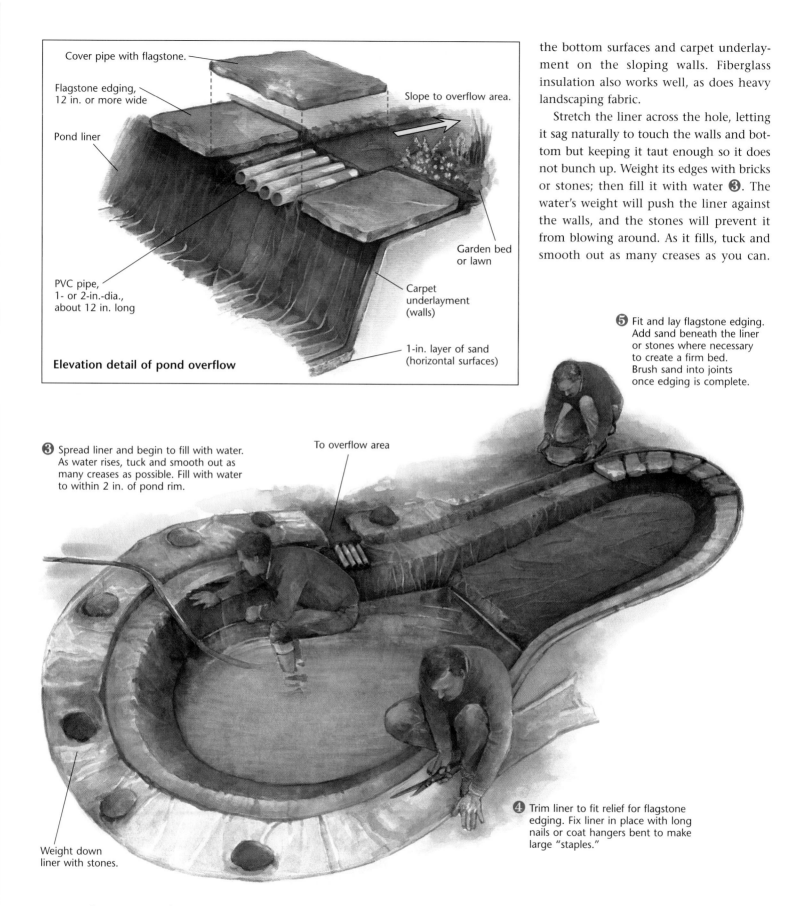

Elevation detail of pond overflow

Cover pipe with flagstone.

Flagstone edging, 12 in. or more wide

Pond liner

Slope to overflow area.

PVC pipe, 1- or 2-in.-dia., about 12 in. long

Garden bed or lawn

Carpet underlayment (walls)

1-in. layer of sand (horizontal surfaces)

the bottom surfaces and carpet underlayment on the sloping walls. Fiberglass insulation also works well, as does heavy landscaping fabric.

Stretch the liner across the hole, letting it sag naturally to touch the walls and bottom but keeping it taut enough so it does not bunch up. Weight its edges with bricks or stones; then fill it with water ❸. The water's weight will push the liner against the walls, and the stones will prevent it from blowing around. As it fills, tuck and smooth out as many creases as you can.

❺ Fit and lay flagstone edging. Add sand beneath the liner or stones where necessary to create a firm bed. Brush sand into joints once edging is complete.

❸ Spread liner and begin to fill with water. As water rises, tuck and smooth out as many creases as possible. Fill with water to within 2 in. of pond rim.

To overflow area

Weight down liner with stones.

❹ Trim liner to fit relief for flagstone edging. Fix liner in place with long nails or coat hangers bent to make large "staples."

The weight of the water would make this difficult after the pond is full. If you stand in the pond to do so, take care not to damage the liner. Don't be alarmed if you can't smooth all the creases. Stop filling when the water is 2 in. below the rim of the pond, and cut the liner to fit into the overlap relief ❹. Hold it in place with a few long nails or large "staples" made from coat hangers while you install the edging.

Edging the pond

Finding and fitting flagstones so there aren't wide gaps between them is the most time-consuming part of this task. Cantilevering the stones an inch or two over the water will hide the liner somewhat.

The stones can be laid directly on the liner, as shown ❺. Add sand where necessary under the liner to level the surface so that the stones don't rock. Such treatment will withstand the occasional gingerly traffic of pond maintenance. If you anticipate heavier traffic, you can bed the stones in 2 to 3 in. of mortar. It's prudent to consult with a landscape contractor about whether your intended use and soil require a footing for mortared stones.

Water work

Unless you are a very tidy builder, you'll need to siphon or pump dirty water out of the pond, clean the liner, and refill the pond. If you're adding fish, you'll need to let the water stand for a week or so to allow any chlorine (which is deadly to fish) to dissipate. Check with local pet stores to find out if your water contains chemicals that require commercial conditioners to make it safe for fish.

Installing the pond and plants is only the first step in water gardening. It takes patience, experimentation, and usually some consultation with experienced water gardeners to achieve a balance among plants, fish, waterborne oxygen, nutrients, and waste that will sustain all happily while keeping algae, diseases, insects, and predators at acceptable levels.

Growing pond plants

One water lily, a few upright-growing plants, and a bundle of submerged plants (which help keep the water clean) are enough for a medium-size pond. An increasing number of nurseries and garden centers stock water lilies and other water plants. For a larger selection, your nursery or garden center may be able to recommend a specialist supplier.

These plants are grown in containers filled with heavy garden soil (*not* potting soil, which contains ingredients that float). You can buy special containers designed for aquatic plants, or simply use plastic pails or dishpans. Line basket-like containers with burlap to keep the soil from leaking out the holes. A water lily needs at least 5 to 10 gal. of soil; the more, the better. Most other water plants, such as dwarf papyrus, need 1 to 2 gal. of soil.

After planting, add a layer of gravel on the surface to keep soil from clouding the water and to protect roots from marauding fish. Soak the plant and soil thoroughly; then set the container in the pond, positioning it so the water over the soil is 6 to 18 in. deep for water lilies, 0 to 6 in. for most other plants.

For maximum bloom, push a tablet of special water-lily fertilizer into the pots once or twice a month throughout the summer. Most water plants are easy to grow and carefree, although many are tropicals that die after hard frost, so you may need to replace these each spring.

Planting water plants

Set water plants in a container of heavy garden soil. Cover soil surface with gravel to keep soil from floating away.

Gravel

1- to 3-gal. dishpan or special container lined with burlap and filled with heavy garden soil

Building a Retaining Wall

Contours and sloping terrain can add considerable interest to a home landscape. But you can have too much of a good thing. Two designs in this book employ retaining walls to alter problem slopes. The wall shown on p. 40 eliminates a small but abrupt grade change, producing two almost level surfaces and the opportunity to install attractive plantings and a patio on them. On p. 72 a retaining wall helps turn a steep slope into a showpiece.

Retaining walls can be handsome landscape features in their own right. Made of cut stone, fieldstone, brick, landscape timbers, or concrete, they can complement the materials and style of your house or nearby structures. However, making a stable, long-lasting retaining wall of these materials can require tools and skills many homeowners do not possess.

For these reasons we've instead chosen retaining-wall systems made of precast concrete for designs in this book. Readily available in a range of sizes, surface finishes, and colors that will coordinate with your house and existing hardscape, these systems require few tools and no special skills to install. They have been engineered to resist the forces that soil, water, freezing, and thawing bring to bear on a retaining wall. Install these walls according to the manufacturer's specifications, and you can be confident that they will do their job for many years.

A number of systems are available in Texas through nurseries, garden centers, and local contracting suppliers (check the Yellow Pages). But they all share basic design principles. Like traditional dry-stone walls, these systems rely largely on weight and friction to contain the soil. In many systems, interlocking blocks or pegs help align the courses and increase the wall's strength. In all systems, blocks must rest on a solid, level base. A freely draining backfill of crushed stone is essential to avoid buildup of water pressure in the retained soil, which can buckle even a heavy wall. (In hilly terrain or where drainage is a concern, experts often recommend installing drainage pipe to remove excess water from behind retaining walls.)

The construction steps shown here are typical of those recommended by most system manufacturers for retaining walls up to 3 to 4 ft. tall; be sure to follow the manufacturer's instructions for the system you choose. For higher walls, walls on loose soil or heavy clay soils, and walls retaining very steep slopes, it is prudent to consult with a landscape architect or contractor. (Some cities and towns have regulations for retaining walls and landscape steps. Be sure to check with local authorities before beginning work.)

Building a wall

Installing a wall system is just about as simple as stacking up children's building blocks. The most important part of the job is establishing a firm, level base. Start by

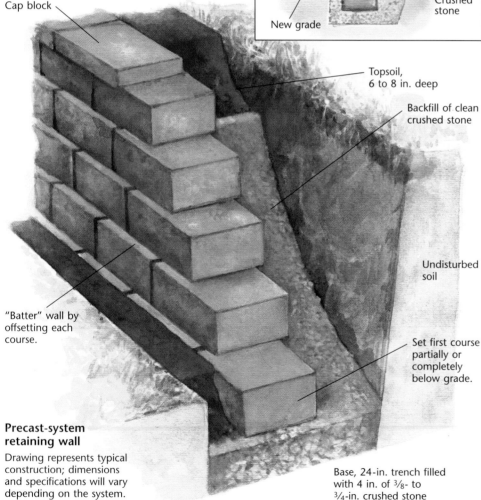

Original slope

New grade level

Excavate for wall. Use soil to fill behind wall.

Soil

New grade

Crushed stone

Cap block

Topsoil, 6 to 8 in. deep

Backfill of clean crushed stone

"Batter" wall by offsetting each course.

Undisturbed soil

Set first course partially or completely below grade.

Precast-system retaining wall
Drawing represents typical construction; dimensions and specifications will vary depending on the system.

Base, 24-in. trench filled with 4 in. of 3/8- to 3/4-in. crushed stone laying out the wall with string and hose (for curves) and excavating a base trench.

As the boxed drawing on the facing page shows, the position of the wall in relation to the base of the slope determines the height of the wall, how much soil you move, and the leveling effect on the slope. Unless the wall is very long, excavate along the entire length and fine-tune the line of the wall before beginning the base trench. When excavating, remember that most sys-

tems recommend a foot of crushed-stone backfill behind the blocks.

Systems vary in the width and depth of trench and type of base material, but in all of them, the trench must be tamped firm and be level across its width and along its length. We've shown a 4-in. layer of ⅜- to ¾-in. crushed stone (blocks can slip sideways on rounded gravel, which also does not compact as well). Depending on the system and the circumstances, a portion or all of the first course lies below grade, so the soil helps hold the blocks in place.

Add crushed stone to the trench, level it with a rake, and compact it with a hand tamper or mechanical compactor. Lay the first course of blocks carefully ❶. Check frequently to make sure the blocks are level across their width and along their length.

Stagger vertical joints as you stack subsequent courses. Set back the faces of the courses so the wall angles back into the retained soil. Some systems design this "batter" into their blocks; others allow you to choose from several possible setbacks.

As the wall rises, shovel backfill behind the blocks ❷. Clean, crushed stone drains well; some systems suggest placing a barrier of landscaping fabric between the stone and the retained soil to keep soil from migrating into the fill and impeding drainage.

Thinner cap blocks finish the top of the wall ❸. Some manufacturers recommend

Building a wall

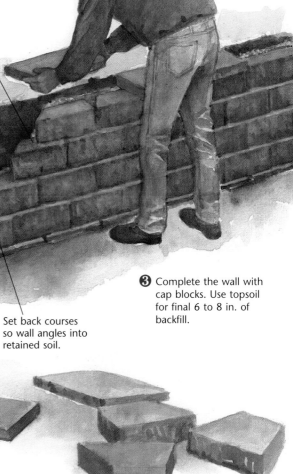

❷ As you add subsequent courses, backfill behind blocks with clean crushed stone.

Stagger joints.

Set back courses so wall angles into retained soil.

❸ Complete the wall with cap blocks. Use topsoil for final 6 to 8 in. of backfill.

Crushed-stone base

Level

❶ After digging and leveling the trench, spread, level, and compact the base materials. Then lay the blocks, checking frequently to see that they are level across their width and length.

Wall parallel to a slope: Stepped base

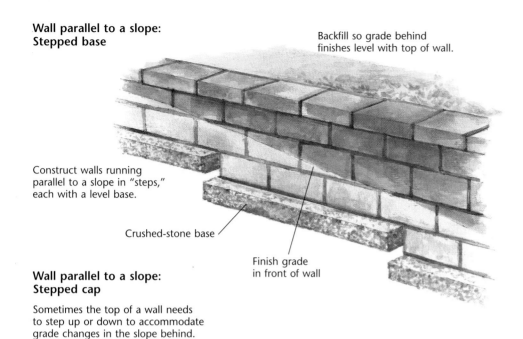

Backfill so grade behind finishes level with top of wall.

Construct walls running parallel to a slope in "steps," each with a level base.

Crushed-stone base

Finish grade in front of wall

Wall parallel to a slope: Stepped cap

Sometimes the top of a wall needs to step up or down to accommodate grade changes in the slope behind.

Cap block

A "return" corner

Where you want the slope to extend beyond the end of the wall, make a corner that cuts into the slope.

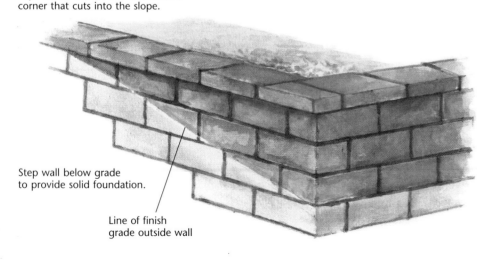

Step wall below grade to provide solid foundation.

Line of finish grade outside wall

cementing these blocks in place with a weatherproof adhesive. The last 6 to 8 in. of the backfill should be topsoil, firmed into place and ready for planting.

If your slope runs parallel to the length of the wall, you can "step" the bottom of the wall and make its top surface level, as shown in the top drawing at left. Create a length of level trench along the lowest portion of the site. Then work up the slope, creating steps as necessary. Add fill soil to raise the grade behind the wall to the level of the cap blocks.

Alternatively, you can step the top of the wall, as shown in the center drawing at left. Here, the base of the wall rests on level ground, but the top of the wall steps to match the slope's decreasing height. This saves money and labor on materials and backfill, while producing a different look.

Retaining walls (such as the one shown on p. 40) are frequently placed perpendicular to the run of a slope. If you want to alter just part of the slope or if the slope continues beyond your property, you'll need to terminate the wall. A corner that cuts back into the slope (shown at bottom left) is an attractive and structurally sound solution to this problem.

Constructing curves and corners

Wall-system blocks are designed so that curves are no more difficult to lay than straight sections. Corners may require that you cut a few blocks or use specially designed blocks, but they are otherwise uncomplicated. If your wall must fit a prescribed length between corners, consider working from the corners toward the middle (after laying a base course). Masons use this technique, which also helps to avoid exposing cut blocks at the corners.

You can cut blocks with a mason's chisel and mallet or rent a mason's saw. Chiseling works well where the block faces are rough textured, so the faces you cut blend right in. A mason's saw is best if you want smooth-faced blocks or if your project requires lots of cutting.

Steps

Steps in a low retaining wall are not diffi-cult to build, but they require forethought and careful layout. Systems differ on construction details. The drawing below shows a typical design where the blocks and stone base rest on "steps" cut into firm subsoil. If your soil is less stable or is recent fill, you should excavate the entire area beneath the steps to the same depth as the wall base and build a foundation of blocks, as shown in the boxed drawing.

These steps are independent of the adjacent "return" walls, which are vertical, not battered (stepped back). In some sys-tems, steps and return walls are inter-locked. To match a path, you can face the treads with the same stone, brick, or pavers, or you can use the system's cap blocks or special treads.

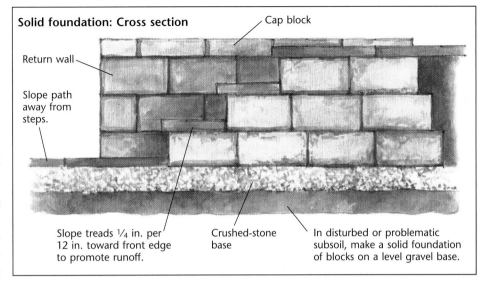

Solid foundation: Cross section

Cap block

Return wall

Slope path away from steps.

Slope treads ¼ in. per 12 in. toward front edge to promote runoff.

Crushed-stone base

In disturbed or problematic subsoil, make a solid foundation of blocks on a level gravel base.

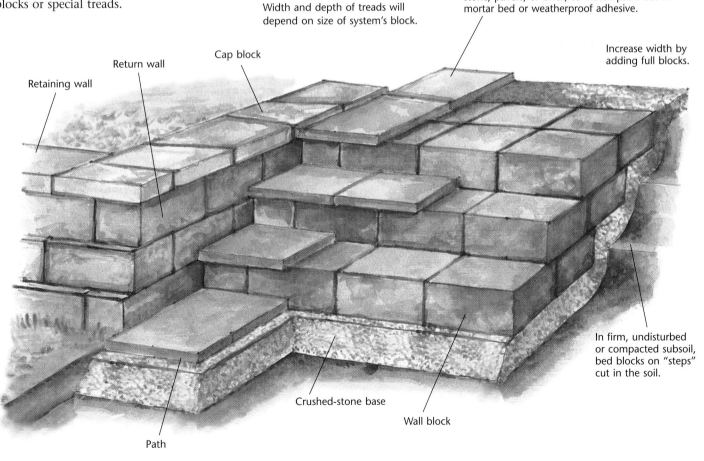

"Stepped" foundation

Width and depth of treads will depend on size of system's block.

Surface steps with system-provided treads or stone, pavers, or brick, to match path. Set in mortar bed or weatherproof adhesive.

Increase width by adding full blocks.

Retaining wall

Return wall

Cap block

In firm, undisturbed or compacted subsoil, bed blocks on "steps" cut in the soil.

Crushed-stone base

Wall block

Path

Fences, Arbors, and Trellises

Novices who have no trouble tackling a simple flagstone path often get nervous when it comes time to erect a fence, an arbor, or even a trellis. While such projects can require more skill and resources than others in the landscape, the ones in this book have been designed with less-than-confident do-it-yourself builders in mind. The designs are simple, the materials are readily available, and the tools and skills will be familiar to anyone accustomed to ordinary home maintenance.

First we'll introduce you to the materials and tools needed for the projects. Then we'll present the small number of basic operations you'll employ when building them. Finally, we'll provide drawings and comments on each of the projects.

Materials

Of the materials offering strength, durability, and attractiveness in outdoor settings, wood is the easiest to work and affords the quickest results. While almost all commercially available lumber is strong enough for landscape structures, most types decay quickly when in prolonged contact with soil and water. Cedar and redwood, however, contain natural preservatives and are excellent for landscape use. Alternatively, a range of softwoods (such as pine, fir, and hemlock) are pressure-treated with preservatives and will last for many years. Parts of structures that do not come in contact with soil or are not continually wet can be made of ordinary construction-grade lumber, but unless they're regularly painted, they will not last as long as treated or naturally decay-resistant material.

In addition to dimension lumber, landscape structures often incorporate lattice, which is thin wooden strips crisscrossed to form patterns of diamonds or squares. Premade lattice is widely available in sheets 4 ft. by 8 ft. and smaller. Lattice comes in decay-resistant woods as well as in treated and untreated softwoods. The strips are typically from $1/8$ to $3/8$ in. thick and about $1\frac{1}{2}$ in. wide, overlapped to form squares ranging from 1 to 3 in. or more on a side. Local supplies vary, and you may find lattice made of thicker or narrower material. Lattice can be tricky to cut; if you're uneasy about this task, many suppliers will cut it for you for a small fee.

Fasteners

For millennia, even basic structures such as these would have been assembled with complicated joints, the cutting and fitting of which required long training to master. Today, with simple nailed, bolted, or screwed joints, a few hours' practice swinging a hammer or wielding a cordless electric screwdriver is all the training necessary.

All these structures can be assembled entirely with nails. But screws are stronger and, if you have a cordless screwdriver, make assembly easier. Buy common or box nails (both have flat heads) hot-dipped galvanized to prevent rust. Self-tapping screws ("deck" screws) require no pilot holes. For rust resistance, buy galvanized screws or screws treated with zinc dichromate.

Galvanized metal connectors are available to reinforce the joints used in these projects. (See the joinery drawings on pp. 128–129.) For novice builders, connectors are a great help in aligning parts and making assembly easier. (Correctly fastened with nails or screws, the joints are strong enough without connectors.)

Finishes

Cedar and redwood are handsome when left unfinished to weather, when treated with clear or colored stains, or when painted. Pressure-treated lumber is best painted or stained to mask the greenish cast of the preservatives; weathered it turns a rather unattractive gray-green.

Outdoor stains are becoming increasingly popular. Clear or lightly tinted stains can preserve or enhance the rich reddish browns of cedar and redwood. Stains also come in a range of colors that can be used like paint. Because they penetrate the wood rather than forming a film, stains don't form an opaque surface—you'll still need paint to make a picket fence white. On the other hand, stains won't peel or chip like paint and are therefore easier to touch up and refinish.

When choosing a finish, take account of what plants are growing on or near the structure. It's a lot of work to remove yards of vines from a trellis or squeeze between a large shrub and a fence to repaint; consider an unfinished decay-resistant wood or an initial stain that you allow to weather.

Tools

Even the least-handy homeowner is likely to have most of the tools needed for these projects: claw hammer, crosscut handsaw, brace-and-bit or electric drill, adjustable wrench, combination square, tape measure, carpenter's level, and sawhorses. You may even have Grandpa's old posthole digger. Many will have a handheld power circular saw, which makes faster (though noisier) work of cutting parts to length. A cordless drill/screwdriver is invaluable if you're substituting screws for nails. If you have more than a few holes to dig, consider renting a gas-powered posthole digger. A 12-in.-diameter hole will serve for 4x4 posts; if possible, get a larger-diameter digger for 6x6 posts.

Setting posts

Most of the projects are anchored by firmly set, vertical posts. In general, the taller the structure, the deeper the post should be set. Arbor posts should be at least 3 ft. deep. Corner and end posts of fences up to

6 ft. tall and posts supporting gates should also be 3 ft. deep. Intermediate fence posts can be set 2 ft. deep.

The length of the posts you buy depends, of course, on the depth at which they are set and their finished heights. When calculating lengths of arbor posts, remember that the tops of the posts must be level. The easiest method of achieving this is to cut the posts to length after installation. For example, buy 12-ft. posts for an arbor finishing at 8 ft. above grade and set 3 ft. in the ground. The convenience is worth the expense of the foot or so you cut off. The site and personal preference can determine whether you cut fence posts to length after installation or buy them cut to length and add or remove fill from the bottom of the hole to position them at the correct heights.

Fence posts

Lay out and set the end or corner posts of a fence first; then add the intermediate posts. Dig the holes by hand or with a power digger ❶. To promote drainage, place several inches of gravel at the bottom of the hole for the post to rest on. Checking with a carpenter's level, plumb the post vertically and brace it with scrap lumber nailed to stakes ❷. Then add a few more inches of gravel around the post's base.

If your native soil compacts well, you can fix posts in place with tamped earth. Add the soil gradually, tamping it continuously with a heavy iron bar or 2x4. Check regularly with a level to see that the post doesn't get knocked out of plumb. This technique suits rustic or informal fences, where misalignments caused by shifting posts aren't noticeable or damaging.

For more formal fences, or where soils are loose or fence panels are buffeted by gusting winds, it's prudent to fix posts in concrete ❸. Mix enough concrete to set the two end posts; as a rule of thumb, figure one 80-lb. bag of premixed concrete per post. As you shovel it in, prod the concrete with a stick to settle it, particularly if

Setting a fence post

❶ Position the end or corner posts; then dig holes for them.

Post — Slope top surface for drainage.

3 ft. (typical)

Concrete and rubble (shown), or tamped earth

Coarse gravel

1 ft. (typical)

❷ Plumb the post, checking on adjacent faces with a level. Hold it in position with stakes and braces.

❸ Fill the hole with concrete and rubble.

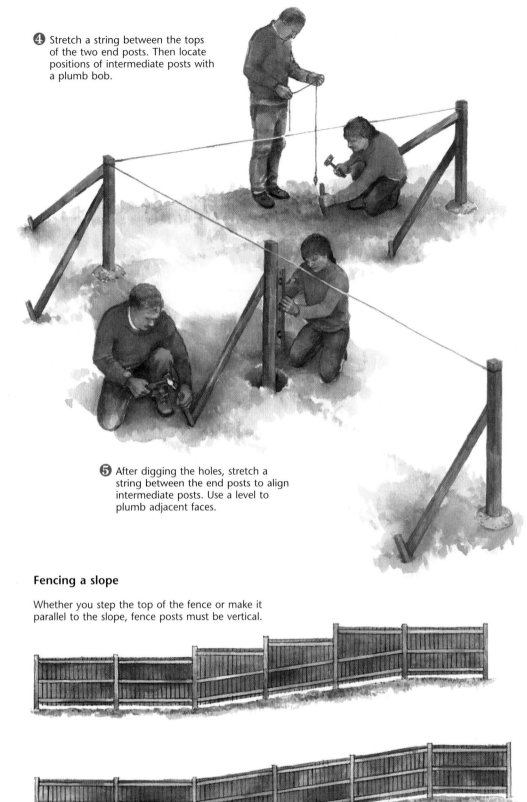

❹ Stretch a string between the tops of the two end posts. Then locate positions of intermediate posts with a plumb bob.

❺ After digging the holes, stretch a string between the end posts to align intermediate posts. Use a level to plumb adjacent faces.

Fencing a slope

Whether you step the top of the fence or make it parallel to the slope, fence posts must be vertical.

you've added rubble to extend the mix. Build the concrete slightly above grade and slope it away from the post to aid drainage.

Once the end posts are set, stretch a string between them. (The concrete should cure for 24 hours before you nail or screw rails and panels in place, but you can safely stretch string while the concrete is still wet.) Measure along the string to position the intermediate posts; drop a plumb bob from the string at each intermediate post position to gauge the center of the hole below ❹. Once all the holes have been dug, again stretch a string between the end posts, near the top. Set the intermediate posts as described previously; align one face with the string and plumb adjacent faces with the carpenter's level ❺. Check positions of intermediate posts a final time with a tape measure.

If the fence is placed along a slope, the top of the slats or panels can step down the slope or mirror it (as shown in the bottom drawing at left). Either way, make sure that the posts are plumb, rather than leaning with the slope.

Arbor posts

Arbor posts are installed just like fence posts, but you must take extra care when positioning them. The corners of the structure must be right angles, and the sides must be parallel. Locating the corners with batter boards and string is fussy but accurate. Make the batter boards by nailing 1x2 stakes to scraps of 1x3 or 1x4, and position them about 1 ft. from the approximate location of each post as shown in the boxed drawing on the facing page. Locate the exact post positions with string; adjust the string so the diagonal measurements are equal, which ensures that the corners of the structure will be right angles.

At the intersections of the strings, locate the postholes by eye or with a plumb bob. (See ❶ on the facing page.) Remove the strings and dig the holes; then reattach the strings to position the posts exactly ❷. Plumb and brace the posts carefully. Check positions with the level and by measuring between adjacent posts and across diagonals. Diagonal braces between adjacent posts will stiffen them and help align their faces ❸. Then add concrete ❹ and let it cure for a day.

To establish the height of the posts, measure up from grade on one post; then use a level and straightedge to mark the heights of the other posts from the first one. Where joists will be bolted to the faces of the posts, you can install the joists and use their top edges as a handsaw guide for cutting the posts to length.

Batter boards

Set L-shaped batter boards at each corner and stretch string to position the posts exactly.

1x2 stakes and 1x3 boards

Taut string

Taut string

18 to 24 in.

For square or rectangular post layout, diagonal measurements should be equal.

Setting arbor posts

❶ Position the posts with batter boards, taut string, and a plumb bob.

Batter board

Plumb bob

❷ Remove the string to dig the holes; then reattach it and align the outer faces of the posts with the string while you plumb and brace them.

Taut string

❸ Check distances between posts at top. Add diagonal bracing between posts to fix positions.

❹ Cement posts in place.

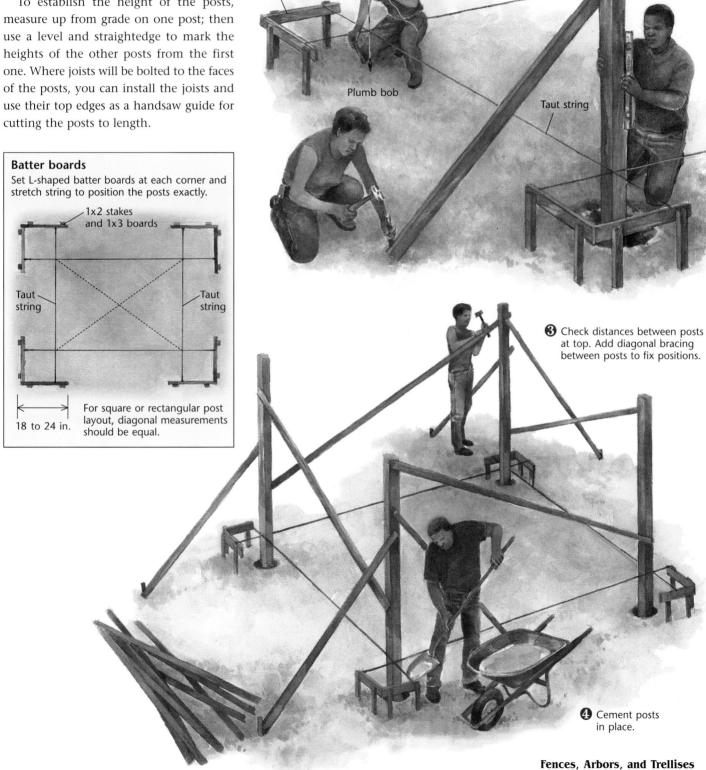

Joints

The components of the fences, arbors, and trellises used in this book are attached to the posts and to each other with the simple joints shown below. Because all the parts are made of dimension lumber, the only cuts you'll need to make are to length. For strong joints, cut ends as square as you can, so the mating pieces make contact across their entire surfaces. If you have no confidence in your sawing, many lumberyards will cut pieces to length for a modest fee.

Beginners often find it difficult to keep two pieces correctly positioned while trying to drive a nail into them, particularly when the nail must be driven at an angle, called "toenailing." If you have this problem, predrill for nails, or use screws, which draw the pieces together, or metal connectors, which can be nailed or screwed in place on one piece and then attached to the mating piece.

In one of the designs, you need to attach lattice panels to posts. The panels are made by sandwiching store-bought lattice between frames of dimension lumber

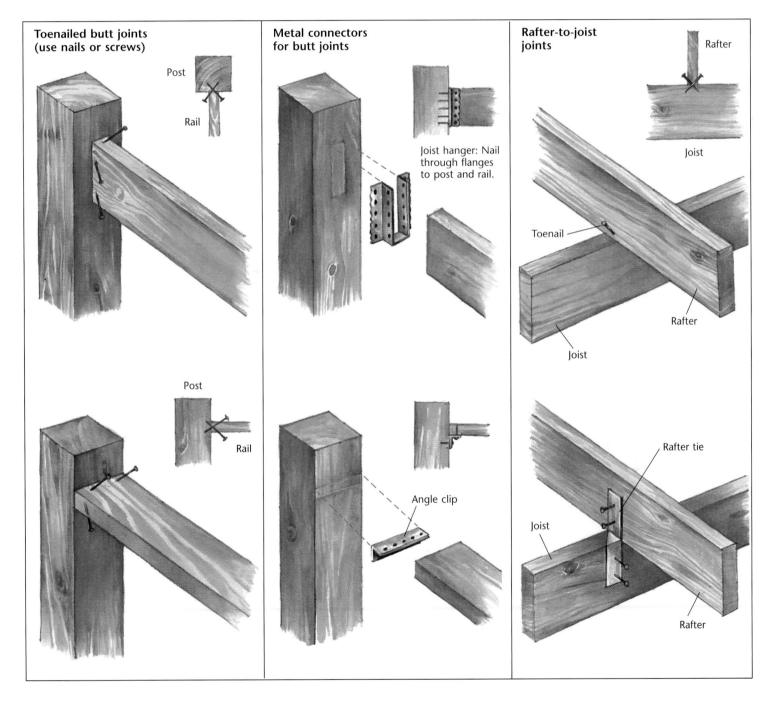

Toenailed butt joints (use nails or screws)

Post
Rail

Post
Rail

Metal connectors for butt joints

Joist hanger: Nail through flanges to post and rail.

Angle clip

Rafter-to-joist joints

Rafter
Joist

Toenail
Rafter
Joist

Rafter tie
Joist
Rafter

(construction details are given on the following pages). While the assembled panels can be toenailed to the posts, novices may find that the job goes easier using one or more types of metal connector, as shown in the drawing at below right. Attach the angle clips or angle brackets to the post; then position the lattice panel and fix it to the connectors. For greatest strength and ease of assembly, attach the connectors with self-tapping screws driven by an electric screwdriver.

In the following pages, we'll show and comment on construction details of the fences, arbors, and trellises presented in the Portfolio of Designs. (The page number indicates the design.) Where the basic joints discussed here can be used, we have shown the parts but left choice of fasteners to you. Typical fastenings are indicated for other joints. We have kept the constructions shown here simple and straightforward. They are not the only possibilities, and we encourage experienced builders to adapt and alter constructions as well as designs to suit differing situations and personal preferences.

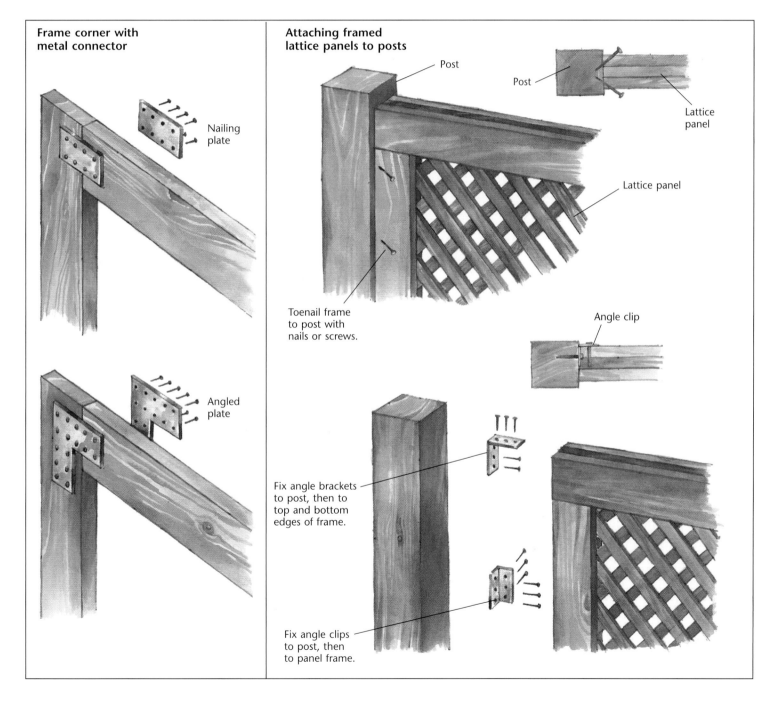

Frame corner with metal connector

Nailing plate

Angled plate

Attaching framed lattice panels to posts

Post

Post

Lattice panel

Lattice panel

Toenail frame to post with nails or screws.

Angle clip

Fix angle brackets to post, then to top and bottom edges of frame.

Fix angle clips to post, then to panel frame.

Homemade lattice trellis
(pp. 44–47)

The trellis shown here supports climbing plants to make a vertical garden of a blank wall (or tall fence). The design can be altered to fit walls of different sizes, while keeping its pleasing proportions. The narrow modules are simpler to make than a single large trellis. Hung on L-hangers, they're easy to remove when you need to paint the wall or fence behind. For the design on p. 45, the trellis is in two separate 32-in.-wide sections. The design on p. 47 uses three narrow sections mounted edge-to-edge.

Start by cutting all the pieces to length. (Here we'll call the horizontal members "rails" and the vertical members "stiles.") Working on a large flat surface, nail or screw the two outer stiles to the top and bottom rails, checking the corners with a framing square. The 2x2 rails provide ample material to house the L-hangers.

Carefully attach the three intermediate stiles, then the 1x2 rails. Cut a piece of scrap 6 in. long to use as a spacer. Fix the L-shaped hangers to the wall or fence. Buy hangers long enough to hold the trellis several inches away from the surface, allowing air to circulate behind the foliage.

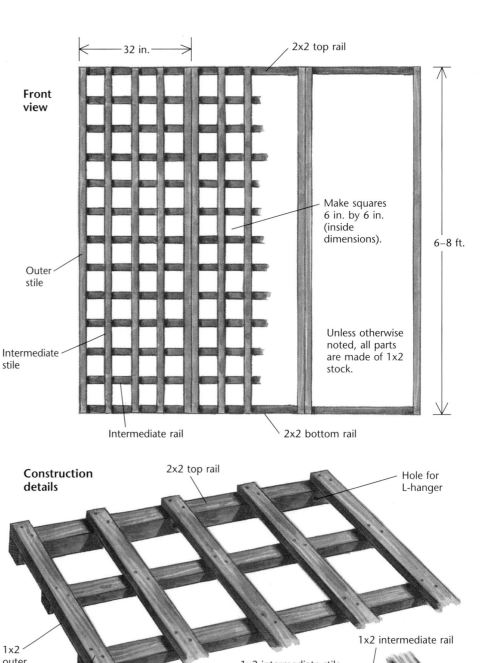

Front view

32 in.

2x2 top rail

Make squares 6 in. by 6 in. (inside dimensions).

6–8 ft.

Outer stile

Intermediate stile

Unless otherwise noted, all parts are made of 1x2 stock.

Intermediate rail

2x2 bottom rail

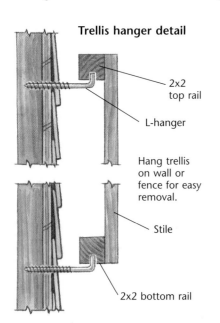

Trellis hanger detail

2x2 top rail

L-hanger

Hang trellis on wall or fence for easy removal.

Stile

2x2 bottom rail

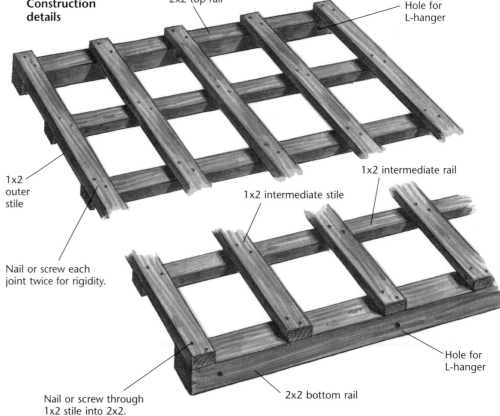

Construction details

2x2 top rail

Hole for L-hanger

1x2 outer stile

Nail or screw each joint twice for rigidity.

1x2 intermediate rail

1x2 intermediate stile

Nail or screw through 1x2 stile into 2x2.

2x2 bottom rail

Hole for L-hanger

Lattice-panel screen
(pp. 30–31)

This screen serves as a decorative embellishment and vine support in the design on p. 30, but it can make an effective enclosure if you wish. The lattice is held in a frame made of 1x2s sandwiched between 1x3s and 1x4s. (The 1x4s add visual weight to the bottom of the screen.) Note how the parts overlap at the corners of the frame to form an interlocking joint.

Panels wider than 6 ft. are awkward to construct and to install. It is easiest to construct the panels on a large flat surface (a garage or basement floor). Lay out the 1x3s and 1x4 that form one face of the panel frame ❶. Then position and nail the 1x2s to them ❷. Add the lattice, then the other layer of 1x3s and 1x4 ❸. As you work, regularly check that the panel is square, its corners at right angles. (Use a framing square or measure across the diagonals to check that they are equal.) Lattice varies in thickness; if yours rattles in its groove, you can add 3/4-in. quarter round as shown in the lower box to tighten the fit.

You can build the panels first and then use them to space the posts, or you can set the posts first (see pp. 124–126) and build the panels to fit. Either way, attach the panels to the posts by toenailing (with nails or screws) or with metal connectors along the lengths of the upright members. Add the 1x4 cap after attaching the panels to the posts. Finials in a variety of styles are available at home and garden stores.

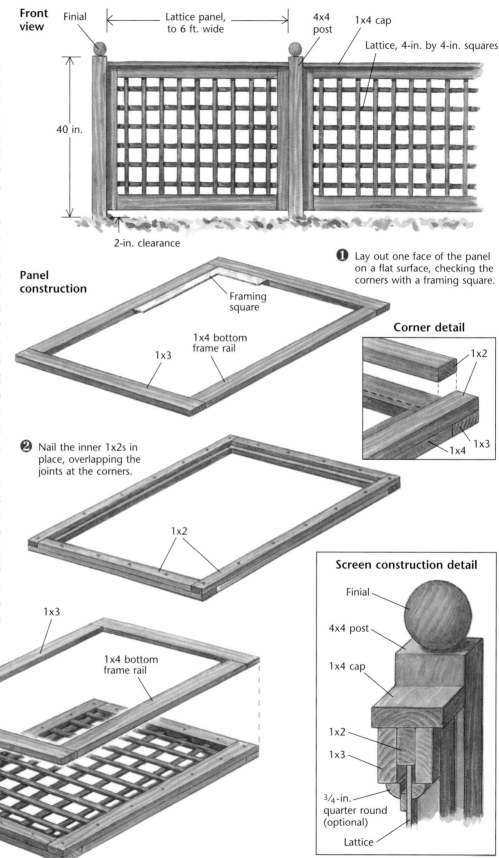

Front view Finial

Lattice panel, to 6 ft. wide

4x4 post

1x4 cap

Lattice, 4-in. by 4-in. squares

40 in.

2-in. clearance

Panel construction

Framing square

1x4 bottom frame rail

1x3

❶ Lay out one face of the panel on a flat surface, checking the corners with a framing square.

Corner detail

1x2

1x3

1x4

❷ Nail the inner 1x2s in place, overlapping the joints at the corners.

1x2

1x3

1x4 bottom frame rail

❸ Place the lattice inside the 1x2 frame. Then nail the other face pieces in place, again overlapping the corner joints.

Screen construction detail

Finial

4x4 post

1x4 cap

1x2

1x3

3/4-in. quarter round (optional)

Lattice

Patio arbor and sun screen

(pp. 52–53)

This simple structure offers relief from the sun on a portion of a backyard patio. The closely spaced 2x4 rafters form a sun screen, while allowing air circulation. Adapt rafter spacing and orientation to accommodate your site. In the design on pp. 52–53, the arbor supports a trumpet vine, which provides additional cooling shade as well as a pleasant leafy ambiance.

If you're building the patio and arbor at the same time, set the 6x6 posts (see pp. 124–127) before you lay the patio surface. If you're adding the arbor to an existing patio, you'll need to break through the paving to set the posts or pour footings to support surface attachments. Consult local building officials or a landscape contractor for advice on how best to proceed.

Once the posts are set, fix the 2x8 beams to pairs of posts with carriage bolts. Nail the 2x8s in place; then make the bolt holes by boring through the 2x8s and the post with a long electrician's bit. Fix the long 2x6 joists and the 2x4 rafters in place with metal connectors. Metal connectors fixed with screws will stand up best to the vigorous growth of the vine.

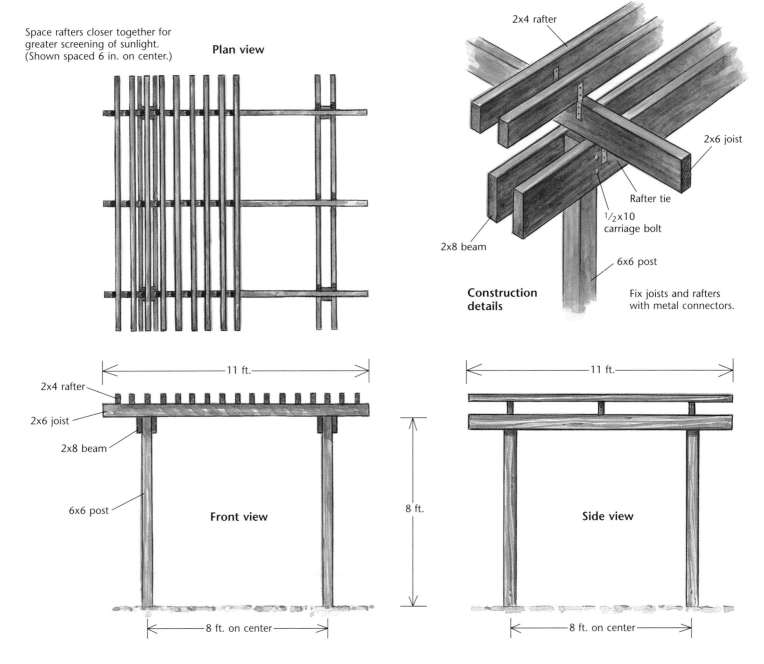

Space rafters closer together for greater screening of sunlight. (Shown spaced 6 in. on center.)

Plan view

2x4 rafter

2x6 joist

Rafter tie

½x10 carriage bolt

2x8 beam

6x6 post

Construction details

Fix joists and rafters with metal connectors.

2x4 rafter

2x6 joist

2x8 beam

6x6 post

— 11 ft. —

Front view

8 ft.

8 ft. on center

— 11 ft. —

Side view

8 ft. on center

Woodland arbor

(pp. 70–71)

Draped with honeysuckle, this shallow arbor helps establish a connection between a mixed border and an adjacent woodland. Once you have gathered the materials together, you should need no more than an afternoon to build the arbor.

Set the posts first, as described on pp. 124–127. The hefty 6x6 posts shown here add presence to the arbor, but cheaper, easier-to-handle 4x4s will make an equally sturdy structure. Cut the joists and rafters to length. The 60° angles on their ends can easily be cut with a handsaw. Bolt or nail the joists in place. Then toenail the short rafters to the joists or attach them with metal connectors.

In addition to the posts, you can provide other supports for the honeysuckle to twine around. Strands of coarse rope or cord work well when stretched between the large screw eyes fixed to the rafters and the base of the posts, as shown here. The vines soon hide the rope or cord from view.

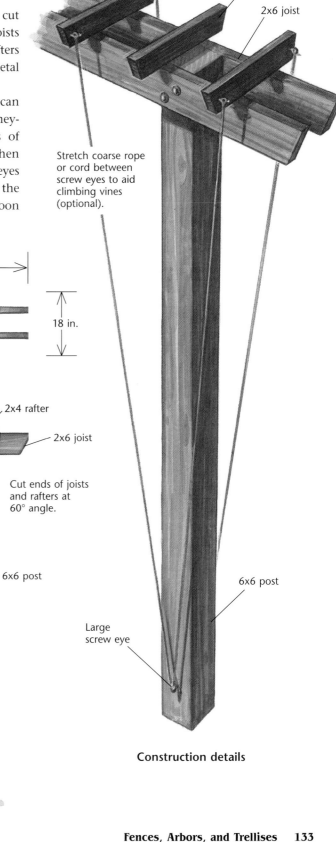

Large screw eye

2x4 rafter

2x6 joist

Stretch coarse rope or cord between screw eyes to aid climbing vines (optional).

Large screw eye

6x6 post

Construction details

Plan view

10 ft.

18 in.

6x6 post

2x6 joist

2x4 rafter

Front view

Large screw eye

Space rafters 12 in. on center.

2x4 rafter

2x6 joist

Cut ends of joists and rafters at 60° angle.

Coarse rope or cord aids climbing vines (optional).

6x6 post

8 ft.

6 ft.

Entry arbor and fence
(pp. 88–91)

This arbor makes an event of the passage from sidewalk to front door or from one part of your property to another. Two versions are shown in the Portfolio. One features the arbor alone; the other adds a picket fence.

Hefty 6x6 posts provide real presence here; the 12-footers you'll need are heavy, so engage a couple of helpers to save your back. You can toenail the 3x6 beams to the tops of the posts and the 2x4 rafters to the beams. (Or you can fix them with long spikes or lag screws, 10 in. or 8 in. long, respectively. This job is easier if you drill pilot holes, with bits slightly thinner than the spikes.) Attach the 2x2 cross rafters with screws or nails. If you can't buy 3x6s, you can nail two 2x6s together face to face.

Sandwich lattice between 1x3s to make the side panels and fix them between posts with nails, screws, or metal connectors.

The fence extends from both sides of the arbor. We've shown 6x6 fence posts to match the arbor. But 4x4s work just as well. Space posts farther apart than 8 ft. You can purchase ready-made lengths of picket fence, but it is easy enough to make yourself. Set the posts; then cut and fit 2x4 rails on edge between them. Space 1x3 picket slats 1½ in. apart. The drawing on the facing page shows large round wooden finials atop the fence posts; you can buy various types of ready-made finials, or you could work a heavy bevel around the top end of the posts themselves.

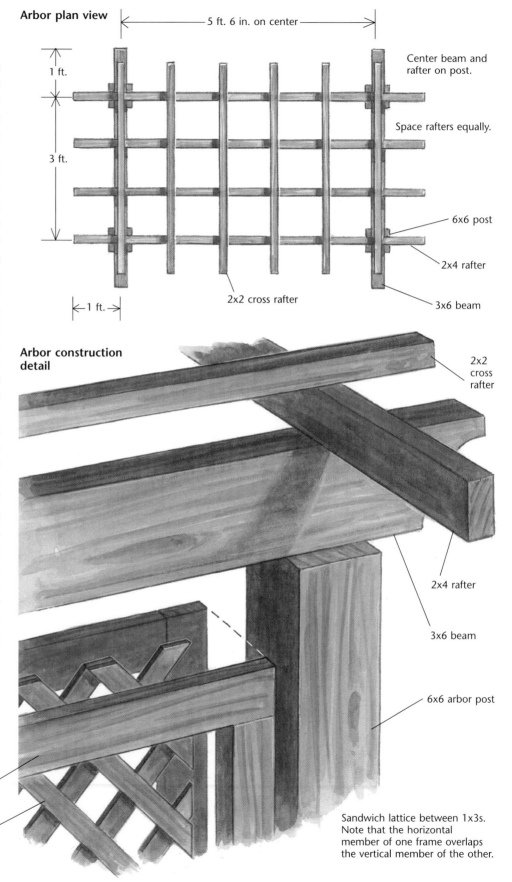

Arbor plan view

5 ft. 6 in. on center

1 ft.

3 ft.

1 ft.

Center beam and rafter on post.

Space rafters equally.

6x6 post

2x4 rafter

3x6 beam

2x2 cross rafter

Arbor construction detail

2x2 cross rafter

2x4 rafter

3x6 beam

6x6 arbor post

1x3 frame

Lattice

Sandwich lattice between 1x3s. Note that the horizontal member of one frame overlaps the vertical member of the other.

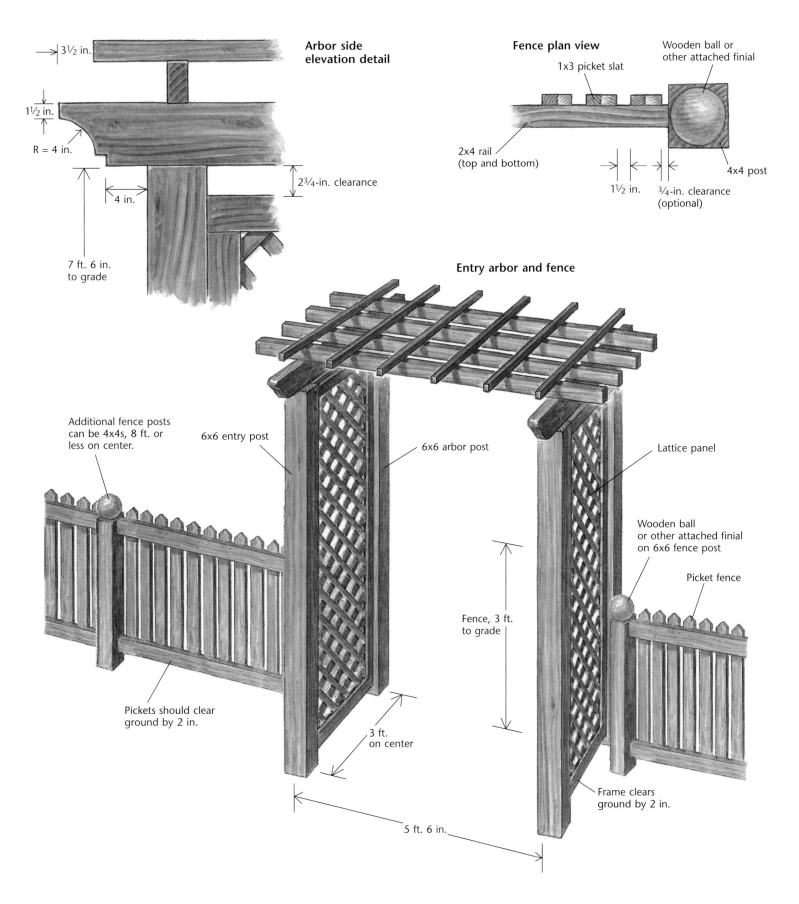

$3\frac{1}{2}$ in.

Arbor side
elevation detail

$1\frac{1}{2}$ in.

R = 4 in.

4 in.

$2\frac{3}{4}$-in. clearance

7 ft. 6 in.
to grade

Fence plan view

Wooden ball or
other attached finial

1x3 picket slat

2x4 rail
(top and bottom)

4x4 post

$1\frac{1}{2}$ in.

$\frac{3}{4}$-in. clearance
(optional)

Entry arbor and fence

Additional fence posts
can be 4x4s, 8 ft. or
less on center.

6x6 entry post

6x6 arbor post

Lattice panel

Wooden ball
or other attached finial
on 6x6 fence post

Picket fence

Fence, 3 ft.
to grade

Pickets should clear
ground by 2 in.

3 ft.
on center

Frame clears
ground by 2 in.

5 ft. 6 in.

Louvered screen
(pp. 92–93)

Made of vertical slats set at an angle, this 6-ft.-tall screen hides trash and recycling bins from view while allowing air circulation in the area.

The slats are supported top and bottom by 2x4 rails; a 2x6 beneath the bottom rail stiffens the entire structure, keeps the slat assembly from sagging, and adds visual weight to the design. Set the posts (see pp. 124–126); then cut the rails to fit between them. Toenailed nails or screws or metal connectors are strong enough, but you can add a 2x4 nailer between the rails (as shown in the drawing at bottom right) to make positioning and assembly easier.

Position the 1x6 slats with a spacer block $1\frac{1}{2}$ in. wide and angled 45° at its ends. Nailing or screwing down through the top rail is easy. Nailing up through the bottom rail is more difficult; instead, you could toenail through the edges or faces of the slats into the bottom rail. You may need to cut the final slat narrower to maintain the uniform spacing.

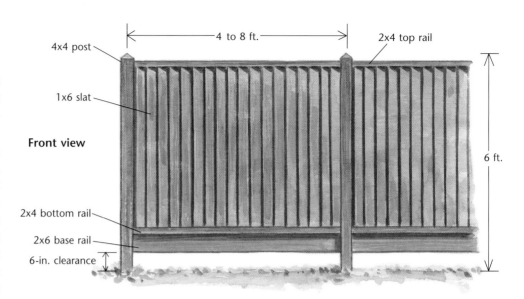

Front view

4x4 post
2x4 top rail
1x6 slat
2x4 bottom rail
2x6 base rail
6-in. clearance
4 to 8 ft.
6 ft.

Construction details

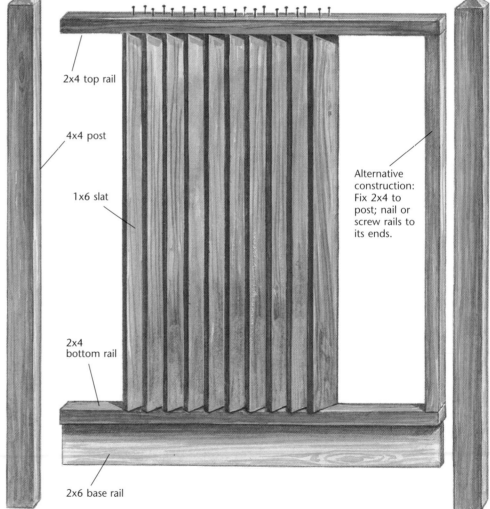

2x4 top rail
4x4 post
1x6 slat
2x4 bottom rail
2x6 base rail
Alternative construction: Fix 2x4 to post; nail or screw rails to its ends.

Slat assembly

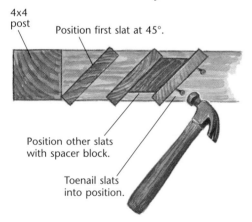

4x4 post
Position first slat at 45°.
Position other slats with spacer block.
Toenail slats into position.

Hideaway arbor
(pp. 48–49)

This cozy enclosure shelters a bench and supports vines to shade the occupants. Once the posts are set in place, this project can be finished in a weekend.

Build the arbor before laying the pavers under it. After setting the posts (see pp. 124–127), attach the 2x10 joists with

carriage bolts. (The sizes of posts and joists have been chosen for aesthetic effect; 4x4 posts and 2x6 or 2x8 joists will work, too.) Tack the joists in place with nails; then bore holes for the bolts through the post and both joists with a long electrician's auger bit. Fix the rafters by toenailing or using rust-protected metal rafter ties. Nail or screw the rafters at each end to the posts for added stability. For more privacy, you can add lattice between the posts at each end. (See p. 130 for a method of lattice panel construction.)

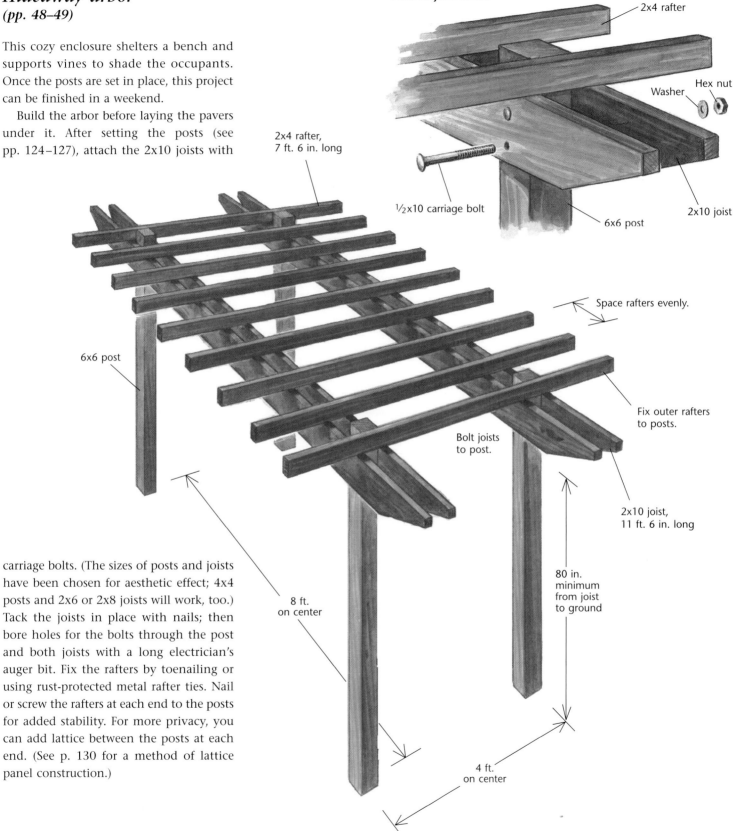

Post-to-joist detail

2x4 rafter

Washer

Hex nut

½x10 carriage bolt

6x6 post

2x10 joist

2x4 rafter, 7 ft. 6 in. long

6x6 post

Space rafters evenly.

Fix outer rafters to posts.

Bolt joists to post.

2x10 joist, 11 ft. 6 in. long

80 in. minimum from joist to ground

8 ft. on center

4 ft. on center

Good-neighbor fence
(pp. 64–67)

A variation on the traditional picket fence, this design provides privacy and good looks to neighbors on both sides, in addition to serving as a backdrop for a perennial border.

This is a simple fence to construct. Just set the posts (see pp. 124–126), cut top and bottom rails to fit between them, and attach the slats. Note that the slats overlap roughly $1/2$ in.; a $4^1/2$-in.-wide spacer block (1 in. narrower than the actual $5^1/2$-in. width of the 1x6s) makes positioning them a snap. Use two screws or nails positioned diagonally for each slat-to-rail connection.

Plan view

Slats overlap on each side $1/2$ in.

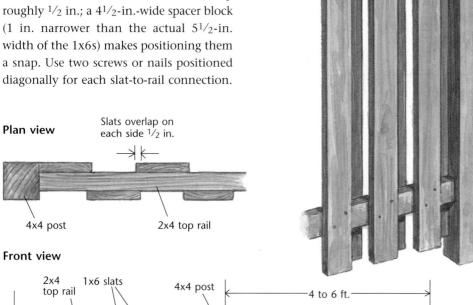

4x4 post

2x4 top rail

Front view

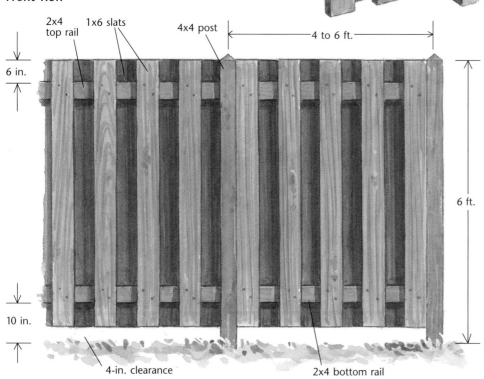

2x4 top rail
1x6 slats
4x4 post
4 to 6 ft.
6 in.
6 ft.
10 in.
4-in. clearance
2x4 bottom rail

Construction details

1x6 slats
4x4 post
2x4 top rail

Position nails or screws diagonally.

Picket fence
(pp. 58–59)

This fence, a variation of the traditional picket fence, supports a profusion of vining foliage and flowers and provides a sense of enclosure to a small pond and planting. The hefty 6x6 posts are used for their visual weight; 4x4 posts are strong enough, if you prefer them.

To build the fence, you can set the posts first (see pp. 124–126) and make fence sections to fit between them. Or make the sections first and set posts accordingly. The pickets are sandwiched between two sets of rails top and bottom and are fixed in place

Side view

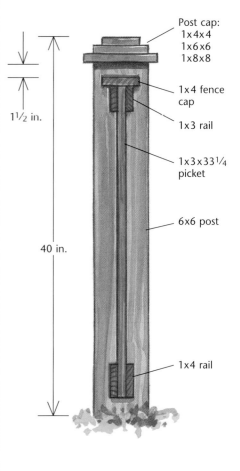

Post cap:
1x4x4
1x6x6
1x8x8
1x4 fence cap
1x3 rail
1x3x33$1/4$ picket
6x6 post
1x4 rail
$1^1/2$ in.
40 in.

with nails or screws. If you're making fence sections to fit a predetermined distance between posts, adjust the gap between pickets to ensure uniform spacing. When you lay out the pickets, make sure that there is a space between each post and the end picket.

You can fasten the rails to the posts by toenailing or with metal fasteners. Adding a spacer between the ends of the rails, as shown in the detail drawing, may make attachment easier. After the fence sections are fixed to the posts, add the cap pieces to the top rails and to the posts.

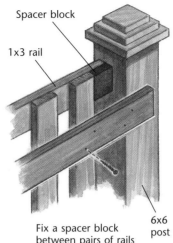

Spacer block

1x3 rail

6x6 post

Fix a spacer block between pairs of rails before attaching fence section to post.

Fence-construction detail

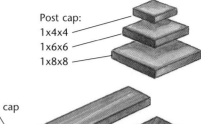

Post cap:
1x4x4
1x6x6
1x8x8

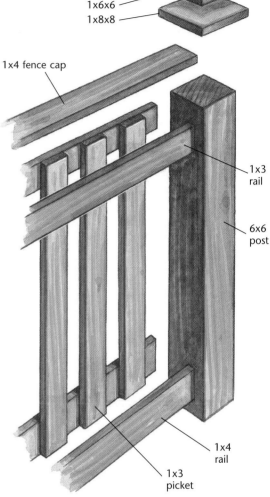

1x4 fence cap

1x3 rail

6x6 post

1x4 rail

1x3 picket

Front view

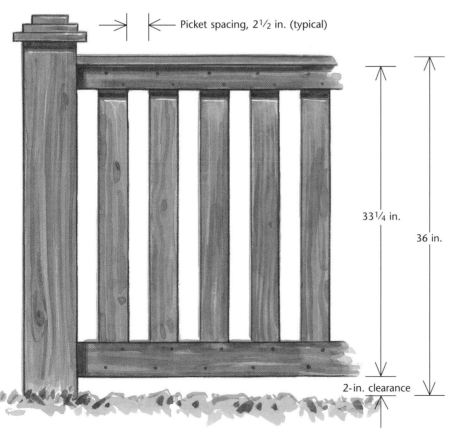

Picket spacing, 2$\frac{1}{2}$ in. (typical)

33$\frac{1}{4}$ in.

36 in.

2-in. clearance

Patio screen
(pp. 52–53)

Draped with vines, this makes an attractive but unobtrusive privacy screen between your patio and an adjacent property.

The screen is a snap to build. After setting the posts (see pp. 124–126), add the top and bottom rails. Cut the ends of those for the angled corners at 45° and toenail or screw them to the posts. Trim the ends of the "pickets" at a 45° angle and fix them with a nail or screw into each rail. Position the pickets before fastening them to ensure even spacing. If you want a more solid-looking screen, offset the pickets so that those on one side fill the gaps left by those on the other. You can vary the size of the screen and the materials shown here. Keep in mind that the proportions are what make this simple design look good.

Construction detail

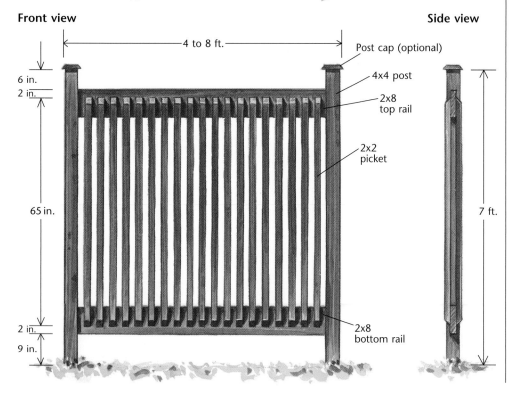

Plan view

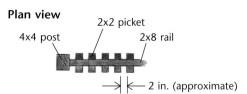

4x4 post
2x2 picket
2x8 rail
2 in. (approximate)

Front view

Side view

4 to 8 ft.

Post cap (optional)
4x4 post
2x8 top rail
2x2 picket
2x8 bottom rail

6 in.
2 in.
65 in.
2 in.
9 in.
7 ft.

Privacy fence
(pp. 80–83)

This design provides privacy between houses and an attractive backdrop for a planting. If the fence is used on a property line, be sure to check local codes for restrictions on placement and height.

This is a simple fence to construct. Assemble the panels on a flat surface, nailing or screwing the slats to the three 2x4 rails. You can lay out the arc at the top of each panel by "springing" a thin strip of wood, as shown on the facing page. Place the strip against a nail driven into a slat at the highest point of the arc in the center of the panel ❶. Enlist a couple of assistants to bend each end of the strip down to nails near the edges of the panel indicating the lowest points of the arc ❷. Pencil in the arc against the strip ❸. Then cut to the line. (A handheld electric jigsaw does the job quickly, but the curve is gentle enough to cut with a handsaw.)

View from back of fence

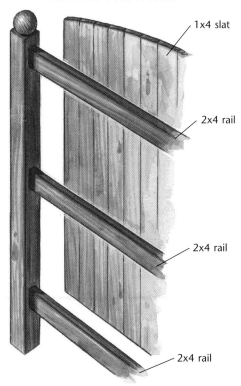

1x4 slat
2x4 rail
2x4 rail
2x4 rail

Set the posts (see pp. 124–126) according to the widths of the finished panels. The 6x6 posts shown here add an eye-pleasing heft to the fence, an effect emphasized by setting the face of the panel 1 in. back from the faces of the posts. (Posts made of 4x4s will work just as well.) Metal connectors are the easiest means of attaching the completed panels to the posts. To allow yourself access to the rails when mounting the metal connectors, leave the last slats at each end off when you assemble the panels. We've shown a spherical finial attached to the top of each post; you can buy finials of various types at home centers.

Springing an arc

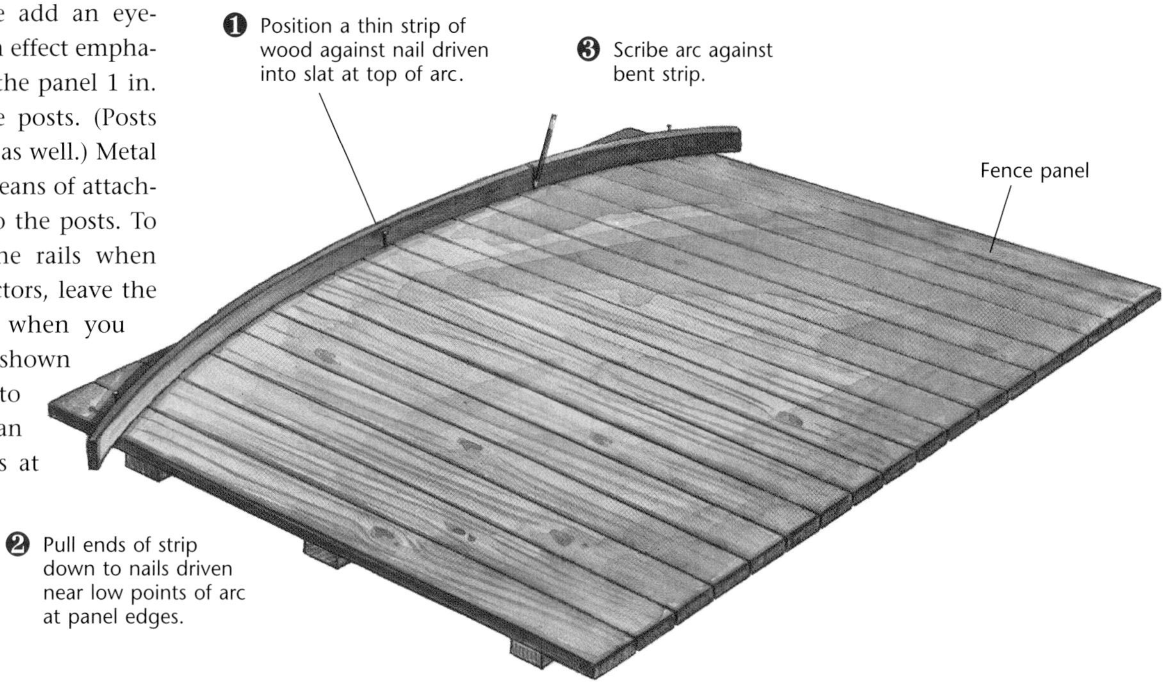

❶ Position a thin strip of wood against nail driven into slat at top of arc.

❸ Scribe arc against bent strip.

Fence panel

❷ Pull ends of strip down to nails driven near low points of arc at panel edges.

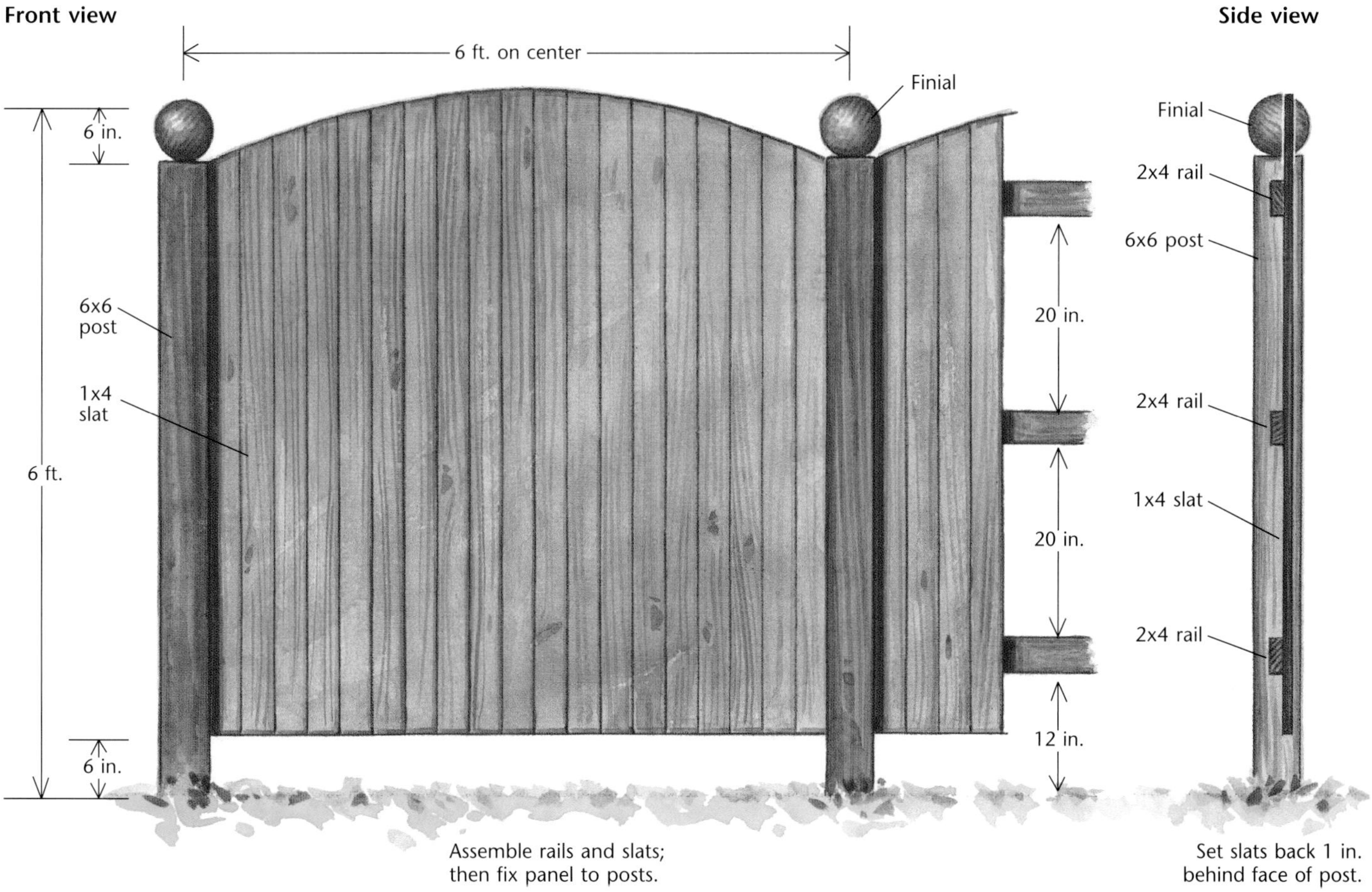

Front view

6 ft. on center

Finial

6 in.

6x6 post

1x4 slat

6 ft.

6 in.

20 in.

20 in.

12 in.

Assemble rails and slats; then fix panel to posts.

Side view

Finial

2x4 rail

6x6 post

2x4 rail

1x4 slat

2x4 rail

Set slats back 1 in. behind face of post.

Preparing the Soil for Planting

The better the soil, the better the plants. Soil quality affects how fast plants grow, how big they get, how good they look, and how long they live. But on many residential lots, the soil is shallow and infertile. Unless you're lucky enough to have a better-than-average site where the soil has been cared for and amended over the years, perhaps for use as a vegetable garden or flower bed, you should plan to improve your soil before planting in it.

If you were planting just a few trees or shrubs, or planting a bed of perennials on a rocky hillside, you could prepare individual planting holes for the plants and leave the surrounding soil undisturbed. However, for nearly all the plantings in this book, digging individual holes is impractical, and it's much better for the plants if you prepare the soil throughout the entire area that will be planted. (The major exception is when you're planting under a tree, which is discussed on p. 144.)

For most of the situations shown in this book, you could prepare the soil with hand tools—a spade, digging fork, and rake. The job will go faster and mix in amendments better if you use a gas-powered rototiller. Unless you grow vegetables, you probably won't use a rototiller often enough to justify buying one yourself, but you can easily borrow or rent a rototiller or hire someone with a tiller to come and prepare your site.

Loosen the soil

After you've removed any sod or other vegetation from the designated area (see pp. 104–105), the first step is digging or tilling to loosen the soil ❶. Do this on a day when the soil is moist—not so wet that it sticks to your tools or so dry that it makes dust. Try to dig down at least 8 in., or deeper if possible. If the ground is very compacted, you'll need to make repeated passes with a tiller to reach 8 in. deep. Toss aside large rocks, roots, or debris. When you're working near a house or other building, be sure to locate buried wires, cables, and pipes. Most local governments and utility companies have a number you can call to request help locating buried utilities.

Preparing the soil for planting

❶ Use a spade, digging fork, or tiller to dig at least 8 in. deep and break the soil into rough clods. Discard rocks, roots, and debris. Watch out for underground utilities.

❷ Spread a 2- to 3-in. layer of organic matter on top of the soil.

❸ Sprinkle measured amounts of fertilizer and mineral amendments evenly across the entire area, and mix thoroughly into the soil.

After this initial digging, the ground will likely be very rough and lumpy. Whump the clods with the back of a digging fork or make another pass with the tiller. Continue until you've reduced all the clumps to the size of apples.

Once you've loosened the existing soil and dug it as deeply as possible, you may need to add clean topsoil or a landscape mix to fill in low spots, refine the grade, or raise the planting area above the surrounding grade for better drainage or to make it easier to see a favorite plant. Unless you need just a small amount, order topsoil or landscape mix by the cubic yard. (Landscape mix is primarily composted pine bark, sometimes with sand, manure, and other composted materials.) Consult the staff at your local nursery to find a reputable supplier of bulk landscape materials.

In many areas of central Texas, only a thin layer of soil covers limestone bedrock, making digging or tilling impossible. In these areas, the best option is to bring in topsoil or landscape mix. Mound it to create a low berm or contain it in a raised soil bed enclose in wood or stone.

Add organic matter

Common soil (and purchased topsoil, too) consists mainly of rock and mineral fragments of various size. One of the best things you can do to improve any kind of soil for landscape and garden plants is to add some organic matter.

Organic materials used in landscaping are derived from plants and animals and include ground bark, peat moss, compost, and composted manures. Organic matter can be bought in bags or in bulk at nurseries, landscape supply companies, and many municipal recycling centers. If possible, buy only composted or aged material to amend your soil. Fresh manure can "burn" plant roots. Fresh bark and sawdust can "steal" nitrogen from the soil as they decay. If you buy uncomposted materials, ask at your nursery how best to use them (some require supplemental nitrogen).

Common soil amendments and fertilizers

The following materials serve different purposes. Follow soil-test recommendations or the advice of an experienced gardener in choosing which amendments and fertilizers would be best for your soil. If so recommended, you can apply two or three of these at the same time, using the stated rate for each one.

Material	Description	Amount for 100 sq. ft.
Compost	Amendment. Decomposed or aged plant parts and animal manures.	1 cubic yard
Wood by-products	Amendment. Finely ground bark or sawdust, composted or not. Add nitrogen to non-composted material.	1 cubic yard
All-purpose fertilizer	Synthetic fertilizer containing various amounts of nitrogen, phosphorus, and potassium.	According to label
Organic fertilizer	Derived from a variety of organic materials. Provides nutrients in slow-release form.	According to label
Composted manure	Weak nitrogen fertilizers. Bagged steer manure is common.	6–8 lb.

How much organic matter should you use? Compost or aged material can be spread 2 to 3 in. thick across the entire work area ❷. At this thickness, a cubic yard (about one heaping pickup-truck load) of material will cover 100 to 150 sq. ft. Composted and aged manures, such as the bagged steer manure sold at nurseries, contain higher concentrations of nitrogen and should be applied at lower rates than other composts. They are more commonly used as slow-release fertilizers than as soil-improving amendments.

Add fertilizers and mineral amendments

Organic matter improves the soil's texture and helps it retain water and nutrients, but these materials usually lack essential nutrients. To provide the nutrients that plants need, you typically need to use organic or synthetic fertilizers. It's most helpful if you mix these materials into the soil before you do any planting ❸, working them into the root zone, but you can also sprinkle them on top of the soil to maintain an established planting.

Testing a sample of soil is the most accurate way to determine how much of which nutrients is needed. (To locate a soil-testing lab, consult the Internet, the Yellow Pages, or your Cooperative Extension Service.) Less precise, but often adequate, is the advice of nursery staff. Test results or an adviser will point out any significant deficiencies in your soil, but large deficiencies are uncommon. Most soil just needs a moderate, balanced dose of nutrients.

The key thing is to avoid using too much of any fertilizer or mineral. Don't guess at this; measure and weigh carefully. Calculate your plot's area. Follow your soil-test results or instructions on a commercial product's package. If necessary weigh out the appropriate amount, using a kitchen or bathroom scale. Apply the material evenly across the plot with a spreader or by hand.

Mix and smooth the soil

Finally, use a digging fork or tiller and go back and forth across the bed again until the added materials are mixed thoroughly into the soil and everything is broken into nut-size or smaller lumps **4**. Then use a rake to smooth the surface **5**.

At this point, the soil level may look too high compared with adjacent pavement or lawn, but don't worry. Once the soil gets wet, it will settle a few inches and end up close to its original level.

Working near trees

Plantings under the shade of stately old trees can be cool lovely oases, like the one shown on pp. 62–63. But to establish the plants, you'll need to contend with the tree's roots. Contrary to popular belief, most tree roots are in the top few inches of

the soil, and they extend at least as far away from the trunk as the limbs do. Always try to disturb as few roots as possible when planting beneath established trees. To do so, it's often best to dig individual planting holes, rather than tilling a bed. Avoid cutting large roots. To start ground covers and perennials, you can add up to 4 in. of loose soil or landscape mix under the canopy of many established trees. Keep the new soil and any mulch away from the trunk. Covering roots with too much soil can starve them of oxygen, damaging or killing them; soil or mulch next to the trunk can rot the adjacent bark.

Plantings beneath existing native post oaks are normally problematic because the additional water needed to maintain the planting may damage or kill these trees. If you're uncertain about whether or how to plant beneath any established tree, or if your landscape plans call for significant grade changes beneath them, consult with a certified arborist.

4 Use a tiller or digging fork to mix everything together, again working as deep as possible.

5 Finish by smoothing the surface with a rake.

Making neat edges

All but the most informal landscapes look best if you define and maintain neat edges between the lawn and any adjacent plantings. There are several ways to do this, varying in appearance, effectiveness, cost, and convenience. Attractive, easy-to-install edges include cut, brick or stone, and strip edgings of plastic, fiberglass, or steel. If you plan to install an edging, put it in after you prepare the soil but before you plant.

Cut edge

Lay a hose or rope on the ground to mark the line where you want to cut. Then cut along the line with a sharp spade or edging tool. Lift away any grass that was growing into the bed (or any plants that were running out into the lawn). Use a rake or hoe to smooth out a shallow trench on the bed side of the cut. Keep the trench empty; don't let it fill up with mulch.

Pros and cons: Free. Good for straight or curved edges, level or sloped sites. But you'll need to recut the edge every four to eight weeks during the growing season; you can cut 50 to 100 ft. in an hour or so. Don't cut the trench too deep; if a mower wheel slips down into it, you'll scalp the lawn. Crabgrass and other weeds may sprout in the exposed soil; if this happens, hoe or pull them out.

Brick mowing strip

Dig a trench about 8 in. wide and 4 in. deep around the edge of the bed. Fill it halfway with sand; then lay bricks on top, setting them level with the soil on the lawn side. You'll need three bricks

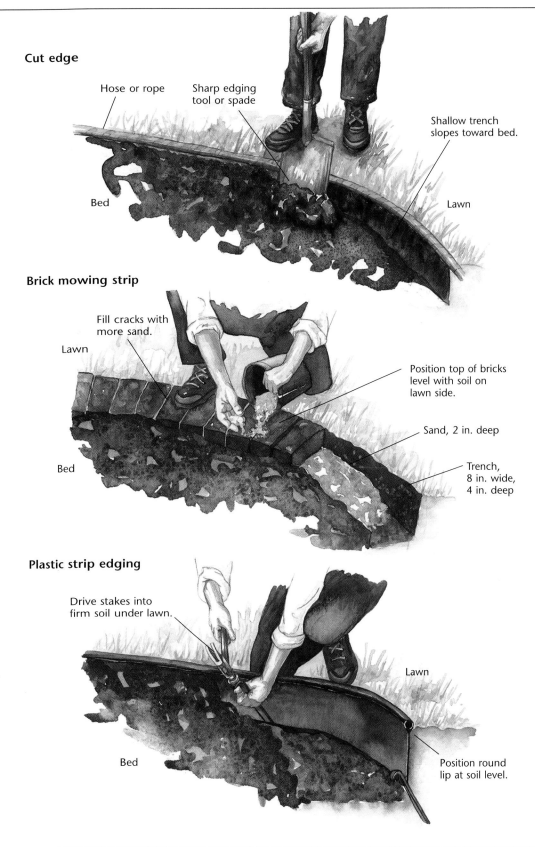

Cut edge

Hose or rope

Sharp edging tool or spade

Shallow trench slopes toward bed.

Bed

Lawn

Brick mowing strip

Fill cracks with more sand.

Lawn

Position top of bricks level with soil on lawn side.

Sand, 2 in. deep

Bed

Trench, 8 in. wide, 4 in. deep

Plastic strip edging

Drive stakes into firm soil under lawn.

Lawn

Bed

Position round lip at soil level.

per foot of edging. Sweep extra sand into any cracks between the bricks. In cold-winter areas, you'll probably need to reset a few frost-heaved bricks each spring. You can substitute cut stone blocks or concrete pavers for bricks.

Pros and cons: Good for straight or curved edges on level or gently sloped sites. Looks good in combination with brick walkways or brick house. Fairly easy to install and maintain. Some kinds of grass and plants will grow under, between, or over the bricks.

Plastic strip edging

Garden centers and home-improvement stores sell heavy-duty plastic edging in strips 5 or 6 in. wide and 20 or 50 ft. long. To install it, use a sharp tool to cut straight down through the sod around the edge of the bed. Hold the edging so the round lip sits right at soil level, and drive the stakes through the bottom of the edging and into the undisturbed soil under the lawn. Stakes, which are supplied with the edging, should be at least 8 in. long and set about 3 ft. apart. Similar strip edging in steel or fiberglass is installed in much the same way.

Pros and cons: Good for straight or curved edges, but only on relatively level sites. Neat and carefree when well installed, but installation is a two- or three-person job. If the lip isn't set right on the ground, you're likely to hit it with the mower blade. Liable to shift or heave unless it's very securely staked. Hard to drive stakes in rocky soil. Some kinds of grass and ground covers can grow across the top of the edging.

Caring for Perennials

Perennials are simply plants that send up new growth year after year. A large group, perennials include flowering plants such as daylilies and purple coneflower as well as grasses, ferns, and hardy bulbs. Although some perennials need special conditions and care, most of those in this book are adaptable and easy to grow. Get them off to a good start by planting them in well-prepared soil, adding a layer of mulch, watering as often as needed throughout the first year, and keeping weeds away. After that, keeping perennials attractive and healthy typically requires just a few minutes per plant each month.

Routine annual care

Some of the perennials that are used as ground covers, such as lilyturf, mondo grass, and vinca, need virtually no care. On a suitable site, they'll thrive for decades even if you pay them almost no attention at all.

Most garden perennials, though, look and grow better if you clean away the old leaves and stems at least once a year. When to do this depends on the type of plant. Perennials such as firebush, cigar plant, and Turk's cap have leaves and stalks that turn tan or brown after they're frosted in fall. Cut these down to the ground in late fall or early spring; either time is okay.

Some perennials, such as oxeye daisy, columbine, yarrow, verbena, and dianthus, have foliage that is more or less evergreen, depending on the severity of the winter. For those plants, wait until after they've bloomed or until the fall; then cut back leaves or stems that are discolored or shabby looking. Don't leave cuttings lying on the soil, because they may contain disease spores. To avoid contaminating your compost, send diseased stems or leaves to the dump.

Right after you've cleared away the dead material is a good time to renew the mulch on the bed. Use a fork, rake, or cultivator to loosen the existing mulch, and add some fresh mulch if needed. Also, if you want to sprinkle some granular fertilizer on the bed, do that now, when it's easy to avoid getting any on the plants' leaves. Fertilizing perennials is optional, but it does make them grow bigger and bloom more than they would otherwise.

Pruning and shearing perennials

Some perennials that bloom in summer or fall respond well to being pruned earlier in the growing season. Aster, chrysanthemum, Mexican sage, garden phlox, and 'Autumn Joy' sedum all form tall clumps of

Pruning a perennial

Prune to create neater, bushier clumps of some summer- and fall-blooming perennials such as garden phlox, chrysanthemums, and 'Autumn Joy' sedum. When the stalks are about 1 ft. tall, cut them all back by one-third. Remove the weakest stalks at ground level.

stems topped with lots of little flowers. Unfortunately, tall stems are liable to flop over in stormy weather, and even if they don't, too-tall clumps can look leggy or top-heavy. To prevent floppiness, prune these plants when the stems are about 1 ft. tall. Remove the weakest stems from each clump by cutting them off at the ground; then cut all the remaining, strong stems back by about one-third. Pruning in this way keeps these plants shorter, stronger, and bushier, so you don't have to bother with stakes to keep them upright.

Purple heart and 'Powis Castle' artemisia are grown more for their foliage than for their flowers. You can use hedge shears to keep them neat, compact, and bushy, shearing off the tops of the stems once or twice in spring and summer.

Remove faded flowers

Removing flowers as they fade (called "deadheading") makes a garden bed look neater, prevents unwanted self-sown seedlings, and often stimulates a plant to continue blooming longer than it would if you left it alone, or to bloom a second time later in the season. (This is true for shrubs and annuals as well as for perennials.)

Pick large flowers such as daisies, daylilies, irises, and hibiscus one at a time, snapping them off by hand. Use pruning shears on perennials such as salvia, gaura, phlox, and yarrow that produce tall stalks crowded with lots of small flowers, cutting the stalks back to the height of the foliage. Use hedge shears on bushy plants that are covered with lots of small flowers on short stalks, such as lantana, Turk's cap, and verbena, cutting the stems back by about one-half their length.

Instead of removing them, you may want to let the flowers remain on black-eyed Susans, 'Autumn Joy' sedum, and the various ornamental grasses. These plants all bear conspicuous seedpods or seed heads on stiff stalks that remain standing and look interesting throughout the fall and winter months.

Dividing perennials

Most perennials send up more stems each year, forming denser clumps or wider patches. Dividing is the process of cutting or breaking apart these clumps or patches. This is an easy way to make more plants to expand your garden, to control a plant that might otherwise spread out of bounds, or to renew an old specimen that doesn't look good or bloom well anymore.

Most perennials can be divided as often as every year or two if you're in a hurry to make more plants, or they can go for years if you don't have any reason to disturb them. Fall is the best time to divide most summer- and fall-blooming perennials, but you can also do it in early spring.

There are two main approaches to dividing perennials, as shown in the drawings at right. You can leave the plant in the ground and use a sharp spade to cut it apart, like slicing a pie, and then lift out one chunk at a time. Or you can dig around and underneath the plant and lift it out all at once, shake off the extra soil, and lay the plant on the ground or a tarp where you can work with it.

Some plants, such as yarrow, and some ferns, are easy to divide. They almost fall apart when you dig them up. Others, such as daylilies and most grasses, have very tough or tangled roots and you'll have to wrestle with them, chop them with a sharp butcher knife, pry them apart with a sharp spade, or even cut through the roots with a hatchet or pruning saw. However you approach the job, before you insert any tool, take a close look at the plant right at ground level, and be careful to divide *between*, not *through*, the biggest and healthiest buds or shoots. Using a hose to wash loose mulch and soil away makes it easier to see what you're doing.

Don't make the divisions too small; they should be the size of a plant that you'd want to buy, not just little scraps. If you have more divisions than you need or want, choose just the best-looking ones to replant and discard or give away the others.

Replant new divisions as soon as possible in freshly prepared soil. Water them right away, and water again whenever the soil dries out over the next few weeks or months, until the plants are growing again.

Hardy bulbs such as narcissus and snowflakes can be divided every few years to plant new areas. Dig clumps after bloom when the foliage turns yellow. Shake the soil off the roots, pull the bulbs apart, and replant them promptly, setting them as deep as they were buried before.

Dividing perennials

You can divide a clump or patch of perennials by cutting down into the patch with a sharp spade, like slicing a pie or a pan of brownies, then lifting out the separate chunks.

Or you can dig up the whole clump, shake the extra soil off the roots, and pull or pry it apart into separate plantlets.

Plant Profiles

Plants are the heart of the designs in this book. In this section, you'll find descriptions of all the plants used in the designs, along with information on planting and maintaining them. These trees, shrubs, perennials, grasses, bulbs, and vines have all proven themselves as dependable performers in Texas. They offer a wide spectrum of lovely flowers and fruits, handsome foliage, and striking forms. Most contribute something of note in at least two seasons. You can use this section as an aid when installing the designs in this book and as a reference for selecting desirable plants for other home-landscaping projects.

Artemisia × 'Powis Castle'

'POWIS CASTLE' ARTEMISIA. A beautiful accent plant, this shrubby perennial is grown for fragrant, silvery, finely divided foliage. Flowers rarely, if ever. It forms a dome-shaped mound 2 ft. tall and 3 ft. wide. Plant in full sun with good drainage. Tolerates dry soil but grows faster when watered during dry summers. Cut back lightly in early spring and fall to encourage new growth and to keep plant compact. Pest free. Pages: 23, 31, 36, 67, 75, 85, 91.

Aspidistra elatior

CAST-IRON PLANT. An unusual evergreen perennial valued for its tolerance of deep shade. It forms a dense patch of stiff, dark, pointed leaves that grow directly from the ground and reach 3 ft. tall. Spreads slowly into a weed-proof colony about 2 ft. wide. Purple to gray-white flowers are solitary and mostly hidden in the foliage. Cast-iron plant grows well in full or partial shade with occasional summer watering. Pest and disease free. Cut back the old growth in early spring before the new leaves emerge. The bold foliage is often used in floral arrangements. Pages: 42, 69, 79, 83.

Aster oblongifolius

FALL ASTER. This carefree native perennial bears showy lavender-purple daisylike flowers from early fall until the first hard freeze. The plant spreads to form a dense clump 2 ft. tall and 3 ft. wide. Fall aster thrives in full sun or partial shade with well-drained soil. It is drought tolerant and has no known pest problems. Prune to the ground after the first hard freeze. In late spring, cut new stems back by one-third to keep plants from getting floppy and to encourage more flowers in fall. Divide plants every few years in early spring. Pages: 22, 29, 36, 40, 55, 65, 91.

Aucuba japonica

AUCUBA. These are showy evergreen shrubs with thick erect stems sporting large, lustrous, leathery leaves. They generally grow around 4 ft. tall and 3 ft. wide. The cultivar 'Variegata', also known as gold dust aucuba (pp. 79, 83), has green leaves sprinkled with yellow dots. The leaves of 'Picturata' (pp. 46, *46*) are splashed with yellow blotches. Aucubas are some of the best shrubs for dark shady areas. They will not tolerate hot, exposed, sunny sites. Provide monthly watering during dry summers. Plants are generally pest free. Prune lightly in late winter to control size.

Artemisia × 'Powis Castle' **ARTEMISIA**

Aspidistra elatior **CAST-IRON PLANT**

Aster oblongifolius **FALL ASTER**

Berberis thunbergii 'Crimson Pygmy'

DWARF JAPANESE BARBERRY. A deciduous shrub grown for its colorful foliage and compact, spreading habit. Stiff, spiny stems are lined with small leaves that are burgundy in summer and bright crimson in fall. Grows into a dense mound 2 ft. tall and 3 ft. wide or can be trimmed into a small hedge. Needs full sun, well-drained soil, and occasional water during dry periods. Expect no insect or disease problems. Shear as needed to maintain a desired shape. Page: 38, *39*.

Bignonia capreolata 'Tangerine Beauty'

'TANGERINE BEAUTY' CROSS VINE. This vigorous evergreen vine grows to a generous 15 ft. tall and wide. In spring the entire plant turns into a mass of beautiful trumpet-like orange flowers with yellow throats. Scattered bloom continues through the growing season. Excellent for covering walls, trellises, and fences. Cross vine is a Texas native and requires little care or water. It is rarely plagued by insects or disease. Pages: 30, 87.

Bulbs

The bulbs recommended in this book are perennials that come up year after year and bloom in late winter or early spring. Buy bulbs from a garden center or catalog in late summer or fall. Plant them promptly in a sunny or partly shaded bed in moderately well-drained soil. As a rule, plant at a depth two times the bulb's height. After bulbs flower in spring, their leaves continue growing until some time in May, when they gradually turn yellow and die down to the ground. In subsequent years, remove (or ignore, if you choose) the old leaves after they turn yellow. Most bulbs can be divided every four to five years if you want to grow them elsewhere. Dig them as the foliage is turning yellow, shake or pull them apart, and replant them right away. Perennial bulbs are great for naturalizing in meadows and borders, for edging flower beds and fences, and as pockets of color among shrubs and ground covers. See the box on p. 170 for information on specific bulbs.

Buxus microphylla

LITTLELEAF BOXWOOD. This evergreen shrub forms a dense mass of small glossy leaves that make it ideal for shearing into formal globes, cones, hedges, or topiary. If left alone, it grows into a neat soft mound 4 to 5 ft. tall. Leaves turn brownish in cold winters. The cultivar 'Green Beauty' (p. 97) forms a

Aucuba japonica
AUCUBA

Bignonia capreolata
'Tangerine Beauty'
CROSS VINE

Recommended bulbs

Narcissus tazetta, Narcissus

This enduring perennial bulb blooms between late fall and early spring. Extremely fragrant white flowers open in dense clusters on 1 to 1½ ft. stalks and make great cut flowers. The dark green foliage occurs in clumps 1 ft. wide and tall, emerging in the fall and going dormant during the summer. 'Avalanche' (pp. 87, *87*) has creamy white flowers with lemon yellow cups. 'Grand Primo' (pp. *50*, 51) is a southern heirloom with creamy white flowers and pale yellow cups; if unavailable, use 'Avalanche' as a substitute. Paperwhite (*N. tazetta papyraceous*) has pure white flowers and can be used as a substitute in the milder areas below Interstate 10. Tazetta narcissus are pest free and require no irrigation. Pages: 61, 69.

Narcissus tazetta
NARCISSUS

Leucojum aestivum
SNOWFLAKE

N. pseudonarcissus 'Ice Follies', 'Ice Follies' daffodil

Along with the golden yellow cultivars 'Carlton' and 'Fortune', this is one of the few daffodils that does well in Texas. A spring-blooming perennial bulb, it has wide, ruffled, yellow trumpets fading to creamy white. The extremely showy blooms rise 1 ft. among blue-green foliage and make great cut flowers. Daffodils require full sun and good drainage. Divide them every 5 to 10 years to keep them blooming. Pages: 21, 80.

N. jonquilla, Jonquil

This early spring bulb has heavenly scented small golden yellow flowers above dark green rushlike foliage. Goes dormant during the summer, re-emerging with fresh foliage in the winter. It has no pest problems and prefers dry summers. 'Trevithian' and 'Sweetness' are commonly available. Page: 77, *79*.

Leucojum aestivum, Snowflake

This dependable perennial bulb delights with clusters of tiny white bells on 1 ft. stalks in early spring. The healthy green foliage emerges in early winter and goes dormant in summer. Snowflakes are great for introducing bright patches of early bloom among ground covers and landscaped beds. They grow in sun or shade and in moist or dry conditions. This foolproof bulb is pest free and requires no supplemental watering. Pages: 27, 71.

Zephyranthes candida, White rainlily

This hardy little bulb produces dark green grasslike foliage during the cool months of the year. In late summer the leaves often die back in exchange for showy white crocus-like flowers in the fall. White rainlily grows less than a foot tall and wide. It will grow in full sun or partial shade and tolerates dry or boggy soil. It has no serious insect or disease problems and can be used to naturalize in beds or as a border substitute for lilyturf or monkeygrass. Pages: 97, *99*.

Narcissus pseudonarcissus 'Ice Follies'
DAFFODIL

Buxus microphylla
LITTLELEAF BOXWOOD

Camellia sasanqua
SASANQUA CAMELLIA

globe 3 to 4 ft. tall and keeps its bright green foliage in winter. Boxwoods grow relatively slowly, so buy the largest plants you can afford. They need well-drained soil and grow best in full or partial sun. Use mulch to protect their shallow roots and water regularly during periods of drought. Shear in late spring to desired shape. 91, *91*.

Callicarpa americana

AMERICAN BEAUTYBERRY. This native deciduous shrub has a lax habit, spreading 4 ft. wide and tall. Tapered dull green leaves line the slightly arching branches. In fall they give way to profuse clusters of vivid violet-purple berries. Beautyberry is pest free and drought tolerant. Irrigation may be needed during periods of drought to maintain attractive foliage. Thin one-third of the older branches to the ground each spring to promote a denser appearance. Pages: 29, 42, 62, 70, 83, 86.

Camellia sasanqua

SASANQUA CAMELLIA. This is a much-sought-after evergreen shrub with glossy foliage and beautiful white, pink, or rose flowers in the fall. There are many cultivars to choose from (pp. 26, *26*). They differ in flower color, size, and form (single or double) as well as in overall plant habit, hardiness, and mature size. They range from 3 ft. tall and wide to 8 ft. tall and 6 ft. wide. The lower-growing forms are useful for mass plantings; the taller forms are ideal for hedges. 'Hana Jiman' (pp. 69, *71*) grows 6 ft. tall and 4 ft. wide and bears semi-double white

Callicarpa americana
AMERICAN BEAUTYBERRY

Cercis canadensis
REDBUD

that turns dark green in the summer. Texas redbud (*C. texensis*, pp. 34, **35**) has thick shiny leaves. Native to central and north Texas, this redbud is adapted to the drier areas of Texas with alkaline soils but performs well throughout the state. Redbuds are generally available with single or multiple trunks and may reach 20 to 25 ft. tall and wide. They require well-drained soil and regular watering in the summer but have few pests. Pages: 21, 62, 69, 86.

Chasmanthium latifolium

INLAND SEA OATS. This is a native perennial grass that forms erect leafy clumps about 2 ft. tall, topped with loose clusters of flat seed heads that dance in the breeze from midsummer through winter. All parts are green in summer and russet or tan in the winter. Grows in sun or shade and adapts to almost any soil. Cut to the ground in spring before the new growth emerges. This vigorous, pest-free plant can reseed and naturalize quite prolifically. To reduce the number of seedlings, pull or hoe them as they appear, apply a heavy layer of mulch in the area, use a selective post or preemergent herbicide, or remove the seed heads before they shatter. The dainty seed heads are great for flower arrangments. Pages: 29, 63, 71, 87, 95.

flowers edged in pink. 'Shi Shi Gashira' (pp. 95, **95**) has rose-colored semi-double flowers and stays a more compact 3 ft. tall and wide. 'Yuletide' (pp. 21, **22**) has red flowers and grows 6 ft. tall by 3 ft. wide. Sasanquas need moist, well-drained, acid soil; a layer of mulch; and a site that is shaded from midday sun. They are relatively pest free and more forgiving than the winter-flowering *C. japonica*. If needed, prune and fertilize immediately after flowering.

Campsis × tagliabuana 'Mme. Galen'

'MME. GALEN' TRUMPET CREEPER. This humming-bird favorite is a vigorous deciduous vine with a stout woody trunk, large compound leaves, and very showy clusters of salmon red flowers from summer until frost. Trumpet vine needs full sun, room to grow, and only occasional watering during summer droughts. Once established, it can climb and cover a trellis, fence, or wall with no further as-sistance or care. It grows at least 10 ft. tall and can reach 20 to 30 ft. Prune in winter to control size, if desired. Pages: 52, **54**.

Cercis

REDBUD. This small, early-spring flowering, decidu-ous tree is native to East Texas and performs best in the piney woods region. It produces clusters of bright purple-pink flowers along bare twigs in early spring before the heart-shaped leaves unfold. Medium-green foliage turns gold in the fall. 'Forest Pansy' (*C. canadensis*, pp. 95, **95**) has purple foliage

Chasmanthium latifolium
INLAND SEA OATS

Chilopsis linearis

DESERT WILLOW. This small native deciduous tree sports narrow willowlike leaves and showy tubular flowers from spring throughout the summer. Flower colors range from pure white to lavender to deeper purple. Desert willow can reach 15 ft. tall and wide and makes a good substitute for crapemyrtle in extremely dry areas. It performs well throughout the state in sunny, well-drained locations. The more compact 'Bubba' (pp. 52, *54*) has greener leaves and dark wine-purple flowers. Desert willow has few pests and is very drought tolerant. Pages: 77, *79*.

× Chitalpa tashkentensis 'Pink Dawn'

'PINK DAWN' CHITALPA. A hybrid of catalpa and chilopsis, this narrow-leaved deciduous tree quickly grows 20 to 30 ft. tall. Large clusters of ruffled, trumpet-shaped pink flowers bloom in early summer. Plant in full sun. Grows best with occasional water in hot-summer climates. Chitalpa may occasionally be defoliated by catalpa worms or fungal leaf spot but survives with little care. Pages: 58, *59*.

Chrysanthemum leucanthemum

OX-EYE DAISY. This vigorous cool-season perennial produces loads of white daisies on 2-ft. stems in spring; the flowers are a great addition to bouquets. Prefers full sun and adequate moisture and has few pest problems. Remove flowers after they finish blooming to encourage more of them. To produce more plants, divide the leafy clumps in fall. Ox-eye daisy is the best substitute for Shasta daisies in Texas. Pages: 23, 73.

Chrysanthemum × 'Country Girl'

'COUNTRY GIRL' DAISY MUM. This daisy mum is a cool-season perennial that produces a profusion of pink daisies on 2 ft. stems in the fall. It is one of the few chrysanthemums that performs as a reliable perennial in Texas. Requires full sun, good drainage, and regular watering in the summer. Plants may need staking when in bloom. After bloom, cut the spent stalks to their base. To promote heavier bloom in fall, shear the plant by half several times during the summer. Daisy mum has no pest problems. Pages: 67, *67*.

Clematis terniflora

SWEET AUTUMN CLEMATIS. One of very few clematis species that perform well throughout Texas. This vigorous perennial vine climbs 25 ft. or higher. It bears medium-green compound leaves and billows

Chrysanthemum leucanthemum
OX-EYE DAISY

Clematis terniflora
SWEET AUTUMN CLEMATIS

Clematis terniflora   **173**

Coreopsis lanceolata
COREOPSIS

Cortaderia selloana 'Pumila'
DWARF PAMPAS GRASS

Cuphea
CUPHEA

of small, very fragrant white flowers in late summer and fall. Grows best in full sun to partial shade in moist soil conditions. It has very few pest problems and only requires supplemental watering during droughts. Prune in early spring, cutting back partway or close to the ground, depending on how far you want it to climb. It can become invasive in East Texas. Often sold under the name *C. paniculata.* Pages: 87, 93.

Coreopsis lanceolata
COREOPSIS. A native Texas wildflower, coreopsis explodes each spring with masses of golden yellow daisylike flowers. Forms a clump 1 ft. tall and 1½ ft. wide of bright green linear leaves and slender flower stalks. A warm-season perennial, coreopsis grows best in full sun with modest irrigation. Tolerates most soil types and has very few pest problems. Looks best if the spent blossoms are sheared off after bloom. Pages: 55, 73.

Cortaderia selloana 'Pumila'
DWARF PAMPAS GRASS. An evergreen clumping grass growing 5 ft. tall and 4 ft. wide with long linear leaves that have very sharp margins. In the summer, plumes of white flowers rise above the foliage. They make excellent dried flowers. Dwarf pampas grass thrives in hot sun and in almost all soil types. Irrigation is only neccessary during prolonged summer droughts. In early spring, you can cut the grass low to the ground to eliminate the old, unsightly foliage. Pages: 65, 73.

Cuphea
CUPHEA. These are showy plants from the tropics that are often grown as perennials or annuals in Texas gardens. Cigar plant (*C. micropetala*, pp. 48, 88) is a warm-season perennial that covers itself with yellow and orange tubular flowers each fall as the days grow short. It makes a bold clump 4 ft. tall and 3 ft. wide. The hybrid 'David Verity' (pp. 53, *54*) grows a more compact 2½ ft. tall and wide and blooms all summer with smaller orange flowers. Both attract hummingbirds in profusion. Mexican heather (*C. hyssopifolia*, p. 31) is a tender perennial that is usually treated as an annual in the northern two-thirds of the state. It grows 1 ft. tall and wide and bears lavender-pink flowers all summer long. Cupheas are very tough plants that prefer full sun and tolerate most soil conditions. They are drought tolerant as well, requiring water only during periods of prolonged drought.

Cyperus alternifolius

UMBRELLA SEDGE. This evergreen perennial forms bold clumps 4 ft. tall and 3 ft. wide, topped with lacy green, leafy umbrellas. It grows extremely well in sun or shade in any soil type including poorly drained. It is often grown as an aquatic. Umbrella plant has no known pests and can become invasive in South Texas. In northern areas or during severe winters it may die back to the ground or not return. Consider using it as an annual or replacing it with a hardy fern. Pages: 57, 59, 79.

Dianthus 'Bath's Pink'

'BATH'S PINK' DIANTHUS. This low-growing perennial forms a dense, grassy mat of gray-green foliage 6 in. tall and 1 to 2 ft. wide. Fragrant flowers like tiny pink carnations carpet the plant during the spring. Needs full sun and well-drained soil. Water only when the soil is dry. After blooming, shear off the flower stalks and cut the plants back halfway. Fresh new foliage will soon develop. Divide every few years during the fall to keep the plants vigorous. Pages: 21, 31, 38, 39, 44, 51, 67, 77, 91, 99.

Euonymus fortunei 'Coloratus'

PURPLE WINTERCREEPER. This shrub is a durable spreading ground cover. Its glossy evergreen leaves turn purplish red during winter. Wintercreeper grows 1 to 2 ft. tall and spreads 5 to 6 ft. wide. It adapts to sun or shade and needs a well-drained soil with regular irrigation during the summer months. Shear or prune at any time to provide a uniform surface. Wintercreeper is relatively pest free and less prone to scale than golden euonymus. Page: 38.

Euonymus kiautschovicus 'Manhattan'

'MANHATTAN' EUONYMUS. An evergreen shrub with thick, glossy, rounded, medium-green leaves and small but showy pink-and-orange fruits that ripen in the fall. It grows naturally as an upright shrub, reaching about 5 ft. tall and wide, but it can be sheared, pruned, or trained as you choose. Tolerates sun or shade and any well-drained soil. It is relatively pest free and requires irrigation only during dry periods. Pages: 70, *71*.

Fatsia japonica

FATSIA. This bold evergreen shrub grows around 4 ft. tall and wide and prefers shade to prevent leaf burn. It sports large, shiny, tropical-looking leaves all year and small rounded clusters of white flowers in early spring; the flowers become black berries.

Cyperus alternifolius
UMBRELLA SEDGE

Fatsia japonica
FATSIA

Dianthus 'Bath's Pink'
DIANTHUS

Fatsia requires well-drained soil and regular watering. It has no common pest problems. It may get leaf burn during severe winters. Pages: 26, 42, 46, 79, 83, 95.

Ferns

These are carefree long-lived perennials. Despite their delicate appearance, several are among the most durable and trouble-free plants you can grow. Most ferns prefer shade, but some do well in partial shade or even full sun. They grow best in well-drained soil that's been amended with extra organic matter. You can divide them every few years in early spring if you want more plants, or leave them alone for decades. If you want to keep the foliage fresh and green, you can cut all the fronds off at the crown each spring before the new fiddleheads start to unfurl.

Holly fern (*Cyrtomium falcatum*, pp. 21, 27, 42, 53, 55, 63, 83, 95) is a showy evergreen fern with fronds divided into large, glossy, hollylike leaflets. It forms dense clumps about 2 ft. tall and wide. Holly fern prefers good drainage, regular watering, and is resistant to most pests. In more northern areas mulch well during cold winters. Wood fern (*Thelypteris kunthii*, pp. 63, 71, 83, 87) is without a doubt the toughest, most versatile fern for Texas; it prefers some shade but will also perform fairly well in full sun. The lacy apple-green fronds grow in clumps 2 ft. tall and wide. Like most ferns, this one requires regular watering during the summer to look its best.

*Cyrtomium
falcatum*
HOLLY FERN

*Thelypteris
kunthii*
WOOD FERN

Gardenia jasminoides 'Daisy'

'DAISY' GARDENIA. An intensely fragrant evergreen flowering shrub, it produces single white blossoms in summer above shiny dark green foliage. Like all gardenias, 'Daisy' prefers partial sun, acidic soil, and regular watering. Feed with acid-type "azalea" fertilizer and apply iron to improve foliage that yellows. In areas that have alkaline soils, amend the soil with sphagnum peat moss, composted pine bark, and sand, or ask at your local nursery about choosing a more suitable alternative. Prune after the plant has bloomed to control size and shape. Gardenias can be somewhat susceptible to white flies and sooty mold, though 'Daisy' is among the easiest to grow. Page: 21, *22*.

Gaura lindheimeri

GAURA. This native Texas perennial forms a loose clump of graceful arched stems bearing pale pink-and-white flowers from spring through fall. Gaura normally reaches about 3 ft. tall and wide. 'Whirling Butterflies' (pp. *54*, 55) is slightly more compact. 'Dauphin' (pp. 36, *39*) is slightly more upright. Gaura needs full sun, well-drained soil, and regular watering during droughts. Too much shade, fertilizer, or moisture makes the stems floppy. Gaura is rarely bothered by insects or disease. Looks best if sheared occasionally after bloom cycles. Cut it to the ground after the first frost. Pages: 33, 61, 65, 85.

Gaura lindheimeri
GAURA

Gelsemium sempervirens
CAROLINA JASMINE

Hamelia patens
FIREBUSH

Gelsemium sempervirens

CAROLINA JASMINE. This is a Texas native evergreen vine beloved for its extremely fragrant and showy display of small bell-shaped yellow flowers in late winter and early spring. The small lancelike leaves are neat and green all year. This vine can climb trees but is usually trained against a fence, trellis, or post. It can also be used as a ground cover but will need pruning yearly to keep it within bounds. Needs full or partial sun. It has few pest problems and requires watering only during periods of drought. Pages: 25, 42, 85, 88.

Hamelia patens

FIREBUSH. This colorful tropical shrub is normally grown in Texas as a tender perennial, usually reaching around 3 to 4 ft. tall and wide. In milder areas it can grow even larger. Firebush bears red-orange trumpet-shaped flowers from summer to frost against red-tinged leaves that turn maroon as cool temperatures set in. Hummingbirds adore this plant. Extremely heat and drought tolerant, it also has very few pests. Cut to the ground after the first frost. In northern areas, mulch the crown heavily or consider growing it as a wonderful summer annual. Firebush has been designated a Texas Superstar™. Pages: 25, 48, 52, 88.

Hedera helix

ENGLISH IVY. This is a vigorous vine with large, lobed evergreen leaves and woody stems that send out roots and cling to any surface they touch. It spreads fast as a ground cover or climbs to cover a fence, wall, or tree trunk. There are slower-growing fancy kinds with fine-cut or variegated leaves, as well as the regular plain green ones. Grows in partial sun or full shade. It has few insect pests but can occasionally encounter leaf spot diseases in heavy shade under frequent irrigation. Water only during drought. English ivy takes a year or two to become established, then lasts forever. Mow or prune it back whenever it grows out of bounds. It can be invasive if left untended. Pages: *46*, 47.

Hemerocallis hybrids

DAYLILY. Among the most popular of perennials, daylilies display large lilylike flowers above dense clumps of narrow, arching leaves. Almost all

Hemerocallis hybrids
DAYLILY

Hemerocallis 'Stella d'Oro'
DAYLILY

Hesperaloe parviflora
RED YUCCA

daylilies today are hybrids (pp. 22, 67) sold as named cultivars. There are many thousands to choose from. Some are evergreen; others die back in winter. Some are low-growing, while others have flower stalks reaching 3 ft. tall. Flowers last only a day but are replaced daily. They come in many shades of white, yellow, orange, red, and purple, and bloom from several weeks to several months. Mix early-blooming, midseason, and late-blooming varieties to ensure months of color. 'Stella d'Oro' has golden yellow flowers (pp. 57, 89) on compact plants 1½ ft. tall and wide. 'Black-Eyed Stella' has gold flowers with a dark reddish eye and grows 1½ ft. tall and wide (pp. 44, **46**). Both Stellas bloom for months. 'Lavender Bonanza' (p. **61**) have pastel-colored flowers. 'Texas Sunlight' has larger gold flowers and grows 2 ft. tall and wide (p. 93). All daylilies prefer full sun and well-drained soil. Water regularly during bloom. Pinch off spent flowers and then cut off flower stalks after blooming is finished. Divide in fall or late winter if you wish to propagate more plants. When planting, space shorter daylilies about 1 ft. apart and taller kinds 2 ft. apart. They will gradually fill in. Daylilies can occasionally be plagued with aphids in the spring and rust disease during humid summers.

Hesperaloe parviflora

RED YUCCA. This native Texas shrub grows in clumps of spiky gray-green succulent foliage. Attractive, coral-pink, trumpet flowers line graceful

3 ft. stalks from late spring to frost. Very heat and drought tolerant, red yucca is adapted to any well-drained soil in full sun. Generally requires no supplemental watering and attracts very few pests. Pages: 33, 53, 65, 75, 77.

Hibiscus coccineus

TEXAS STAR HIBISCUS. A tall, striking native perennial that bears large, brilliant red, star-shaped flowers above leafy stalks from early summer to frost. Foliage is medium green and deeply lobed. Plant can reach 6 ft. tall and 4 ft. wide with the right conditions. Prefers full sun and regular watering. Cut back after bloom cycle to promote bushy plants. It has no common insect or disease problems. Pages: 48, 52, 69.

Hibiscus syriacus

ALTHEA. Also known as rose of Sharon, this is a showy deciduous shrub when in full summer-to-fall bloom. Flowers may be white, pink, or lavender and single or double. Medium-size leaves are dull green and slightly lobed. 'Diana' (pp. 96, **99**) has large single white flowers. Altheas grow 6 to 8 ft. tall and 3 to 4 ft. wide. They need full sun and well-drained soil. They have few pest problems but are subject to cotton root rot in alkaline areas. Prune in early spring to give desired shape and size. Page: 22.

Hypericum calycinum

ST. JOHN'S WORT. A semi-evergreen mounding shrub that grows 2 ft. tall and wide. Its small oval leaves are green all year in mild climates and reddish purple to bronze where winters are cold. Bears five-petaled golden yellow flowers with long stamens in summer. Grows well in full sun to partial shade and prefers well-drained soils. It has few insect or disease problems and only requires watering during dry periods. Cut all stems by two-thirds in early spring. If you want to keep the plants shorter and more compact, prune all new shoots by half again in June. Pages: 38, 42, 56, 87, 97.

Ilex

HOLLY. An extremely versatile group of shrubs and trees, hollies are used for foundation plantings, hedges, and specimens. The attractive leaves can be small or large, smooth or spiny, dull or glossy. Holly plants are either male or female. If a suitable male is planted within a few hundred yards, females bear heavy crops of small round berries that ripen in fall and last through the next spring. All tolerate sun and

Hibiscus coccineus
TEXAS STAR HIBISCUS

Hibiscus syriacus
ALTHEA

Hypericum calycinum
ST. JOHN'S WORT

Recommended hollies

Ilex cornuta 'Burfordii', Burford holly

A large evergreen shrub that generally grows about 10 ft. tall and wide if left unpruned. It has shiny green foliage with a single spine at the leaf tip and attractive clusters of large red berries. Pages: 66, *67*.

I. cornuta 'Burfordii Nana', Dwarf Burford holly

This smaller cultivar grows a 5 ft. tall and 3 ft. wide. It has small leaves and berries. Pages: 29, *31*.

I. decidua, Possumhaw holly

A small Texas native deciduous tree with lustrous dark green leaves. Berries are very showy after the leaves fall. They can be yellow, orange, or red depending on the cultivar. Designated a Texas Superstar™. Pages: 48, 70.

I. decidua 'Warren's Red'

This possumhaw cultivar has small, bright red berries and an upright habit to 15 ft. tall and 6 ft. wide. Pages: 29, *31*.

I. vomitoria 'Nana', Dwarf yaupon holly

A dwarf version that reaches only 3 ft. tall and wide. Commonly used as a substitute for boxwood in Texas and the South. Pages: 21, 30, 35, *35*, 36, 71.

Ilex vomitoria 'Nana'
DWARF YAUPON HOLLY

Ilex decidua
POSSUMHAW HOLLY

partial shade and almost any well-drained garden soil. Hollies are generally pest free. Prune or shear at any season to keep them at the desired size. See the box for more information about specific hollies.

Iris × germanica

BEARDED IRIS. This popular perennial blooms in early spring, with large elegant flowers in shades of blue, lavender, pink, yellow, or white, on stalks 2 ft. tall. Flowers open above an attractive clump of stiff, bladelike, gray-green leaves. Bearded iris needs full sun and extremely well-drained soil and grows best with little to no irrigation. If you live close to the coast, plant heirloom and species types; they perform better because they are less likely to suffer root rot. Pages: 44, 67, 91.

Iris × Louisiana hybrids

LOUISIANA IRIS. This cool-season perennial forms a clump of straplike foliage 2 ft. tall and 3 ft. wide. Large delicate flowers rise on 3 ft. stalks in early spring. Cultivars come in almost every color of the rainbow. Tolerates wet soil or a well-drained soil with winter and spring moisture. Louisiana iris has few, in any, pests. Goes somewhat dormant in summer. Pages: 42, 57, 69.

Juniperus

JUNIPER. These needle-leafed evergreens are tough, hardy shrubs for exposed sites. 'Blue Pacific' shore juniper (*J. conferta* 'Blue Pacific', pp. 57, *59*) makes a good ground cover, staying around 1 ft. tall and spreading 5 to 6 ft. wide. It has short, soft, blue-green needles. Dwarf Japanese garden juniper (*J. procumbens* 'Nana', pp. 59, *59*) grows 1 to 2 ft. high, spreads 5 to 6 ft. wide, and has blue-green foliage. Junipers prefer full sun and excellent drainage. They suffer blighted foliage from excess watering. Limit pruning to maintain a natural shape and to avoid brown-tipped foliage.

Lagerstroemia

CRAPEMYRTLE. An extremely popular deciduous shrub or small tree usually grown with multiple trunks. It blooms for several months in the heat of summer, with large clusters of papery red, pink, purple, lavender, or white flowers at the end of each stem. Leaves typically turn red, orange, or yellow in the fall. Exfoliating bark reveals wonderful, smooth mottled trunks in winter. There are many cultivars to choose from, ranging from dwarf types that grow 3 ft. tall to tree types that reach 30 ft. Look for the

Iris × *germanica*
BEARDED IRIS

Iris × Louisiana hybrids
LOUISIANA IRIS

powdery mildew-resistant cultivars that are named for American Indian tribes. The showy 'Catawba' (*L. indica*, pp. 25, *26*) is a purple-flowered cultivar that grows a standard 12 ft. tall and 6 ft. wide. It has excellent fall color and resists mildew. 'Natchez' (*L.* × *fauriei*, pp. 30, *31*) is a vigorous tree-type cultivar that reaches 25 ft. tall and 15 ft. wide. It has fragrant white flowers, spectacular tan and cinnamon bark, and is especially resistant to powdery mildew. 'Tonto' (*L.* × *fauriei*, pp. 80, *82*) is a semi-dwarf cultivar that stays less than 10 ft. tall and 5 ft. wide and has watermelon pink flowers. All crapemyrtles need full sun, well-drained soil, and a modest amount of irrigation during severe droughts. Prune them in late winter if at all, removing dead branches and basal suckers only. We discourage the common practice of topping crapemyrtles because it ruins their naturally beautiful shape, scars their trunks, causes them to flop over when blooming, and leads to basal suckering.

Lantana

LANTANA. These tough colorful plants are usually grown as tender perennials or summer annuals. Clusters of small flowers, each one a magnet for butterflies, top the plants from late spring until frost. Cultivars come in white, yellow, pink, orange, red, and purple flowers. Depending on the selection, they grow 1 to 3 ft. tall and spread 2 to 5 ft. wide. Lantanas make great bedding plants, container plants, or ground covers. They are exceptional choices for hot sites and poor soils, requiring full sun and little water. Shear after bloom cycles to keep them compact and encourage more flowers. See the box on p. 182 for information on specific kinds.

Leucophyllum frutescens 'Compactum'

COMPACT TEXAS SAGE. A dwarf cultivar of the striking, silver-leaved, drought-tolerant Texas native shrub. It has a dense, slightly irregular shape and reaches 3 to 4 ft. tall and wide. Following summer

Recommended lantanas

Lantana camara 'Dallas Red'
'Dallas Red' lantana
This bush-type cultivar has striking orange-red flowers. It grows 2 ft. tall and 3 ft. wide. Pages: 52, *54*.

Lantana camara 'Confetti'

Lantana camara 'Radiation'

L. camara 'Confetti'
Another bush-type lantana, this one has eye-catching pink and yellow flowers and grows 2½ ft. tall and wide. Pages: 22, 61, 66.

L. camara 'Radiation'
This bush lantana has orange and yellow flowers and grows 2½ ft. tall and wide. Pages: 33, 69, 88.

L. × hybrida 'Lemon Drop'
This vigorous cultivar of spreading lantana has creamy yellow flowers and grows 3 to 4 ft. wide. It sets little fruit, which contributes to increased flower production. Page: 53.

L. × hybrida 'New Gold'
The most popular of all spreading lantanas, 'New Gold' has golden-yellow flowers on vigorous plants that reach 2 ft. tall and spread 3 to 4 ft. It sets little fruit so it doesn't need deadheading. It is designated a Texas Superstar™. Pages: 33, 48, 53, 77.

L. montevidensis 'Trailing Lavender'
A low-growing, trailing species that stays under 1 ft. tall and spreads 5 ft. or more. It drapes a profusion of fragrant lavender flowers over steps and containers from spring through the first hard freeze. Not uncommon for it to bloom year-round in coastal areas and during mild winters. It sets no fruit, so it doesn't require deadheading. Designated a Texas Superstar™. Pages: 55, 73, *74*, 97.

L. montevidensis 'Weeping White'
This vigorous trailing selection spreads 5 to 6 ft. wide and has pure white flowers. It blooms almost year-round and needs no deadheading. Designated a Texas Superstar™. Page: 38, *39*.

Lantana × hybrida 'Lemon Drop'

Lantana × hybrida 'New Gold'

Lantana montevidensis 'Trailing Lavender'

Leucophyllum frutescens 'Compactum'
COMPACT TEXAS SAGE

Liriope muscari
LILYTURF

Lonicera
sempervirens
**CORAL
HONEYSUCKLE**

rains, it becomes flushed with orchid pink flowers. Texas sage demands full sun and excellent drainage and requires little, if any, supplemental watering. Expect few if any insect or disease problems. Does not grow well in East Texas; 'Old Blush' China rose (*Rosa chinensis* 'Old Blush') makes a good flowering substitute there. Pages: 40, 55, 58, 66, 77.

Liriope muscari

LILYTURF. This perennial ground cover forms dense tufts of dark green grasslike leaves that stay green throughout the year. Clusters of slender lavender flower spikes bloom among the foliage in summer. Lilyturf makes a fine small-scale ground cover near walks and patios, and is frequently used as an edging around borders or as a lawn substitute (p. 35). 'Big Blue' (pp. 47, 57, 79, 80, 83, 97) has larger flowers and foliage than the species and grows about 1 ft. tall and wide. 'Evergreen Giant' (pp. *74*, 75) is the largest cultivar. It grows 2 ft. tall and wide and is often used as a specimen clump. Variegated lilyturf ('Variegata', pp. 31, *31*) has attractive striped foliage in creamy white and green and normally grows 1 ft. tall and wide. 'Silvery Sunproof' is very similar to 'Variegata,' and may be the same plant. Lilyturf can tolerate sun or shade, has few pest problems, and requires water only during dry summers. Mow or shear off old foliage in early spring.

Lonicera sempervirens

CORAL HONEYSUCKLE. This native Texas evergreen vine twines around any support, climbing 10 to 15 ft. or higher. The smooth, oval, blue-green leaves are arranged in neat pairs on the stems. Blooms heavily in early summer and continues off and on until fall. The slender, tubular red-orange flowers are scentless but attractive to hummingbirds. Songbirds eat the bright red berries that follow the flowers. Grows in shade but blooms best when planted in full or partial sun. Prune in winter if at all, thinning out some of the older stems. Unlike Japanese honeysuckle (*L. japonica*), this species is not aggressive or invasive. Pages: 48, 71, 88.

Recommended Japanese maiden grasses

Miscanthis sinensis 'Adagio'
This dwarf grass has gray-green foliage and grows 2 ft. tall and wide. Blooms reach 3 ft. Pages: 48, 55, 93.

M. sinensis 'Gracillimus'
The most common miscanthus cultivar, 'Gracillimus' has narrow gray-green foliage and grows 3 ft. tall and wide. Blooms rise to 4 ft. Pages: 40, 56, 59, 88.

M. sinensis 'Morning Light'
This selection has very slender, white-striped leaves that look silvery from a distance. It forms a clump 3 ft. tall. Blooms reach 4 ft. Pages: 31, 85, 99.

M. sinensis 'Strictus'
Commonly called porcupine grass, this striking cultivar has wide green leaves with yellow horizontal banding. Grows 4 ft. tall and wide. Blooms reach 5 ft. Page: 29, *31*.

Miscanthis sinensis 'Gracillimus'

Miscanthis sinensis 'Morning Light'

Miscanthis sinensis 'Adagio'

Loropetalum chinense rubrum

CHINESE FRINGE FLOWER. This is a popular large evergreen shrub or small tree for a woodland garden or shrub border. It bears lovely, bright pink, fringe-like flowers among layers of small purple-tinged leaves. Blossoms occur during the spring and again in the fall. Doesn't do well where soils are extremely alkaline; a good substitute is American beautyberry. Page: 42.

Malvaviscus arboreus drummondii

TURK'S CAP. One of the easiest perennials for Texas gardens, Turk's cap performs well in sun or shade, acidic or alkaline soils, and in wet or dry situations. Plants grow a bushy 2 ft. tall and 3 ft. wide in shade but can reach 5 ft. tall in full sun. The fairly coarse-textured foliage is medium green and slightly lobed. Small red Turk's turban flowers keep on coming from summer until frost, attracting a stream of sulfur butterflies and hummingbirds, especially in the fall. Turk's cap has few pest problems and requires little water. Shear throughout the growing season to keep tidy and cut to the ground after the first frost. Pages: 29, 34, 48, 53, 62, 69, 73, 87.

Miscanthus sinensis

JAPANESE MAIDEN GRASS. This showy grass forms a vase-shaped clump of long, arching, light green leaves. Silvery blooms rise above the foliage in late summer or fall and last through winter. For best flowering results, plant in bright sunny spots. Japanese maiden grass has very few insect or disease pests. Water regularly during periods of drought. Cut old leaves and stalks close to the ground in late winter or early spring before the new growth emerges. Page: 25.

Myrica cerifera

WAX MYRTLE. A Texas native evergreen shrub that naturally maintains an upright and bushy profile. It can also be pruned into a small tree. The slender twigs are densely covered with glossy leaves that have a delicious spicy aroma. Historically, the leaves were used as a flavorful subtitute for bay leaf. In fall and winter, clusters of small gray berries line the stems of female plants. Wax myrtle needs full or partial sun and tolerates most soil conditions, including fairly wet ones. It has few pest problems. Water only during periods of drought. It grows quickly and can reach up to 20 ft. tall if left alone. Prune in winter if you want to keep it small or control its shape. Pages: 38, 50.

Malvaviscus arboreus drummondii
TURK'S CAP

Myrica cerifera
WAX MYRTLE

Nandina domestica 'Gulf Stream'
HEAVENLY BAMBOO

Nandina domestica

HEAVENLY BAMBOO. This versatile evergreen shrub forms a clump of slender erect stems and fine-textured compound leaves that change color with the seasons, from bronze to green to red. Common nandina (pp. 25, *26*) grows 4 to 5 ft. tall and 3 ft. wide. It bears fluffy clusters of white flowers in summer and sporadically throughout the year, followed by long-lasting red berries. Cultivars are available in smaller sizes. 'Harbour Dwarf' (pp. 71, *71*) makes a bushy mound 2 ft. tall and wide but produces few fruit. 'Gulf Stream' (pp. 29, 34, 71, 93) is an outstanding dwarf form, 3 ft. tall and 2 ft. wide, that turns beautiful shades of orange and red during the winter months. It rarely produces fruit. All nandinas do well in shade or full sun, have virtually no pest problems, and require only sporadic irrigation during the summer months. In spring, prune to remove old, weak, or winter-damaged stems. To keep the plant full, cut some of the stems to the ground each year. This will encourage new growth from the base.

Nerium oleander 'Petite Salmon'

'PETITE SALMON' OLEANDER. A dwarf variety of a tough evergreen shrub bearing slender leaves and clusters of showy flowers. Grows 3 to 4 ft. tall and wide. Salmon pink flowers bloom from spring to frost. Performs best in full sun and tolerates most soil conditions. Water only when severely dry. It has few pest problems. In early spring, cut out dead wood and shape into desired form. In northern areas consider replacing it with a more cold-hardy shrub such as althea. Page: 74, *74*.

Ophiopogon planiscapus
'Ebony Knight'
BLACK MONDO GRASS

Opuntia lindheimeri
SPINELESS PRICKLY PEAR

Ophiopogon japonicus
MONDO GRASS

Ophiopogon japonicus

MONDO GRASS. This perennial ground cover resembles unmown grass. It grows in clumps of narrow, shiny, dark green leaves 1 ft. tall and wide. Flowers are inconspicuous. The miniature 'Kyoto Dwarf' (pp. *46*, 47) grows only 4 in. tall and 6 in. wide. It is often used between individual flagstones. Black mondo grass (*O. planiscapus* 'Ebony Knight,' pp. 42, 47, 83) has purple-black foliage and grows 1 ft. tall and wide. Both do best in full to partial shade; foliage can burn in the hot sun. Start with a number of small plants instead of a few large ones. They'll grow more quickly to fill a spot. Mow or shear off the top of old foliage in early spring before new growth appears. The new leaves will look fresh and neat the rest of the year. Pages: 29, 79, 97.

Opuntia lindheimeri

SPINELESS PRICKLY PEAR. This popular cactus has smooth, succulent, gray-green leaf pads. Called "spineless," the leaves actually have tiny hidden spines, so wear gloves when handling them. The plant grows to 4 ft. tall and wide over time, on occasion producing showy yellow flowers in spring, followed by purple fruit in fall. Spineless prickly pear rarely needs water and has no major insect or disease problems. It makes a great living sculpture in the garden. Pages: 73, 77.

Parthenocissus quinquefolia

VIRGINIA CREEPER. This native woody vine is a great climber, growing up to 30 ft. or more. The deciduous leaves are dark green in summer and vivid orange or red in autumn. The plant adapts to sun or shade and has few pest or disease problems. Water only in periods of drought. Once established, prune as needed to control its size. Pages: 87, *87*.

Perovskia atriplicifolia

RUSSIAN SAGE. A shrubby perennial with an open, vase-shaped habit. Straight, fairly stiff stems are lined with sparse silver-gray foliage and tiny, but abundant, powdery blue flowers for many weeks in the summer. Grow in full sun and well-drained soil. It needs little water and is rarely bothered by insects or disease. Cut old stems down to the ground in spring. The plant will reach 3 ft. tall and 2 ft. wide by fall. To control its size, cut stems back by one-third in early summer. Pages: 65, 73, 85, 88.

Phlox paniculata 'John Fanick'

'JOHN FANICK' GARDEN PHLOX. This is a beautiful and dependable pink-flowering perennial. It grows into a tidy 2 ft. clump of leafy flower stalks that produce dense clusters of fragrant pale pink flowers with dark pink eyes starting in early summer and continuing until frost. Garden phlox needs full or partial sun and adapts to most ordinary garden soil. Water regularly during dry conditions. To promote continuous bloom, cut off the flowers after they fade. Named for the late San Antonio nurseryman John Fanick. Designated a Texas Superstar™. Pages: 67, 85.

Phyllostachys aurea

GOLDEN BAMBOO. An evergreen bamboo with bright green leaves rising from golden canes. Grows 8 ft. tall and spreads by running rhizomes. Plant in full sun to partial shade. Golden bamboo can be very invasive. To control its spread, plant in heavy clay soil and prune the rhizomes each year, or surround the planting with a barrier 2 to 3 ft. deep. Make sure the barrier extends 2 to 3 in. above the soil to keep the rhizomes from growing over it. To thin the planting, cut some culms to the ground each spring. Pages: 46, *46*.

Pittosporum tobira 'Wheeler's Dwarf'

'WHEELER'S DWARF' PITTOSPORUM. This is a compact evergreen shrub with tufts of glossy leaves and fragrant white flowers in spring. It rarely exceeds 2 ft. in height and 3 ft. in width. It adapts to sun or shade and only needs occasional watering. Prune anytime, though it rarely needs it. In northern areas consider choosing a more cold-hardy species like dwarf yaupon holly. Pages: *26*, 27.

Plumbago auriculata

TROPICAL PLUMBAGO. A tropical ever-blooming shrub that is often grown as a tender perennial in Texas. Plumbago mounds to 2 ft. tall and 2 to 3 ft. wide or can be grown as a climber. It is smothered with baby-blue flowers from summer to frost. Rarely

Perovskia
RUSSIAN SAGE

Phlox paniculata 'John Fanick'
'JOHN FANICK' GARDEN PHLOX

Plumbago auriculata
TROPICAL PLUMBAGO

Punica granatum
POMEGRANATE

Prunus caroliniana
'Compacta'
**COMPACT CAROLINA
CHERRY LAUREL**

flowers are held among the shiny leaves in spring. The widely grown cultivar 'Wonderful' (pp. 44, 93) has a fountainlike shape and reaches 6 to 8 ft. tall. Its flowers are followed by large, bright red, edible fruit. Compact pomegranate (*P. granatum* 'Nana', pp. 48, *50*) makes an excellent container plant. It grows 3 ft. tall and 2 ft. wide and bears small inedible fruit. Plant pomegranates in full sun and well-drained soil. They need little water once established and are generally pest free. They can be sheared at any time to a desired shape.

Quercus

OAK. Among the most majestic and long-lived shade trees in Texas landscapes. The state is home to many deciduous and evergreen species. Texas red oak (*Q. buckleyi*, p. 29) is a small deciduous oak native to the Hill Country and adapted throughout Texas. It normally grows a modest 20 to 30 ft. tall and wide. Its pointed multi-lobed leaves turn shades of brilliant red and orange in the fall. Often available in both single and multitrunked forms.

Live oak (*Q. virginiana*, p. 54) is a slow-growing evergreen oak that achieves a height of 25 ft. and a width of 30 ft. in a person's lifetime but is capable of reaching immense proportions over the centuries. It has gnarled branches and small, hollylike deep olive green leaves that don't drop until the new leaves emerge in the spring. This oak casts dense shade, making it difficult to grow turfgrass underneath. Ground covers are often a better option.

When buying oaks, ask where the trees were grown. Texas red oaks and live oaks native to central Texas are smaller, more alkaline tolerant, and more drought tolerant than their cousins in east and southeast Texas.

All Texas oaks grow best in full sun and well-drained soils. They require supplemental watering only during periods of drought. They have few serious insect or disease problems. In areas of central Texas where oak wilt disease is a problem, prune the trees only during the dormant period of winter to avoid attracting disease-spreading insects to the fresh cut wounds. Applying a pruning paint is also recommended.

Rhaphiolepis indica

INDIAN HAWTHORN. A low, spreading, evergreen shrub bearing thick dull green leaves, small pink or white flowers in spring, and purple-black berries that last through the summer and fall. It grows 2 to 4 ft. tall and wide. There are many fine cultivars to

plagued by insects or disease. Only needs occasional watering during dry spells. Cut to the ground after the first hard freeze and mulch well. In northern areas, use it as a summer annual for a long season of blue flowers, or consider replacing it with a cold-hardy substitute such as daylily. Pages: 21, 51, 59, 80, 99.

Prunus caroliniana 'Compacta'

COMPACT CAROLINA CHERRY LAUREL. A very useful shrub for hedge or screen. Glossy green leaves look fresh all year. Small spikes of lightly scented white flowers appear in spring, followed by black berries in summer. Berries can be messy if the shrub is planted near a patio or walk. Although cherry laurel will grow larger, it is often pruned to about 10 ft. tall and 8 ft. wide. It does best in full sun but can take partial shade. Prefers moist well-drained soil but tolerates dry sites. Shear anytime to desired size and shape. Pages: 86, 96.

Punica granatum

POMEGRANATE. This is a very ornamental deciduous fruiting shrub. Bronze new growth turns green in summer, and bright yellow in fall. Vibrant orange

Quercus buckleyi
TEXAS RED OAK

Quercus virginiana
LIVE OAK

choose from, including larger forms and those with single or double flowers. Indian hawthorn needs full sun and good drainage. Requires minimal pruning or care and has few pest problems. Fungal leaf spot may occur in shady, humid sites. Pages: 80, *82*.

Rhododendron × 'Gumpo White'

'GUMPO WHITE' DWARF EVERGREEN AZALEA. A low-growing evergreen shrub with very showy white flowers in spring. Small elliptic leaves are borne on a compact plant 2 ft. tall and wide. All azaleas do best with partial shade and need fertile, moist, well-drained, acidic soil. When planting, mix ample amounts of sphagnum peatmoss into the planting bed. Be sure not to plant too deep. The top of the root ball should be level with, or a little higher than, the surrounding soil. Azaleas are shallow rooted, so cover with a layer of mulch to keep the soil cool and damp. Water regularly in summer. Prune and apply an acid azalea fertilizer after the plant finishes blooming. Azaleas are most adapted to the acid soils of east Texas. In other areas, plant in raised beds of a peat, pinebark, and sand mixture or consider an alternative such as dwarf nandina, boxwood, or dwarf yaupon holly. Pages: *26*, 27.

Rosa

ROSE. Texans love roses. Most of the roses that do well in Texas are evergreen shrubs with glossy compound leaves, somewhat thorny stems or canes, and showy, sometimes fragrant, flowers. The classes that perform best include teas, Chinas, polyanthas, and the old-fashioned ramblers. All these roses are often referred to as "antique roses" in the nursery. They are grown and sold in containers and can be planted year round.

All roses grow best in full sun and well-drained soil topped with a few inches of mulch. Once established, the roses recommended in this book require no more care than many other shrubs. Prune them lightly once a year in early spring, before new growth starts. (See p. 156 for more on pruning.) Apply a light application of lawn fertilizer, manure, or compost after pruning. The roses we've selected have good resistance to various fungal diseases. They may have problems during years that are especially moist, but each has shown that it will survive and recover without chemical sprays. Aphids, soft-bodied insects the size of a pinhead, may attack new growth, especially in the spring. Wash them away with a blast from the water hose

Recommended roses

Rosa chinensis 'Climbing Old Blush'
The climbing form of the wonderful old China rose, 'Old Blush'. It has a heavy flush of loose double-pink blooms in spring and then a scattering of repeat blooms until fall. Grows vigorously up to 15 ft. tall and wide. There are legendary 'Old Blush' roses in front of the Admiral Nimitz Hotel in Fredericksburg. Pages: 90, *91*.

R. chinensis 'Martha Gonzales'
This dwarf China rose has brilliant red semi-double blooms all season. It grows about 3 ft. tall and 2 ft. wide and occasionally larger. The new growth in spring is a brilliant plum color. Named for the late Martha Gonzales of Navasota. Pages: 90, *91*.

Rosa × 'Belinda's Dream'

R. chinensis 'Mutabilis', Butterfly rose
This popular landscape rose produces showy single flowers all season in everchanging shades of yellow, orange, and pink. Flowers resemble a swarm of butterflies hovering about the bush. Grows to a generous 5 ft. tall and wide, and occasionally larger. New growth is plum colored. Designated an Earth-Kind™ rose. Pages: 54, 98.

R. × 'Belinda's Dream'
This showy shrub rose produces large, very double pink flowers all season. Generally grows around 4 ft. tall and 3 ft. wide. The fragrant flowers are great for floral arrangements. Designated a Texas Superstar™ and an Earth-Kind™ rose. Pages: 22, 61.

R. × odorata 'Gilbert Nabonnand'
This healthy tea rose makes a profusion of loosely double pink blooms all season, with the heaviest bloom in spring and fall. It grows 4 ft. tall and wide and has thornless stems. If you can't find it, try 'Belinda's Dream'. Pages: 90, *91*.

R. × polyantha 'Climbing Pinkie'
This is the climbing form of the polyantha, 'Pinkie'. It can be grown as a loose shrub or as a climber to 8 ft. Pink semi-double blooms smother the canes in spring and repeat the performance in fall. The stems are mostly thornless. Designated an Earth-Kind™ rose. Pages: 30, *31*.

R. × polyantha 'Marie Daly'
This is the pink sport of the popular polyantha, 'Marie Pavie'. It produces a profusion of very fragrant light pink, semi-double flowers all season. Grows 3 ft. tall and 2 ft. wide, on mostly thornless stems. Named for the late Marie Daly of Longview. Designated both a Texas Superstar™ and an Earth-Kind™ rose. Pages: *50*, 51.

R. × polyantha 'Marie Pavie'
This dwarf shrub rose produces clusters of small white blooms all season. It grows 3 ft. tall and 2 ft. wide. If you can't find it, another polyantha, such as 'Marie Daly', makes a good substitute. Pages: 97.

Rosa × *polyantha* 'Marie Pavie'

Rosa chinensis 'Mutabilis'
BUTTERFLY ROSE

or shear off the infected new growth. Deer eat rosebushes, despite the thorns. Where deer are a problem, consider planting oleander, Texas sage, or pomegranate instead of roses.

The Texas Cooperative Extension program (a branch of Texas A&M University) has conducted extensive research to identify the roses that perform best in Texas without pesticides. Those that pass the test are designated Earth-Kind™ roses.

Rosmarinus officinalis

ROSEMARY. This classic Mediterranean evergreen is a tough and attractive herbal shrub. The gray-green needlelike leaves combine a lovely fragrance with a tasty flavor. Small blue flowers bloom in late winter and early spring and sporadically throughout the year. Most rosemary species grow upright to a dense 3 ft. tall and wide (pp. 22, 25). 'Hill's Hardy' (pp. 36, 77, 85, 93) is a cold-hardy selection named for Texas herb expert Madeline Hill. Trailing rosemary (the low-growing *R. officinalis* 'Prostratus') has curved stems and grows 1 ft. tall and 3 ft. wide (pp. 65, 75). Rosemaries do best in full sun and very well-drained soil. They need little water once established and can be pruned or sheared lightly during any season, though they suffer if cut back hard.

Rudbeckia fulgida 'Goldsturm'

'GOLDSTURM' BLACK-EYED SUSAN. This is a popular perennial that bears daisylike flowers with bright

Rosmarinus officinalis **ROSEMARY**

Rosmarinus officinalis 'Hill's Hardy'

Rudbeckia fulgida 'Goldsturm' **BLACK-EYED SUSAN**

Rosmarinus officinalis 'Prostratus'

Ruellia brittoniana 'Katie'
DWARF MEXICAN PETUNIA

Salvia farinacea
MEALYCUP SAGE

gold petals and prominent brown conical centers in early summer. It forms a robust clump 2 ft. tall and wide, with dark green leaves at the base and stiff, erect, branching flower stalks. Plant in full sun or partial shade in a fairly well-drained soil. It looks best with regular watering. Remove spent flowers and cut down all the flower stalks in fall or early spring. Pages: 25, 35, 48, 61, 69, 88.

Ruellia brittoniana 'Katie'

DWARF MEXICAN PETUNIA. An extremely durable and attractive perennial ground cover with narrow dark green leaves. Grows in low dense clumps 1 ft. tall and wide and offers a profusion of small light-purple petunia-like flowers from spring until frost. Grows in full sun or partial shade and tolerates most soil types. It is also quite tolerant of both drought and excess moisture. It has few if any pest problems. It self-seeds; pull out unwanted seedlings. Cut to the ground after the first frost. Designated a Texas Superstar™ because of its beauty and low maintenance requirements. Pages: 21, 27, 42, 63, 95, 97.

Salvia farinacea

MEALYCUP SAGE. A popular native Texas perennial. Clusters of medium-blue flower spikes are borne on upright plants that grow vigorously to 3 ft. tall and wide. Flowers top the gray-green foliage in spring and continue until frost. Improved cultivars are purple, blue, or white and grow to a compact $1\frac{1}{2}$ ft.

tall and wide. Requires little water and is generally pest free. Shear off old blooms to stimulate new ones and to keep the plants tidy. Pages: 35, 40, 44, 56, 73, 75, 77, 89.

Salvia greggii

AUTUMN SAGE. This shrubby perennial is native to Texas and Mexico. It produces small, oval, sage-scented leaves and a profusion of two-lipped flowers, especially in spring and fall. Flowers are white, pink, red, and other colors, depending on the cultivar. 'Alba' (pp. 40, *42*) has pure white flowers. 'Pink' (pp. 77, 80, *82*, 85) is a large and dependable vivid pink cultivar, one of many pink ones available. 'Cherry Chief' (pp. 36, 53, 55) offers bright red flowers. Autumn sage generally grows $2\frac{1}{2}$ ft. tall and wide, has few pests, and is very tolerant of dry spells, requiring supplemental watering only during prolonged droughts. Plant autumn sage in full sun and well-drained soil and shear between flower cycles to keep the plants full and blooming. Pages: 44, 59, 65.

Salvia leucantha

MEXICAN BUSH SAGE. This perennial blooms in the fall with hundreds of spikes of purple and white flowers above handsome gray-green foliage. Grows upright to 4 ft. tall and wide. For a bushier plant with more flower spikes, cut the stems back by half several times during the growing season. Requires full sun and good drainage. It has very few pests and needs little watering. Cut to the ground after the first frost. Designated a Texas Superstar™. Pages: 29, 33, 40, 61, 77, 91.

Salvia × 'Indigo Spires'

'INDIGO SPIRES' SALVIA. A vigorous perennial that grows a bushy 5 ft. tall and 3 ft. wide. It puts out a plethora of long, deep blue-purple spikes all season. See mealycup sage (*S. farinacea*, p. 192) for growing requirements and care. Pages: 51, 66.

Santolina chamaecyparissus

GRAY SANTOLINA. A bushy little shrub grown for its soft, fragrant, fine-textured, silver-gray foliage. Often sheared to make an edging or a formal specimen, it is also useful as a ground cover. If left unsheared, it bears round yellow flowers in summer.

Salvia greggii
AUTUMN SAGE

Salvia greggii 'Cherry Chief'
AUTUMN SAGE

Salvia × 'Indigo Spires'
'INDIGO SPIRES' SALVIA

Salvia leucantha
MEXICAN BUSH SAGE

Santolina needs full sun and well-drained, dry soil. Prune every year in early spring, before new growth starts, cutting the old stems back by half. It generally grows a little more than a foot tall and wide. Pages: 36, 44, 65, 75, 99.

Santolina chamaecyparissus
GRAY SANTOLINA

Sedum 'Autumn Joy'

'AUTUMN JOY' SEDUM. This hardy perennial forms clumps of succulent foliage on thick stems topped with flat clusters of tiny flowers in the fall. 'Autumn Joy' grows 18 in. tall and wide, with erect stems and gray-green foliage. The flowers change color from pale to deep salmon pink to rusty red over a span of many weeks in late summer and fall as they open, mature, and go to seed. Most sedums, including 'Autumn Joy', need full sun. They have few pest problems and only require occasional watering in periods of drought. Cut down the old stalks in winter or early spring. Pages: 25, 35, 93.

Setcreasea pallida 'Purple Heart'

PURPLE HEART. This Mexican perennial is among the easiest of all plants to grow. The thick succulent stems sport showy purple foliage from spring to frost. Small pink flowers throughout the growing season are an added bonus. Purple heart has no insect or disease problems and requires little to no watering. It will grow in sun or shade but has better coloration in full sun. Tolerates almost any soil type. It is sometimes sold as purple Jew or *Tradescantia pallida*. Pages: 27, 42, 95, 99.

Sophora secundiflora

TEXAS MOUNTAIN LAUREL. This native shrub or small tree boasts beautiful blossoms as well as shiny evergreen foliage. It generally grows 10 ft. tall or better and 7 ft. wide. The extremely fragrant flowers hang like clusters of purple wisteria each spring. Requires full sun and good drainage. It may occasionally suffer attack from leaf-eating caterpillars but generally recovers. It requires little to no supplemental irrigation or pruning. Do not prune during the winter because flower buds are present at that time. Pages: 73, 80, 85.

Spiraea × *bumalda*

JAPANESE SPIREA. A deciduous shrub, it creates a low mound of thin, graceful, arching stems that bear sharply toothed leaves and, from late spring into summer, round flat clusters of tiny flowers. 'Anthony Waterer' (pp. 38, *39*) has carmine pink flowers. 'Goldflame' (pp. 69, *71*) has bright gold leaves that are tinged with orange in spring and turn red in fall. Flowers are pink. Both cultivars grow about 2 to 3 ft. tall and wide. Plant them in full or partial sun. Prune every year after bloom, removing some of the older stems at ground level and cutting the others

Sedum 'Autumn Joy'
'AUTUMN JOY' SEDUM

back partway. In summer, shear off faded flowers to promote possible reblooming. Water during periods of drought. Rarely suffers from insects or disease.

Tagetes lemmonii

COPPER CANYON DAISY. A shrublike perennial with small finely divided, dull-green aromatic leaves and bright orange-yellow, marigold-type flowers in fall. It grows 2 to 3 ft. tall and wide. Trim back by one-third several times during the growing season to maintain a compact habit and to prevent sprawling in bloom. Plant in full sun. Rarely needs water and has no pest problems. Late blooms can be damaged by a hard frost. Page: 73.

Tagetes lucida

MEXICAN MINT MARIGOLD. This Mexican perennial has aromatic foliage and clusters of small golden yellow marigold-like flowers in the fall. The scented foliage (tasting of licorice or anise) can be used as a culinary substitute for French tarragon. Generally grows $1\frac{1}{2}$ ft. tall and wide and requires full to partial sun. Shear the plants back by one-third several times during the growing season to maintain a compact habit and to promote heavier bloom. It has few pests and requires watering only during dry periods. Pages: 40, 48, *50*, 85.

Setcreasea pallida
'Purple Heart'
PURPLE HEART

Tagetes lemmonii
COPPER CANYON DAISY

Sophora secundiflora
TEXAS MOUNTAIN LAUREL

Tecoma stans 'Gold Star'

'GOLD STAR' ESPERANZA. This showy Texas native can be grown as a deciduous shrub in the lower third of the state. In the middle section, it may be grown as a perennial, pruned to the ground after the first hard freeze. In the northern third, it may be grown as an annual. It bears bright shiny green pecanlike leaves, extremely showy clusters of yellow bell-shaped flowers from summer until frost, and green bean pods after the flowers fade. Generally grows to a bushy 5 ft. tall and wide. Esperanza requires full hot sun and only occasional watering during the summer. It has no major insect or disease problems. Cut off bean pods or shear plants to encourage repeat bloom. Plant it in a protected area or mulch heavily to protect it from freezing. In the northen half of the state, consider using it as an annual or potted specimen, or use a more cold-hardy substitute like the butterfly rose. A designated Texas Superstar™. Pages: 25, 33, 61, 98.

Trachelospermum asiaticum

ASIAN JASMINE. This common ground cover is dense and low growing, forming a thick mat of small, shiny evergreen leaves. It grows less than 1 ft. tall and spreads to about 3 ft. Asian jasmine has few pest problems and only requires watering when it's dry and the leaves turn dull green. Shear as needed to keep tidy or mow each spring with the mower on the highest setting. Page: 29.

Trachelospermum jasminoides

STAR JASMINE. This is an evergreen vine with woody, twining stems lined with pairs of small, glossy green, oval leaves. It bears dangling clusters of sweetly scented creamy white flowers in spring. It can climb 10 to 15 ft. if given a pillar or fence for support but is also useful as a sprawling ground cover, 1 to 2 ft. tall. Prune anytime to keep within bounds. If used as a ground cover, shear as needed to keep it compact. Plant in full sun or partial shade and water during periods of drought. Also sold as star jasmine. Pages: 44, 52, 83.

Trachycarpus fortunei

WINDMILL PALM. This is one of the more cold-hardy palms. It forms a small tree with somewhat drooping, dark green palm-shaped leaves and a matted burlaplike trunk. It commonly grows 8 to 10 ft. tall and 4 to 5 ft. wide. It has no insect or disease problems and needs watering only during dry spells. Pages: 79, 98.

Tecoma stans 'Gold Star'
'GOLD STAR' ESPERANZA

Trachelospermum asiaticum
ASIAN JASMINE

Trachelospermum jasminoides
STAR JASMINE

Verbena bonariensis

PURPLE VERBENA. This perennial forms a low mound of basal foliage topped by a thicket of stiff, erect, much-branched but almost leafless flower stalks. They bear countless little clusters of lavender-purple flowers throughout the season. The heaviest bloom comes before the heat of summer, beckoning butterflies and floral arrangers. Purple verbena needs full sun and tolerates most soil conditions. Shear as needed during the growing season to promote new bloom stalks. It may occasionally be attacked by flea hoppers. Generally self-sows but isn't weedy. Pages: 55, 80, 97.

Verbena × hybrida

VERBENA. These are sprawling perennials with evergreen leaves and round clusters of showy flowers. 'Blue Princess' (pp. 25, 31, 40, 51, 59, 93) has lightly fragrant lavender-blue flowers and is designated a Texas Superstar™. 'Homestead Purple' (pp. 22, 33, 37, 55, 57, 61, 67) has vibrant purple flowers. Plant them in full sun and they will bloom nonstop from early spring until hard frost if regularly deadheaded. Plants generally grow about 1 ft. tall and spread 3 ft.

Trachycarpus fortunei
WINDMILL PALM

Verbena bonariensis **PURPLE VERBENA**

Verbena × hybrida 'Blue Princess'
VERBENA

Verbena × hybrida 'Homestead Purple'
VERBENA

Verbena × hybrida **197**

or wider. Prune any damaged or frosted shoots in early spring, and shear throughout the growing season to keep tidy. Water regularly during hot spells. Plants may suffer attack from flea hoppers during summer heat.

Viburnum tinus 'Spring Bouquet'

'SPRING BOUQUET' VIBURNUM. A compact evergreen shrub with dark green leaves borne on reddish stems. It produces clusters of fragrant white flowers in spring and metallic-blue berries in late summer. Generally grows 5 ft. tall and about 4 ft. wide and has few pest problems. Water well during periods of drought. Shear anytime after blooming to maintain desired shape but do not prune in the late fall or winter, because flower buds will be present. Pages: 22, 50, 69.

Vinca major

PERIWINKLE. A spreading evergreen ground cover with medium green heart-shaped leaves and five-petaled lavender-purple flowers in the spring. The plants normally grow about 1 ft. tall and 2 to 3 ft. wide before rooting to form new plants. Periwinkle performs best in shady situations and well-drained soil. Water regularly during periods of drought or when the leaves turn dull green. It may suffer occasional attacks from leaf feeding insects but almost always recovers. Pages: 74, *74*.

Vitex agnus-castus

CHASTE TREE. This is a tough deciduous shrub or small tree that can reach up to 20 ft. and more with age. It generally grows with multiple trunks and has an open habit. The aromatic, narrowly palmate leaves are dull green on top and grayish underneath. Showy flower spikes bear small, tubular, lavender-blue flowers. They bloom in summer and attract many butterflies. Plant in full sun and well-drained soil. Chaste tree isn't bothered by pests and is able to survive dry periods. Cut off lower limbs in winter if you want to develop a tree shape; otherwise it will be shrubby and dense. To keep it small, cut it back to 1 to 2 ft. in early spring, when new growth starts. Then shear with hedge clippers or power shears between bloom cycles to prevent seed set and promote new blooms. Pages: 61, 65, 74.

Water plants

Many garden centers offer a limited selection of water plants. Specialty nurseries and mail-order water-garden specialists often offer dozens of kinds. Most water plants are fast-growing, sometimes even weedy, so you need only one of each to start. Some water plants are tender to frost, but you can overwinter them indoors in a pot or aquarium. There are three main groups of water plants: marginal, floating, and oxygenating. Choose one or more of each for an interesting and balanced effect.

Marginal plants grow well on the edge of the pond or in containers covered with 2 in. or more of water. Their leaves and flower stalks stand above the water surface while their roots stay submerged. Louisiana iris (see *Iris* × Louisiana hybrids, p. 180) and umbrella sedge (see *Cyperus alternifolius*, p. 175) are two common examples that are easy to grow and readily available.

Floating plants have leaves that rest on the water and roots that dangle into it. Water lettuce (*Pistia* species) is a floater that forms saucer-size rosettes of iridescent pale green leaves.

Oxygenating, or submerged, plants grow completely under water. They help keep the water clear and provide oxygen, food, and shelter for fish.

Viburnum tinus 'Spring Bouquet'
VIBURNUM

Anacharis (*Elodea* species) is a popular oxygenator with tiny, dark green leaves.

Water lilies (*Nymphaea* species, pp. 57, 59) are the most popular plants for pools and ponds. The best selection is available from specialty nurseries. There are two main groups of water lilies. Hardy water lilies survive outdoors from year to year and bloom in midsummer. They are usually the easiest to grow. Tropical water lilies, such as Dauben water lily, (*N. × daubenyana*, 99, **99**) need warm water and bloom over a longer season from summer through fall but are cold tender and often treated as annuals. Both kinds are available in dwarf-size plants, suitable for small pools, with fragrant or scentless flowers in shades of white, yellow, and pink. Tropicals also come in shades of blue and purple. All water lilies need full sun. Plant the roots in a container of heavy, rich, garden soil, and set the container in the pool, making sure that about 6 in. of water covers the soil. (See p. 119 for more on planting.)

Wisteria sinensis

CHINESE WISTERIA. This is a vigorous woody vine with deciduous compound leaves that turn yellow in fall. Dangling clusters of very fragrant lavender-purple flowers appear in early spring. The vine climbs by twining around a trellis, tree, or other support and may exceed 30 ft. if not controlled. To flower well, it needs full sun along with well-drained soil. A young plant may not bloom for several years after you plant it, but it should bloom as the new growth matures. Wisteria has few pest problems and only requires irrigation during dry summers. To keep it in bounds, prune the long vining shoots during summer. Major pruning should be done immediately following bloom. Do not prune during winter, when flower buds are present. Wisteria can be invasive in East Texas. Pages: 80, *82*.

Yucca

YUCCA. These are bold architectural plants with pointed swordlike leaves and tall stalks of showy creamy white flowers. *Y. filamentosa* (pp. 73, **74**) has narrow leaves with hairy filaments along the margins and generally grows 3 ft. tall and wide. Soft-tip yucca (*Y. gloriosa*, pp. 40, 65, 99) has somewhat flexible gray-green leaves and grows 4 to 5 ft. tall and 3 ft. wide. Yuccas require full sun and good drainage and no supplemental irrigation. Maintenance is limited to removing dead leaves at their base and cutting down dead flower stalks. Yuccas have few if any pest problems.

Vitex agnus-castus
CHASTE TREE

Yucca gloriosa
SOFT-TIP YUCCA

Glossary

Amendments. Organic materials or minerals used to improve the soil. Peat moss, pinebark, and compost are commonly used.

Annual. A plant that grows from seed, flowers, produces new seeds, and dies during a single growing season; a tropical plant treated like an annual in that it is grown for only a single season's display and then removed after it freezes.

Balled-and-burlapped. Describes a tree or shrub dug out of the ground with a ball of soil intact around the roots, the ball then wrapped in burlap and tied for transport.

Balled-and-burlapped

Bare-root

Bare-root. Describes a plant dug out of the ground and then shaken or washed to remove the soil from the roots.

Chlorosis. Yellowing of the foliage usually due to a lack of iron uptake in alkaline soils.

Compound leaf. A leaf consisting of two or more leaflets branching from the same stalk.

Container-grown. Describes a plant raised in a pot that is removed before planting.

Crown. That part of a plant where the roots and stem meet, usually at soil level.

Cultivar. A cultivated variety of a plant, often bred or selected for some special trait such as double flowers, compact growth, cold hardiness, or disease resistance.

Deadheading. Removing spent flowers during the growing season to improve a plant's appearance, prevent seed formation, and stimulate the development of new flowers.

Deciduous. Describes a tree, shrub, or vine that drops all its leaves in winter.

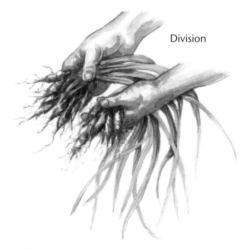

Division

Division. Propagation of a plant by separating it into two or more pieces, each piece possessing at least one bud and some roots. Plants commonly divided include perennials, bulbs, grasses, and ferns.

Drainage. Movement of water through soil. If water poured into a foot-deep hole drains completely in a few hours, the drainage is good.

Drip line. An imaginary line beneath a tree that marks the perimeter of the tree's canopy. This area benefits from direct rainfall and "drip" from leaves. Because many of the tree's feeder roots are found along the drip line and beyond, this area is the best for fertilizing and watering.

Dry-laid. Describes a masonry path or wall that is installed without mortar.

Edging. A barrier that serves as the border between lawn and a planting bed. Edgings may be shallow trenches or barriers of plastic, brick, or metal.

Exposure. The characterization of a site according to the sun, wind, and temperature acting upon it.

Formal. Describes a style of landscaping that features symmetrical layouts, with beds and walks related to adjacent buildings, and often with plants sheared to geometric or other shapes.

Foundation planting. Traditionally, a narrow border of evergreen shrubs planted around the foundation of a house. Contemporary foundation plantings often include deciduous shrubs, grasses, perennials, and other plants as well.

Full shade. Describes a site that receives no direct sun during the growing season.

Full sun. Describes a site that receives at least eight hours of direct sun each day during the growing season.

Garden soil. Soil specially prepared for planting to make it loose enough for roots and water to penetrate easily. Usually requires digging or tilling and the addition of some organic matter.

Grade. The angle and direction of the ground's slope in a given area.

Ground cover. A plant providing continuous cover for an area of soil. Commonly a low, spreading foliage plant such as Asian jasmine, vinca, or lilyturf.

Habit. The characteristic shape of a plant, such as upright, mounded, columnar, or vase-shaped.

Hardiness. A plant's ability to survive the winter temperatures in a given region without protection.

Hardscape. Parts of a landscape constructed from materials other than plants, such as walks, walls, and trellises made of wood, stone, or other materials.

Herbicide. A chemical used to kill plants. Preemergent herbicides are used to kill weed seeds as they sprout, and thus to prevent weed growth. Postemergent herbicides kill plants that are already growing.

Hybrid. A plant with two parents that belong to different species or genera.

Interplant. To use plants with different bloom times or growth habits in the same bed to increase the variety and appeal of the planting.

Invasive. Describes a plant that spreads quickly, usually by runners or seeds, and mixes with or dominates the adjacent plantings.

Landscape fabric. A synthetic fabric, sometimes water-permeable, spread under paths or mulch to serve as a weed barrier.

Loam. Soil rich in organic matter and with mineral particles in a range of sizes. Excellent for many garden plants.

Microclimate. A small-scale "system" of factors affecting plant growth on a particular site, including shade, temperature, rainfall, and so on.

Brick mowing strip

Mowing strip. A row of bricks or paving stones set flush with the soil around the edge of a bed, and wide enough to support one wheel of the lawn mower.

Mulch. A layer of organic or other materials spread several inches thick around the base of plants and over open soil in a bed. Mulch conserves soil moisture, smothers weeds, and moderates soil temperatures. Where winters are cold, mulches help protect plants from freezing. Common mulches include compost, shredded leaves, pine straw, lawn clippings, gravel, cotton-seed hulls, and landscape fabric.

Native. Describes a plant that is or once was found in the wild in a particular region and was not imported from another area.

Nutrients. Elements needed by plants. Found in the soil and supplied by organic matter and fertilizers, nutrients include nitrogen, phosphorus, potassium, calcium, magnesium, sulfur, iron, and other elements, in various forms and compounds.

Organic matter. Partially or fully decomposed plant and animal matter. Includes leaves, trimmings, and manure.

Peat moss. Partially decomposed mosses and sedges. Dug from boggy areas, peat moss is often used as an organic amendment for garden soil.

Perennial. An herbaceous plant with a life span of more than two years, usually much longer. Cool-season perennials usually go dormant during the summer. Warm-season perennials go dormant during the winter.

Pressure-treated lumber. Softwood lumber treated with chemicals that protect it from decay.

Propagate. To produce new plants from seeds or by vegetative means such as dividing plant parts, taking cuttings, and grafting stems onto other plants.

Retaining wall. A wall built to stabilize a slope and keep soil from sliding or eroding downhill.

Rhizome. A horizontal underground stem from which roots and shoots emerge. Some swell to store food. Branched rhizomes (those of iris, for instance) can be divided to produce new plants.

Root ball. The mass of soil and roots dug with a plant when it is removed from the ground; the soil and roots of a plant grown in a container.

Selective pruning. Using pruning shears to remove or cut back individual shoots in order to refine the shape of a shrub, maintain its vigor, or limit its size.

Severe pruning. Using pruning shears or loppers to cut away most of a shrub's top growth, leaving just short stubs or a trunk.

Shearing. Using hedge shears or an electric hedge trimmer to shape the surface of a shrub or hedge, or to deadhead annuals or perennials.

Soil pH. The alkalinity or acidity of the soil, which affects plant growth and nutrient uptake. Alkaline soils in the western two thirds of Texas are often amended with sulfur and iron products.

Specimen plant. A striking plant, often providing year-round interest, placed for individual display.

Spike. An elongated flower cluster on which individual flowers are attached directly to the main stem or are on very short stalks attached to the main stem.

Tender. Describes a plant that is damaged by cold weather in a particular region.

Underplanting. Growing short plants, such as ground covers, under a taller plant, such as a shrub.

Variegated. Describes foliage with color patterns in stripes, specks, or blotches that occur naturally or result from breeding.

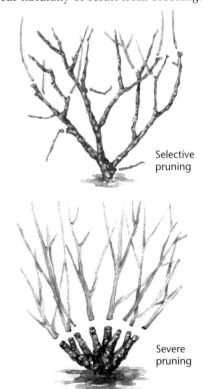
Selective pruning

Severe pruning

Index

Note: Page numbers in ***bold italic*** refer to illustrations.

Have a home gardening, decorating, or improvement project? Look for these and other fine Creative Homeowner books wherever books are sold.

An impressive guide to more than 100 flowering plants. More than 500 color photos. 208 pp.; 9"×10"
BOOK #: 274032

How to prepare, cultivate, and harvest a successful garden. Over 400 color photos. 176 pp.; 9"×10"
BOOK #: 274244

A four-season step-by-step guide to growing flowers. Over 500 photos & illustrations. 224 pp.; 9"×10"
BOOK #: 274791

A comprehensive tool for the aspiring water gardener. Over 400 color photos. 208 pp.; 9"×10"
BOOK #: 274452

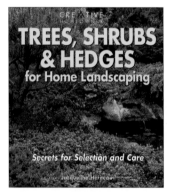

How to select and care for landscaping plants. Over 500 illustrations. 208 pp.; 9"×10"
BOOK #: 274238

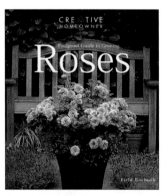

A growing guide for beginners and experienced gardeners. Over 400 color photos. 160 pp.; 9"×10"
BOOK #: 274055

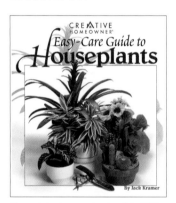

Complete houseplant guide 200 readily available plants; more than 400 photos. 192pp.; 9"×10"
BOOK #: 275243

Home landscaping guides that cover six other regions: Mid-Atlantic (274537); Midwest (274385); Northeast (274618); Southeast (274762); Northwest (274344); California (274267). 400 photos & illustrations each.

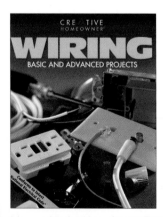

New, updated edition of best-selling house wiring manual. Over 700 color photos. 256 pp.; 8½"×11"
BOOK #: 277048

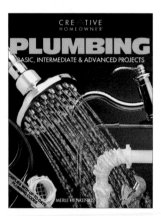

Take the guesswork out of plumbing repair. More than 750 illustrations. 272 pp.; 8½"×10⁷⁄₈"
BOOK #: 27820

How to work with space, color, pattern, texture. Over 400 photos. 288 pp.; 9"×10"
BOOK #: 279672

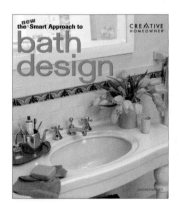

All you need to know about designing a bath. Over 260 color photos. 208 pp.; 9"×10"
BOOK #: 279234